PERGAMON INTERNATIONAL LIBRARY
of Science, Technology, Engineering and Social Studies

The 1000-volume original paperback library in aid of education,
industrial training and the enjoyment of leisure

Publisher: Robert Maxwell, M.C.

Village Women of Bangladesh

PROSPECTS FOR CHANGE

THE PERGAMON TEXTBOOK
INSPECTION COPY SERVICE

An inspection copy of any book published in the Pergamon International Library will gladly be sent to academic staff without obligation for their consideration for course adoption or recommendation. Copies may be retained for a period of 60 days from receipt and returned if not suitable. When a particular title is adopted or recommended for adoption for class use and the recommendation results in a sale of 12 or more copies, the inspection copy may be retained with our compliments. The Publishers will be pleased to receive suggestions for revised editions and new titles to be published in this important International Library.

Women in Development Series
Volume 4

Editors: T. Scarlett Epstein and S. Rosemary Watts, *School of African and Asian Studies, University of Sussex, UK*

WOMEN IN DEVELOPMENT is the result of the "Action-oriented Study of the Role of Women in Rural Development", a research project directed by the editors of this series. This new and imaginative series is concerned with the world-wide movements for economic development and female emancipation, with particular emphasis on the role of women in changing rural societies. Books planned for the series will review existing research and literature, report on the problems and successes of current research projects, highlight the main research lacunae, and outline recommendations for the future role of women in rural societies.

Volume 1
NELSON, N.
Why has Development Neglected Rural Women?
A Review of the South Asian Literature

Volume 2
SEARLE-CHATTERJEE, M.
Reversible Sex Roles
The Special Case of Benares Sweepers

Volume 3
EPSTEIN, T. S. and WATTS, R. A.
The Endless Day
Some Case Material on Asian Rural Women

The World Employment Programme (WEP) was launched by the International Labour Organisation in 1969, as the ILO's main contribution to the International Development Strategy for the Second United Nations Development Decade.
The means of action adopted by the WEP have included the following:
• Short-term high-level advisory missions;
• Longer-term national or regional employment teams; and
• A wide-ranging research programme.
Through these activities the ILO has been able to help national decision-makers to reshape their policies and plans with the aim of eradicating mass poverty and unemployment.
A landmark in the development of the WEP was the World Employment Conference of 1976, which proclaimed inter alia that "strategies and national development plans should include as a priority objective the promotion of employment and the satisfaction of the basic needs of each country's population". The Declaration of Principles and Programme of Action adopted by the Conference have become the cornerstone of WEP technical assistance and research activities during the closing years of the Second Development Decade.
This publication is the outcome of a WEP project.

Village Women of Bangladesh

PROSPECTS FOR CHANGE

A study prepared for the International Labour
Office within the framework of the World
Employment Programme

by
TAHRUNNESSA A. ABDULLAH
and
SONDRA A. ZEIDENSTEIN

PERGAMON PRESS

OXFORD · NEW YORK · TORONTO · SYDNEY · PARIS · FRANKFURT

U.K.	Pergamon Press Ltd., Headington Hill Hall, Oxford OX3 0BW, England
U.S.A.	Pergamon Press Inc., Maxwell House, Fairview Park, Elmsford, New York 10523, U.S.A.
'CANADA	Pergamon Press Canada Ltd., Suite 104, 150 Consumers Rd., Willowdale, Ontario M2J 1P9, Canada
AUSTRALIA	Pergamon Press (Aust.) Pty. Ltd., P.O. Box 544, Potts Point, N.S.W. 2011, Australia
FRANCE	Pergamon Press SARL, 24 rue des Ecoles, 75240 Paris, Cedex 05, France
FEDERAL REPUBLIC OF GERMANY	Pergamon Press GmbH, 6242 Kronberg-Taunus, Hammerweg 6, Federal Republic of Germany

Copyright © 1982 International Labour Organisation

First edition 1982

British Library Cataloguing in Publication Data

Abdullah, Tahrunnessa A.
Village women of Bangladesh: prospects
for change.—(Women in development).
—(Pergamon international library)
1. Woman—Bangladesh—Social conditions
I. Title II. Zeidenstein, Sondra A.
III. Series
305.4'2'095492   HQ1745.6
ISBN 0-08-026795-5

In order to make this volume available as economically and as rapidly as possible the authors' typescripts have been reproduced in their original forms. This method unfortunately has its typographical limitations but it is hoped that they in no way distract the reader.

Printed in Great Britain by A. Wheaton & Co. Ltd., Exeter

Dedicated
to the rural women
of Bangladesh

FOREWORD

by Ester Boserup

The process of economic and social development is a gradual
shift from a stage at which people use all their time to produce
goods and services for family use to a stage when they produce
for others, either as self-employed or as employees. Most often,
men are the first to take the step from production for family
use to production for others, while women continue to spend all
their time working for their own families. If this difference
in the work pattern of the sexes becomes an important part of
the traditional culture, as is the case in Bangladesh, the
possibilities for development may become severely restricted.

In countries with *purdah* systems women lose status if they
perform work which requires them to leave the confines of their
own household. Therefore, they cannot make a rational choice
between different types of money earning activities nor can they
decide how to allocate their time between income earning and
domestic work. For lack of acceptable alternatives, they are
forced to continue low productivity domestic activities and
self-production of household equipment, i.e. activities, which
have long ago been replaced by purchase of goods and services
in societies in which women have more freedom of choice. In
Bangladesh the degree of self-sufficiency of rural households is
still so high, that rural women must perform hard work for long
hours every day, although they confine their work, exclusively
or mainly, to activities for family use. Because of this lack
of specialisation and the consequently low productivity of
female work, the rural households remain poor and unable to
purchase either industrial goods or specialized food or artisan
products. Thus, the market for agricultural and non-agricultural
products remains too small to provide sufficient encouragement to

either industrial or rural development.

To break this vicious circle of rural self-sufficiency and lack of market outlets for specialized production is a complicated matter. Of course, both men and women in such countries want to raise family incomes, but if rigid sex-segregation is the generally accepted ideal, at least in rural areas, neither women nor men want to raise family incomes by means which imply a radical break with the accepted status system. Therefore, the primary goal for women's projects in such areas is to create opportunities for rural women to contribute to family income by means which are acceptable both to themselves and to the male villagers on whom they depend.

The present study describes and evaluates an attempt in Bangladesh to increase incomes of rural households by the establishment of self-governed credit co-operatives for rural women. The credits are used to start or expand individual small scale animal husbandry, crop raising and other productive activities in or around the homes of the women. The Project aims not only to obtain a badly needed improvement in the living standards of the poorest families, but also and possibly more important to bring about a change in customary norms: to substitute work for idleness as a status symbol. In the words of the authors, women's projects "must address the complex problem of how to enable status-bound women to maintain and even raise their status through regular income producing work. It is not easy, but it is the only viable way".

The experience gained from the work in Bangladesh, as recorded in this book, is extremely valuable for women and men who are engaged in or concerned with rural projects in other parts of the world where sex-segregation predominates in rural areas. But the message of this book is highly relevant also to countries unaffected by purdah systems, because it deals extensively with the problem of self-government of rural projects and the inter-relationship between villagers and experts. It is emphasized that experts must first learn from the rural women before they can teach them, and that they must stay long enough in the villages to be able to do both.

While it is encouraging to find that not only many rural women took an active part in the Bangladesh Project but also many male village leaders were willing to accept and even support the innovations it involved, it is sad to hear of the resistance against such programmes that exists among educated urban males,

both in the national administration as well as among the staff
of international aid agencies. To overcome this obstacle it is
necessary to give books of this kind wide publicity to ensure
that not only women but also male development experts will be
attracted to learn more about the benefits and problems of
involving the large mass of Third World rural women in development programmes.

PREFACE

The Programme of Action adopted by the World Employment
Conference in 1976 noted that women constitute the group at the
bottom of the ladder in many developing countries in respect of
employment, poverty, education, training and status. The Rural
Employment Policies Branch of the Employment and Development
Department of the ILO has underway a substantial research and
action Programme on Rural Women aimed at increasing knowledge
and providing guidelines for policy makers and planners concerned
with the amelioration of working conditions and employment and
income-earning opportunities for women, particularly poor and
otherwise disadvantaged women, in rural areas.

The present study on Village Women of Bangladesh which this
Programme supported, is divided into two distinct parts. Part I,
which is a description of the various aspects of the lives of
rural women, attempts to explain how rural women determine their
priorities and to identify some of the pivotal issues which limit
their options. It gives, in particular, a detailed description
of the productive work performed by secluded, purdah women behind
their compound walls. In respect of the rice crop, for example,
women's several operations take long hours of intensive application and involve the crucial responsibility of ensuring the
quality and quantity of the rice produced as well as the condition of next year's seed. Some of this work, such as seed
selection and processing, requires a high level of expertise,
developed over long years of experience. Food scientists
attached to research institutes, who are looking for ways to
process rice commercially with minimal losses, are trying to
understand how women dry the rice so they can replicate it.

Part II is a detailed case study of the first few years of a
national programme in Bangladesh to integrate rural women in
the development process. It draws attention to some of the
problems which arise in the course of project implementation,
including the recruitment of female staff: their training and
orientation to work with the rural poor, the incorporation of
the women's component into the over-all Integrated Rural
Development Programme, and, the change in attitudes which this
requires on the part of the men working in the Programme at all
levels, men who previously held that village women did little
else than "serve their husbands, take care of the children and
animals, and do a little of this and that around the house".

This study is especially pertinent in the context of the
Programme of Action recently adopted in Copenhagen (July 1980)
by the World Conference of the United Nations Decade for Women,
which stressed the importance of grass-roots organisations.
The project described in this volume seeks to initiate change
through village-based institutions, referred to as co-operatives,
but "different from Western-originated co-operatives in fundamental ways". A variety of problems are experienced by these
community-wide organisations which attempt to serve all categories of rural women, whilst at the same time having as the
major concern "exploring ways for rural women to earn real
income through work on a regular basis". Obviously, an organisation which caters to both rich and poor in rural areas finds
it difficult to reflect the felt needs of the majority of rural
women who are poor and preoccupied with earning an additional
income. This study reveals the contradictions in the original
project design and the need to revise it in the light of
additional information about rural women collected in the course
of project implementation and experimenting with and evaluating
new approaches. There are many lessons which development
planners, researchers and rural women themselves can and should
draw from the study.

Zubeida Ahmad,
Rural Employment Policies Branch,
Employment and Development Department,
International Labour Office.

ACKNOWLEDGMENTS

This study was commissioned by the Rural Employment Policies
Branch within the framework of the ILO World Employment
Programme.

The authors are especially grateful for the encouragement of
Ingrid Palmer and Joan Dunlop as well as for the technical
assistance provided by the members of the Employment and
Development Department of the International Labor Office.

Additional financial support was provided by the Australian
Government and John D. Rockefeller III.

The authors want to thank the dozens of rural women of
Bangladesh who took time from their busy lives to answer our
questions. All names used in the text are fictitious.

CONTENTS

List of Tables   xix

List of Plates   xix

THE SETTING   1

PART ONE   RURAL WOMEN OF BANGLADESH

   I   Introduction   7

   II   Bangladesh Background   11

           Population   12
           History   12
           Religion   13
           National Economy   13
           The Household as an Economic Unit   15
           The Village   16
           The "Bari"   18
           Administration   19

   III The Work of Women   21

           Rice Production   24
           Other Kinds of Home-Based Production   33
           The Value of Women's Work   35

   IV   Women and Income   41

   V   Reproduction and Health   49

           Reproduction   49
           Health   52

   VI   Purdah   55

   VII Status   65

VIII	Life Crises	71
	Widowhood	82
	Divorce, Polygamy and Abuse	83
	Problems of Young Women	84
IX	Family Strategy and Female Strategy	87
	Family Strategy	87
	Female Strategy	89
X	Co-operation and Conflict	92
XI	Change	95
	A Look Ahead	101
	A Vision	102
PART TWO	THE PROJECT	
I	Description of the Project	107
	Context	108
	Institutional Framework	109
	Rural Women's Co-operatives	113
II	Staff	116
	Roles	116
	Training	123
III	Co-operatives	139
	Orientation of the Community	139
	Formation of Co-operatives	143
	Co-operative Leaders	146
	Membership	162
	Meetings	164
	Economic Program	166
	Recent Developments	173
	Specialized Training	174
	Case Studies of Co-operatives and Co-operative Members	178

IV	Family Planning	186
	Training in Family Planning	189
	Results	191
	Reasons for Accepting or Opposing Contraception	195
V	The Paradox of Women's Programs	202

PART THREE OVERVIEW   215

Glossary of Abbreviations and Vernacular Words   221

Appendix A. Sample Questionnaires   222

Appendix B. The Basic Structure of the Project   231

References   234

Related Readings   239

LIST OF TABLES

Table 1   Marital Status of Co-operative Leaders   149

Table 2   Educational Status of Co-operative Leaders   150

Table 3   Age of Co-operative Leaders   150

Table 4   Landholding Status of Co-operative Leaders   150

Table 5   Profession of Male Guardians of   151
                        Co-operative Leaders

LIST OF PLATES (BETWEEN pp.108-109)

I.   A woman turning rice with her feet to dry it
        evenly. On the line behind her is the house-
        hold bedding, hung out to absorb warmth.

II.   Two women are husking rice with traditional
        technology. One woman pedals; the other stirs
        and checks what is being husked.

III.   Taking care of livestock is women's respon-
        sibility. Women often control the distribution
        of milk for household consumption and market.

IV.   A woman is drying dung for fuel, perhaps for
        the next day's cooking.

V.   These dung cakes and sticks of dung have been
        collected, arranged and dried by women. They
        are used as fuel.

VI.   A woman is repairing the door step with a
        mixture of mud and cow dung. Such repair is
        women's responsibility.

VII.   Women make fishnets.

VIII. Women make mats for regular household use as bedding and for drying rice.

IX. Women are in charge of storage. They make the hanging containers to keep food and other precious things where there is air and away from rodents.

X. A traditional skill of women is making fans for special and household use.

Credit for all photographs: ULLA FORNAEUS

THE SETTING

The attainment of the priorities of national development in Bangladesh and most developing countries depends on enabling rural women to change their behavior. In Bangladesh two priorities are increasing food production and lowering the birth rate. One way to lower the birth rate is to practice contraception. Obviously this involves a change in the motivation and practice of rural women. Another way to lower the birth rate, according to many demographers, is to lower the rate of infant mortality. Since nutrition, health, and sanitation are in the control of women, improvement in these practices depends on changes in their behavior. With regard to increasing food production, since women participate in critical aspects of rice production and are responsible for some or all aspects of the production of most other foods eaten in rural areas, changes in the practices of rural women would again seem to be indicated.

One alternative to enabling rural women to change their behavior might be to take these activities out of their control. It is difficult to consider such an alternative in the realms of health, nutrition and sanitation. For complex reasons (including Western and urban biases against rural women and the orientation of Western agriculture and economics toward the exclusion of women), it is less difficult to consider it in terms of food production. Historically, the consequences of such conversion from female-dominated subsistence food production to commercial technologies under the control of men include: the dislocation of poor women from their traditional means of survival; the lowering of the perceived value of all rural women as their contribution to the family is removed; and the waste of time,

1

money, and food as traditional methods of food production and processing employed by women are neglected as a base for improved commercial technology, while expensive experiments and research are often undertaken with little connection to what is already being done. These processes are under way in Bangladesh - but they are not, we think, an alternative to be deliberately chosen.

Since policy-makers and planners cannot wisely choose this alternative, they must create programs directed specifically towards rural women in order to enable women to make changes in their behavior. If successful, such programs would lead not only to improved nutrition, sanitation, and health, lower birth rate and more food, but also to an increase in the social status of women and in the likelihood of their participating in all national efforts.

Once one chooses to create programs directed specifically towards rural women, it is essential that one recognizes that such programs must be *suited* to rural women. That is, they must be based on the awareness that any single manifestation of rural women's behavior is part of their response to their total situation as they experience it. Programs that take a partial view - i.e., the view that specific forms of behavior are independent of the total culture and can be addressed independently - are not likely to succeed. This may seem to be a truism, not worth repeating. But if one looks at the design of most programs for rural women in nutrition, health, family planning, handicrafts, or whatever, one recognizes the necessity to keep repeating it.

In designing programs for women, one must recognize that women, like the rest of people, act out of self-interest. That is, they act in terms of needs they experience or perceive as priorities. For rural women in poor countries these needs are, not surprisingly, survival and security for themselves and their families. Women are seeking, to the best of their abilities in society *as it exists*, to satisfy these needs. Like rural men, rural women are calculating in pursuit of their goals and have little margin for risk. No one involved in development work questions these statements about rural men. They are equally true for rural women. However, those in development must recognize that the culture or socio-economic context experienced by rural women as a sex (varying with, but not negated by, class), as they pursue security and survival, is different from that of men.

In other words, programs directed towards rural women cannot accomplish their objectives unless they address the practices of rural women, recognizing what women want, what risks they cannot take, how these risks differ by class and status, and what their culture values. Nor, obviously, can they accomplish their objectives unless women directly participate in the direction the program will take.

The purpose of this study is to describe how change for village women has been *initiated* in one specific setting; the organizing principle of the study is "action" or the initiation of change. The setting is rural Bangladesh; the action project is the Women's Program of the Integrated Rural Development Program (IRDP) of Bangladesh. The authors have been involved in implementing this Women's Program. Tahrunnessa Abdullah has been Joint Director of IRDP in charge of the Women's Program since its inception in 1974. Sondra Zeidenstein was Advisor to the Women's Program from 1974-1976. From discussions with our counterparts in other projects and other countries, we believe that many of the issues arising out of the experience described in the study will have relevance to those concerned with initiating change for rural women in other countries.

The study is divided into two parts. The first section is a description of various aspects of the lives of rural women. Although these sections are presented sequentially, it would be erroneous to think that the information came first and the project second. Rather they are part of the same process: the need for information has been dictated by the initiation of change through the project.

Because it is required for the specialized work of initiating change - i.e. "action-oriented" - the information presented in Part One has a special character. It attempts to explain how rural women determine their priorities and to identify some of the pivotal issues which limit their options, but which can, at the same time, be addressed within the scope of a *project*, as opposed to a *policy*. Getting such information requires paying close attention, through interviews, observation, and discussion, to how rural women of varying backgrounds respond to certain issues or problems, since a woman's behavior or choice of action reflects the range of options she perceives in a situation. It also requires close attention to the subtle differences between normative behavior prescribed by the social ideology of the village and projected in certain situations, and the actual behavior of women which indicates the acceptable range of options

for manipulating those norms. With this approach one is able
to begin to get a sense of the socio-economic situation *as rural
women perceive it.* This perception is the primary concern of
this kind of action-oriented research, and needs to be understood as such, so that its particular emphasis will not be
misinterpreted or mistaken for other forms of research.

The second part is the detailed case study of the first few
years of a national program to integrate rural women in the
development process - apparently, one of the first such efforts.
The case study also has a special character, we feel, because
its focus is the *process* of translating program objectives into
action in rural areas through the medium of a national institution. This process is rarely described, with the result that
it is rarely understood or evaluated and supported in appropriate, constructive ways.

Unless the role of project work is correctly valued and
supported for what it *can* (and *cannot*) do, the process of
development becomes distorted. One way of viewing that process
is to see policy, which is an expression of ideology, both
giving direction to and learning from issue-oriented research
on the one hand and project work and action-oriented research
on the other. In this model, project work cannot take the place
of or go beyond ideology and policy, nor can it collect data to
meet the scientific standards of research. Nevertheless, it has
an essential and distinctive function in the total process since,
whatever the ideology and however fine the research, there can
be no change without those who know how to translate policy
into action. Projects *work directly* with rural people in
villages, and are guided by how rural people perceive their
situation and accommodate themselves to it in order to survive.
Because of this, project workers can help planners and policy-
makers understand, among other things, what approach is practicable and realistic in moving toward goals, what the critical
pivots for change are at different stages, how long it takes to
create new alternatives, given the rural situation and the
institution, as well as how expensive the process will be.

PART ONE

RURAL WOMEN OF BANGLADESH

CHAPTER I

INTRODUCTION

No matter how long-range the objectives of a rural project may be, one always starts with the first step, which is taken *from where one is* - i.e., the situation as rural people see it. Because almost no one else has been addressing this body of knowledge and because, in the case of rural women, there is little available information, the project has been both a focus for identifying information needs and an instrument for collecting it. The focus is operational; that is, information is valued for the light it throws on how to direct resources to women so that they are able to take advantage of them and so that the resources are used in ways consistent with national priorities. For example, some of the early project needs for information were: a comprehensive picture of the role of women in the household economy; a sense of the cultural and economic forces affecting women *as women*; and a sense of the range of choices a rural woman considers for improving her situation. Once the project had been under way for a year or two and women were joining co-operatives and applying for loans, other issues began to demand attention. Two of these were: the geographical and social extent of groups with whom women identify and to which they feel loyal; and the patterns of dependency, co-operation and exploitation that exist among women of different economic backgrounds. Thus the coming into existence of a project offering new resources for rural women has identified questions which need to be answered so that the project can move toward its objectives.

8

The project is also an instrument for collecting information.(1)
At the time it was taking shape (1973-74), the misinformation
about rural women was pervasive and persistent, but there was
very little data about the lives and work of such women with
which to counter it. The reasons for the extreme dearth of
information about rural women were, no doubt, complex, but they
probably included: a general reticence, based in history and
culture, to ask for and give information about women; a lack of
motivation for learning about rural women; and the lack of a
conceptual framework for looking at women as a separate culture
or sub-culture.

Yet, even when such motivation and conceptualization exist,
there are real difficulties in learning about rural women. In
a sexually segregated society, male researchers often cannot
gain direct access to women or to women in the absence of men.
When men answer for women or when women answer questions in the
presence of men, information that goes beyond basic facts may
be distorted to reflect the male picture of the female world.
Female researchers are themselves restricted by segregation
customs and often cannot stay in a village long enough to gain
the confidence of rural women or fully understand their situation.
Surveys and questionnaires which can be managed in short stays
often have limited value in creating a picture of the world of
rural women as they themselves see it. Foreign women researchers
have not been affected as much by segregation practices and have
had a somewhat easier time of it, but, to the extent that their
approach is dictated by foreign institutions, it may be somewhat
irrelevant or inaccessible to the project. And, of course, being
foreign, their view of another culture may be partial and their
hypotheses sometimes inaccurate.

There have been significant exceptions to these limitations in
the past, and the situation may improve in the future, but even
so, the project retains certain advantages in learning about
rural women for its own needs and in providing hypotheses for
other kinds of research. One advantage is the project's ability
to identify specifically the information it needs as problems
arise or as unexplained patterns seem to emerge. Another is the
presence of educated women staff members living in rural areas,
often in their own homes, and working over long periods of time
with rural women through a project that is providing them access

(1) See our "Finding Ways to Learn about Rural Women: Experience
of a Pilot Project in Bangladesh"

to new resources. These staff women have a greater potential
than almost anyone else for *understanding the context* in which
new information is being sought and is to be interpreted. And
a third is the involvement of the project (since it is a
catalyst for change) in a dynamic process that reveals or
focuses on aspects of rural behavior that are not obvious in a
more static situation. The information the project can provide
is often not highly technical or quantitative but it is usually
an adequate basis for action. When it is not, the project,
because of its continuing interaction with rural women, can
provide hypotheses for the more in-depth research that may be
required.

The description of rural women in Part One is, therefore, an
integral part of a continuing and evolving process. Details of
the description come from two sources. One is the group of
already available studies of rural women, limited in number and
scope, but not in value, which have largely been written in the
last few years. The other is the project-stimulated research
in the form of interviews, case studies, and discussions with
more than 200 rural women of varying ages, localities, and
economic conditions, conducted by staff of the project.(2) The
research followed a basic pattern. As points arose about
aspects of rural women's lives that were relevant to project
policy or about responses of co-operative members to project
guidelines, questions were developed and tested on a small
sampling of rural women, individually or in groups depending on
the nature of the issue. The answers to these initial questions
provided hypotheses which were then tested mainly through in-
depth interviews or group discussions with rural women from all
over Bangladesh and, where appropriate, of varied ages and
economic backgrounds. The opportunities for this stage of the
research were provided in a number of ways: in some cases,
questions were asked of rural women who came from different
parts of Bangladesh to Dacca or Comilla or some other location
for training; in others, field staff located throughout Bangladesh were asked to collect information from women of specific
backgrounds in villages where they were working; in others,
Headquarters staff, on their visits to projects around the
country, conducted interviews and group discussions. The women
who were questioned were not necessarily members of project
co-operatives, but access to rural women was generally

_____

(2) See Appendix A for some of the interview and case study
questions.

provided by the contacts and mobility of the project staff, and by the fact that they had been accepted by these women. It is from this project-oriented research and the long-term contact with rural women provided by projects that the framework for the details has emerged. We include the words of the respondents themselves when they are representative of a large number of responses because we think they come closer to conveying the perspective of rural women than our own restatement would.

The following pages provide a picture of the traditional situation of rural women, which we hope will not be mistaken for a static situation. The potential for change is latent and can only be revealed when the opportunities for change - i.e. new options - are introduced. That is the subject of Part Two. Although the description that follows is tentative in the sense of leaving gaps to be filled and generalizations to be quali-fied,(3) we believe that it has importance in providing the working hypotheses needed for guiding first steps.

(3) The absence of numbers is especially frustrating. The *project* is not in a position to collect new statistics, but it is in a position to claim that many of the existing ones - i.e. in relation to women's employment, productive labor, economic condition, and marital status - do not accurately reflect the rural situation.

CHAPTER II

BANGLADESH BACKGROUND

To understand the description of women's lives in rural Bangladesh and the project that has been evolved to help them enter
the mainstream of development, one must, of course, understand,
as much as possible, the situation of Bangladesh. This brief
introduction to Bangladesh cannot begin to convey the complexity
of its historical, political, economic, or even geographical
conditions, the variety of points of view through which these
conditions have been interpreted, or the process of change that
is affecting them. It is meant to suggest, rather than explain,
the country. Readers who want a better knowledge of Bangladesh
should turn to the books and articles that explore aspects of
the country in depth and, especially, to what is currently being
written by Bangladeshi social scientists(1).

Physical Setting

Bangladesh is a South Asian country of 55,598 square miles,
bounded by India, Burma and the Bay of Bengal. It is largely
made up of the delta of three great rivers and an immense system
of tributaries and distributaries. The condition of the delta

_____

(1) See especially articles and monographs from the Bangladesh
Institute of Development Studies, the Institute for Bangladesh
Studies at Rajshahi University, the Institute of Education
Research at Dacca University, the Comilla Academy for Rural
Development, Dacca University, and Chittagong University, as
well as the ILO publication.

varies in different parts of the country from active to moribund, with consequent effects on crops, settlement, and population. The land is, for the most part, plains, rising in only a few places to more than 50 feet above sea level. The climate is tropical monsoon. The winter months are relatively cool and dry with the temperature around 60°-80^oF. The rest of the year, the temperature is usually in the 80s and 90s and the humidity is in the 70s and 80s. The monsoon runs from June to October with rainfall varying, in different parts of the country, from 47" to 136"(2). During this season, about one-third of the country is under water.

Population

Bangladesh has a population of about 75 million people reflecting an increase of at least 20 million since 1960. The annual growth rate is 2.9%. This rapid increase in numbers without a corresponding increase in production is contributing to conditions of widespread poverty. The population is predominantly youthful with 57% of the people under 20 years. About 90% of the people live in rural areas. The rural literacy rate is 18.5% (with a breakdown of 25.7% for males and 10.9% for females)(3).

History

Bangladesh became an independent nation in 1971 after the Liberation War. Its history before that had included about 25 years as a province of Pakistan, about 200 years as part of the British Empire, and about 200 years as part of the Moghul Empire. This history has contributed to many features of present-day Bangladesh, including its one-crop agriculture, its large population, its rural character and its low level of modernization. The high degree of seclusion among Bangladeshi women, rare among rural populations in Asia regardless of religion, is popularly thought to be the result of attempts to protect them from foreign rulers. Since the Liberation, efforts to develop national policy have had to face the destruction of physical resources as well as the dislocation of international markets caused by the War, internal political unrest, inflation, flood and famine.

(2) *Statistical Yearbook of Bangladesh*, 1975
(3) Alamgir, S., 1977

Religion

The predominant religion of Bangladesh is Islam, comprising
about 85% of the population; Hindus comprise about 13%,
Buddhists 0.61% and Christians 0.31%.(4) In this study,
emphasis will be on the culture of Moslem women.

National Economy

The economy is largely *agricultural*, with 55% of the GDP coming
from agriculture and involving 75% of the labor force. Another
10% of the GDP is made up of transportation and marketing of
agricultural products. About 9% comes from industry of all
sizes, with 6% of that from large-scale industry. Half the
value added in manufacturing industries comes from processing
domestically produced agricultural goods.(5)

The major crop grown in Bangladesh is rice. It is grown on
about 80% of cropped acreage.(6) Although an exact figure is
not known, many sources suggest that a large percentage of rice,
perhaps as much as 70% or 80%, is consumed by its producers.
Probably it is more accurate to say that this much remains very
close to the area where it was produced. The rest enters the
larger commercial market. Bangladesh has not been self-
sufficient in rice for many years and currently imports large
quantities of food grains.(7) Jute is the main cash crop of
Bangladesh and accounts for about 8% of total cropped acreage.
Other cash crops include sugar-cane and oil-seed.

Although landholdings vary in size, plots which make up landholdings are for the most part fragmented, often about one-tenth
to one-fifth of an acre in size. A small percentage (16%) of
cropped acreage is farmed with modern inputs such as high-
yielding variety rice, chemical fertilizer, insecticide and
mechanized irrigation.(8) The rest is basically rain-fed and is
farmed by traditional patterns of cultivation, using either
manual or bullock power and implements such as plough, yoke and
harrow. Labor requirements are intensive, but seasonal. The

---

(4) *Statistical Yearbook of Bangladesh*, 1975
(5) Khan, A.R., 1972
(6) Ahsan and Haque, 1975
(7) Statistical Pocket Book of Bangladesh
(8) Ahsan and Haque, 1975

14

average cropping intensity in 1975-76 was 149 per cent.(9)

With regard to landholding patterns the figures vary, but
suggest the following picture. There are about 7 million farms.
A quarter of these are of one acre or less.(10) More than 50%
are of two and a half acres or less.(11) A quarter are over
four acres.(12) Many farmers lease in land and sharecrop it.
In 1968, it was estimated that about 32% of farm households were
involved in some form of tenancy. According to Alamgir, new
data indicates that the percentage is "far greater" than that.(13)
Most sharecropping arrangements give 50% of the yield to the
cultivator.

For the most part, families cannot feed themselves from the land
if they farm less than one acre. They must find other sources
of income for food as well as other necessities. Families who
farm two and a half acres may, depending on cropping intensity
and kind of seed, be able to feed themselves from the land and,
in some situations, have a surplus. Usually, however, they also
depend on other sources of income besides land for some of their
needs.(14) The number of rural families that are landless, i.e.
that have no more than, at best, a homestead, is not precisely
known but some individual village studies give figures ranging
from 16% to 44%.(15) It is suggested by most sources that the
number of landless is steadily increasing.

Cultivating one's own land provides for the needs of relatively
few farm families. Depending on need, opportunity and status
aspirations, rural people work at a variety of occupations.
Probably those who can afford to do so educate their children
to be qualified for occupations and professions that anchor
them in the non-rural, money-based economy. The poorest are
laborers in agriculture and other available laboring jobs.

(9) Statistical Pocket Book of Bangladesh, 1978.
(10) Faaland and Parkinson, 1976.
(11) Pakistan Master Survey of Agriculture, 1968.
(12) Faaland and Parkinson, 1976.
(13) Alamgir, S., 1977.
(14) Judging productive capacity by how much land a family owns
can sometimes be misleading because land in some parts of Bangladesh is much less productive than in other parts.
(15) See especially: Qadir, S.A., 1960; Khan, A.A., 1968; Huq, N.,
1973; Adnan, S. et al., 1975, 76, 77; Cain, M., 1976.

About 16% of the rural population are landless laborers.(16)
Other rural employed include: physical laborers such as boatmen,
cart-drivers, earth-cutters and brick-layers; fishermen; workers
in family industries like potters, weavers and oil-pressers;
petty traders in various commodities; artisans like goldsmiths
and blacksmiths; those in "professions" like barbers or tailors;
hakims(17), fakirs and homeopathic doctors; school teachers;
religious men; and government workers. At all levels there are
not enough jobs to meet the needs of all those who must depend
on income from sources other than land.

Although rural people engage in many occupations besides farming,
land is still the secure base they seek. There are always enough
scattered examples of people with little or no land working their
way up to positions of importance and acquiring land to provide
models for their aspirations. Recently, families with members
in Government service who are able to direct resources to their
village and thereby gain in influence in the village have
provided examples of upward mobility. Downward mobility is much
more common. In many cases credit is the mechanism, and is a
major part of the rural scene. All classes - except the poorest
- borrow and much of the borrowing is from money lenders who
exact high interest in kind or hold land in mortgage, or from
relatives. Small farmers may sell their crops from the fields
to pay money lenders. In marginal situations, if the crops are
bad, for example, they may lose their land.

The Household as an Economic Unit

The household economy has been studied even less than the rural
economy. Lack of information about the household as an economic
unit creates a major gap in understanding the behavior of rural
people in response to *their perception* of their social and
economic situation. In our study of rural women, we make the
following assumptions about the rural household economy in
Bangladesh which we think warrant further study and testing:
that the family is experienced as a basic economic unit on which
its members depend for economic survival and advancement; that
it is the institution through which rural people seek to satisfy
their basic needs; that its resources are human as well as
material; that the family deploys its members, female, male,

---

(16) Salimullah and Islam, 1976.
(17) Indigenous medical practitioners.

child and elderly, for maximum socio-economic advantage; and, that how it deploys its members depends on *its resource base*, including the number and status of its members, the available opportunities, and the social ideology of the village, which is sustained by those of power and influence. The following examples of variations in the ways rural families deploy their sons illustrate one range of possibilities: in some families, sons will begin working as laborers for food or wages at an early age; in other families, sons will work on the family's land from an early age and will receive little or no education; in others, sons will get a level of primary or secondary education that enables them to qualify for a low-level job in the monetary sector; finally, in others, sons will get education to a much higher level to compete for prestigious jobs beyond the rural area. In each case, the son is being deployed to serve the needs of the family as perceived by the family, but the specific course he pursues is determined by the socio-economic factors referred to above. The same holds true for each other member of the family.(18)

With regard to food, to the extent that there is a resource base for doing so, members of a rural household are deployed to contribute to the production and processing of food. Men and children perform the work that takes place outside the homestead, and women the work that can be done inside or close by. If there is no resource base for subsistence production, family members are of necessity deployed to "earn" food, in cash or kind.

The Village

Although the village is by no means self-contained or self-sufficient, it is the base of rural life. The area that rural people identify as their village or *gram* may be different from the area officially defined as village for census or revenue purposes. It is the villager's concept of the *gram* that we will sketch in very general terms.

A typical village is approached by a narrow dirt path raised a little from rice fields or ponds on either side, and protected from erosion by hedges. From the main path, subpaths lead off

---

(18) See Mead Cain's work for detailed examination of the deployment of children in rural Bangladesh and variations depending on the socio-economic conditions of the family (1977a).

to neighborhoods or *paras*, which are made up of groups of home-
steads or *baris*. The whole *para* is often hidden by vegetation
from the surrounding fields, water or other open space. The
para, more than the village, is likely to be the group of people
a villager feels identified with.

The *baris* are made up of a number of *ghors* or huts around a
courtyard which may be square or rectangular. Each *bari* may be
sheltered by vegetation or its entrance screened in some way to
give shelter to those in the courtyard. The *ghors* are made of
a variety of local materials depending on the area. Commonly,
they have a floor of cow dung and mud, walls of mud, woven
bamboo or leaves woven with wood, and roofs of woven bamboo,
thatch or, less often, tin. They are usually small shelters
with floors raised a little above the courtyard, and divided by
a screen or wall into two rooms or spaces, one for sleeping and
the other for cooking and storage, or sometimes for housing a
dependent relative; in winter the cooking is done outside.
There is usually one doorway and no windows. Ventilation is
through the thatch or, if the shelter is constructed of solid
material, space is left between the walls and roof for air to
circulate. Furnishings commonly include bedding, storage containers, and a clay oven or *chula*.

The courtyard has a surface of cow dung and mud. If the family
has a cow, there is likely to be a shed near the house. There
may be small patches of arable land accessible to the *bari* without exposure to the outside world. There will probably be a
pond, well or river that all women of the *para* have access to by
sheltered paths. Except during the winter women usually do not
have to travel far for water.

Often the people living in the same *para* are related to each
other through the men. They may, through varying fortunes, be
of different classes, as defined by landholdings. Sometimes
most of the people in a *para* have the same basic occupation, in
agriculture, or as fishermen, weavers or potters. Although there
is a variation in size among *paras*, *baris* and *ghors*, a typical
para may include 100-200 people in five or six *baris*. Each *bari*
may have 20-30 people in four to six *ghors* or households. Each
household may have five or six members.

Within the *para*, then, are basically a number of *baris* concealed
by vegetation and interconnected by fairly sheltered by-paths.
Outside the *para* but within the village are the fields. Some
villages include a mosque and a primary school. There is almost

always an open space for communal prayer. At the entrance to
some villages there may be a post office or shop. If the village
meets a road, there may be a market or shops at the junction.
Within the *para* there may or may not be a shop or *dhokan*.
Usually pedlars or *bepari* bring wares to the *para*. Beyond the
village are bi-weekly or weekly markets where men gather to trade
and discuss prices, politics and news.

Transport and communication differ for men and women. Men move
freely by foot or boat across open spaces outside the *para*.
Women move within the courtyard or inner courtyard or the *bari*
with freedom, and in many cases can visit from one *bari* to
another within the *para* moving along the sheltered by-paths.
They can do this more easily when men are in the fields, or at
night. During monsoon, however, in flooded areas, *baris* are cut
off from each other by water and women are further isolated.
Women cannot move easily outside the *para*. Therefore they
usually have *direct* access only to those resources that are within the neighborhood. For what is in the village but outside the
para, they may need the services of a child, an older woman or
a male servant. To reach beyond the village they usually depend
on boys or men. Men can have access to news and information
wherever it is disseminated or wherever they gather, for example,
at the market or mosque. Women hear news from men, from each
other, from relatives who are visiting or from pedlars. They
usually have detailed knowledge of what is of interest to them
in their village and nearby villages.

The "Bari"

The residents of a *bari*, divided into households living in
separate *ghors*, are members of a patrilineal family at varying
stages of the family life cycle. Potentially it includes a
father, a mother, sons and their wives and children, daughters
until they marry or return home and, occasionally, servants.
In most families, sons separate their "kitchens" or economic
identity from their fathers' within a few years after marriage,
though they continue to reside in the *bari* and contribute to
family units, strength and financial support. In a smaller
number of cases, usually among those with more than average
resources, the family remains "joint" as long as the father is
alive, with sons contributing their income to the father who

manages the family resources.(19) Whether the *bari* is joint or
the households have separate kitchens, the women of the *bari*
share the same courtyard.

Lines of authority within the family vary considerably with
class, age, and individual circumstances, but still certain
general patterns may be observed. The father makes the major
decisions about family affairs (including education and
marriage), land use, and important expenditures, though he will
usually consult with certain people before reaching these
decisions. If the father is old and not contributing to the
household, the oldest son may consult with the father, but make
the decisions himself. The woman's sphere of activities is
controlled by the mother, though when her husband dies she loses
power. She distributes resources and sets tasks for the other
women and children. To a great extent, male and female spheres
of activity are separate. Men may not know what food there is
in the house, how much there is, or where. Nor are they likely
to know how to carry out the agricultural activities which are
typically women's work. Women try not to "bother" men, who have
access to the outside world, except when necessary. The father
controls the women's world through his wife and she represents
the women when communicating with the father, though sometimes
a daughter or daughter-in-law may actually be more influential
with him.

As much as possible, families resolve their own conflicts. In
important matters they depend on each other and rarely act without consultation with each other as well as with influential
members of the village. Conflicts within the village may be
resolved by the decision of a council of leading men in the
village. This is considered preferable to going beyond the
village for help in maintaining order.

Administration

Since most services and modern resources are channelled to
rural people through the Government, it is important, in order
to understand to what services or resources *rural women have
access*, to look at the administrative structure. Bangladesh is
administered centrally from Ministries through 19 Districts,
which are divided into Subdivisions, which are, in turn, divided

---

(19) In Ellickson's study (1972), 17% of the households were
joint, while in Bertocci's study (1972), 30% were joint.

into *Thanas*. The *Thana* is the important administrative unit
for extending Government services to the villages. Extension
agents of many Ministries and Departments have offices at the
Thana, usually in the same complex or *Thana* Center. The number
of *Thanas* in a District varies from nine to 42. Each *Thana* is
responsible for reaching about 170 villages (or 170,000 people)
which may be as far distant as ten miles from the *Thana* Center.

Thanas are subdivided into about ten Unions. Some Ministries
have employees at the Union level also and there are plans to
extend health and family planning clinics to the Union, with
workers making visits to the villages. However, at present the
Government services for rural people including medical facilities,
family planning clinics and poultry or horticulture farms, have
not reached significantly closer than the *Thana*, and if one
considers only those with full staff, services and supplies, in
many cases not even that close.

CHAPTER III

THE WORK OF WOMEN

The work of rural women is an integral part of the rural economy,
which means, since Bangladesh is predominantly rural, an important part of the national economy. It relates mostly to food
production, household manufacture, household maintenance and
child-raising; i.e. the production and maintenance of labor. It
has to do mainly, but not exclusively, with non-monetary production of goods and services for family use - the subsistence
sector of the economy. Women's work also has a range of connections with the local market economy as it redistributes production among local consumers, and with more distant markets.

Rural women work under several constraints. Firstly, there is
a sexual division of labor, which is interpreted with varying
degrees of strictness depending on social class, family size and
composition that makes the burden of women's work, including as
it does agricultural and domestic tasks, especially heavy. Women,
according to the findings of the study *The Hard Working Poor* by
A. Farouk and M. Ali, work longer hours at productive work than
do men. They carry out their work using traditional, time
consuming technology. Secondly, women work under the restraint
of *purdah* which means that for the most part they feel compelled

---

(1) Rural women, according to this study, work at least 12 hours
a day. At harvest times their normal work load increases considerably. On a daily basis, women work fairly constantly,
though at varying paces, from 4.30 or 5.30 a.m. to 8 or 9 p.m.,
with a period of slackness after the noon meal.

to stay within the boundaries of their *bari* and a few adjoining *baris*, if they are interconnected, to avoid being seen by men who are not in the family, as defined by local criteria. Unless driven by necessity, rural women are not usually seen in the fields or on public roads. This segregation from men often involves isolation from women outside the immediate area and from direct access to most services.

The following description of rural women's work does not examine regional variations which, though Bangladesh is small and relatively homogeneous, count for a lot in terms of social and economic responses to ecology, and therefore influence the kind and amount of work women do. There are, for example, important ecological variations between northern and eastern parts of Bangladesh which determine how many and which kinds of rice crops are grown and what other crops are customary. Regional variations in land-holding patterns and variations in use of high yielding variety rice influence the intensity with which land is cultivated. Intra-regional variations, like degree of access to town or urban centers, also influence women's work.

This description does not exclude the situations in which women, who are confined by *purdah*, delegate work to sons and daughters, servants, or, in very small nuclear families, husbands. When we describe "women's" work, we do not mean that it is done exclusively by adult women, but rather that this work is typically and traditionally the *responsibility* of women. They know what is to be done and how it should be done. If they do not do it themselves, because it involves leaving the *bari* or, in fewer cases, because they can call on male servants to do it, they supervise the work, set the standards for its performance, and evaluate it.

Our information is not exhaustive. We are leaving out a lot of detail because it seems irrelevant to the purpose of this study. But, at the same time, there is a lot that we do not yet know which would make this picture of women's work more accurate and true to life. We hope new information will be forthcoming from a variety of sources, including, of course, the project. Some, we know, might say there is too much detail in the following description of women's work, that it is too long and tedious. But, even at that risk, we feel that it is necessary to include as much information as we do. We have heard for years, from every source imaginable, that rural women do "nothing", or we have heard "nothing" expanded generously to "the work of the house". We know from the experience of Bangladesh and other countries the harmful effect that lack of knowledge on the part

of policy makers about the work of rural women is likely to
produce on rural women, and especially, but not merely, on
poorer women.

Several issues are involved. One is the widespread ignorance
about the *kind* of work farm women do. We think that the collection, in one place, of this much detail about the work they
do should help planners and program implementors at all levels,
as well as donors, to learn about the aspects of household and
rural economy that women are in charge of. Such information not
only establishes the fact of women's integration in the household and rural economy, but it indicates why they must be included in rural development efforts to increase production and
provide equitable distribution. At a very practical level, it
indicates which rural extension services must be directed to
women in order to be effective in increasing food production.

A second important issue is the lack of knowledge about the *way*
women do their work - what are their methods, their technology,
their level of knowledge. The failure to recognize that the
very poor women depend on certain labor intensive techniques to
earn food has led to their increasing displacement by machines.
Knowing *how* rural women are doing their work might enable
modernization to take place by building on what rural women already know, rather than by taking away work from poor women and
undermining the value of all women by shifting to mechanization
under male control. Rural development that builds on the existing involvement of rural women in production will be much more
conducive to equitable distribution than the more conventional
development practice of removing women from production, because
it can provide opportunities for poorer women to remain in
agricultural work, and, rather than become destitute, to continue to have opportunities as this sector becomes modernized.
It will also be much more conducive to efficiency. In working
with *male* farmers, policy usually involves trying to improve
production by building on the system used by these farmers. If
theory or research concerning new technology has not accounted
for the constraints that farmers face, their attempts to use
more modern methods quickly identify the constraints which can
then be addressed. It is inconceivable that *anyone other than
farmers* would be able to reveal the problems in new technologies, on the basis of which changes can be made. We think the
same policy is relevant for women farmers. In this regard,
information about *how* women work provides a basis for appropriate research on modernization.

Among those for whom this section is intended, because he seems
representative of so many people, foreign and Bengali, is the
young educated man from rural Bangladesh who, when asked in a
written assignment to describe the work of village women, wrote
"they serve their husbands, take care of the children and animals,
and do a little of this and that around the house."

Rice Production

All of Bangladesh's rice production is consumed in Bangladesh.
As already mentioned, it is generally estimated that 60% to 80%
of rice is produced for home consumption. The rest is sent to
market, by surplus farmers for profit, by poor farmers who need
cash more urgently than rice and by farmers who "trade" it to
supply their other needs. If possible, farmers keep aside what
is needed for the family and sell only if there is excess.
Although rural women traditionally do not go to the fields where
rice is growing,(2) they play key roles in certain aspects of
rice production whether as homeworkers or laborers.

Seed Germination: It is the responsibility of rural women to
test the seed, which they have stored, for germination quality
before men take it to the fields to sow. Women have described
the following steps to us. Several days before it is time to
sow, they take several samples of each variety of seed that is
needed from the storage containers where they have distributed
them (so that if one container suffers severe spoilage the whole
amount of that variety will not have been lost), soak them for a
while and then spread them on straw to see which sample is
germinating the best - if one sample indicates severe spoilage
as far as seed use is concerned, then the whole container is
converted to food use. From the containers that produce good
germination, women take the amount of the kind of seed required
for each plot and prepare it for sowing, again by soaking for
the requisite amount of time (which varies according to seed
variety), straining the water and spreading the seeds on layers
of straw or banana leaves for from 24 to 36 hours until the
seeds split and are ready to be sown. If the weather is
inappropriate when the seeds are at this stage, they have to be
dried and the process repeated. The skill and judgment of women
in this phase of rice cultivation contribute to the germination
rate of seeds in the field.

_____

(2) In recent years, there have been instances of poor women
doing field work, but this is still the exception rather than
the rule.

Field Work: Most rural women have little to do directly with the field procedures of rice cultivation: land preparation, planting and transplanting, irrigating and spraying for high-yielding variety rice, cultivating, and harvesting. Still, though they do not go to the fields and in many cases will never have seen the family land (their husbands' family), their knowledge of rice growing is likely to be quite extensive and they are often in a position as widows to supervise laborers and/or to advise their grown sons on proper management of the land.

Within the *bari*, the rural woman contributes to the field work in at least two ways. Firstly, she cooks for the laborers who are hired by many farmers, or for the neighbors with whom her household is exchanging labor in order to do the concentrated field work of rice cultivation. It is her job to feed these laborers two or three meals a day. Since the laborers' day starts unusually early and the preparation of a meal (not counting husking and grinding which are the heavy, time-consuming parts of food preparation) takes about two hours, this form of payment for laborers is made up of the heavy work of women. Most women regard it in this light.

The second contribution to the field work has to do with the year round responsibility of many women for the feeding and health of the bullocks which are among the most valuable assets a farmer has. Such a woman's daily responsibilities involve feeding the bullocks properly three times a day, cleaning the sheds where they sleep (and storing the manure for fuel or fertilizer), seeing that they are bathed daily and securing them properly for the night. She must be on constant watch for signs of ill-health and respond to them with traditional or modern remedies depending usually on the cost, availability, and history of her success with either approach. All the heavy work with the animals and the work that involves taking them out of the compound will be done when possible by sons or hired help, but nevertheless the responsibility for the care of the bullocks is hers. She may have a say in which animals are purchased (her husband or son brings them home to show her), since they have to be manageable enough for her to work with them.

Rice Processing: What follows is a description of a day in the life of a farm wife during the harvest of the *boro* rice crop - that is, not the main rice crop. In the family are her husband, her mother-in-law, two sons, one daughter, and a servant. Although she is from the minority of rural families that can feed themselves from their land, this description is fairly typical

of the kind of work women do at harvest, the conditions under
which they work, the expertise and management skills they
exercise, and the care they take to avoid waste:(3)

Shamila wakes up before daybreak. She looks at the sky to
see if it is cloudy, takes the broom from beside the door
and sweeps the courtyard. She goes to the stack of paddy
brought in last night from the field, unbinds some stalks
and spreads them in the courtyard to dry, working alone
because her mother-in-law is too old to help her. She
spreads the paddy and arranges it on the ground for threshing, afterwards shaking out the bits and pieces that have
clung to her sari. Her servant brings the cows from the
cowshed and yokes them together to do the threshing.

Shamila goes to the cooking room, collects the ashes from
the oven into a broken basket and, with a little ash and
mud, plasters the outside of the pot that is used to parboil
paddy, putting the pot in the oven. She fetches dry cakes
of dung, husks, and jute sticks from her store in the cooking room and puts them near the oven. She brings grain that
has already been threshed and cleaned, puts some straw at
the bottom of the pot, fills it with water and adds the
grains. After starting a fire to heat the oven, she cleans
the dirty utensils and plates from last night's meal, picks
up the water pitcher and an old basket and goes out to clean
the cowshed. She gathers the fresh dung, throws it outside
the shed and spreads it to dry. Then taking the pitcher to
the pond, with her muddy hands, she scours it, rinses it in
the pond and fills it with water.

When her mother-in-law wakes, Shamila lets the chickens out
of their enclosure and brings out the goat and calf, tying
the calf and the goat to a tree near the pond. She returns
and serves her husband and children last night's rice cold.
Meanwhile, she removes the parboiled grains from the pot,
empties them on to a torn mat in the courtyard and puts a
fresh supply of paddy in the pot, adding jute sticks to the
fire. When her husband finishes eating, she serves her

---

(3) This description is taken from that recorded by Saleha
Khatun, a staff member of the project, on May 19, 1977. It is
included in "*Bari*-Based Post Harvest Operations and Livestock
Care: Some Observations and Case Studies", Ford Foundation,
Dacca, December, 1977.

mother-in-law and, taking a plate of food for herself, she
goes and sits near the oven. She puts her child at her
breast, tends the fire and eats. Still carrying the baby,
she takes several baskets of paddy to the *dheki* (husking
paddle) and pushes the pedal, while her mother-in-law
alternately stirs the grain in the *dheki* and winnows what
has been husked. Once in a while, Shamila stops husking,
goes to the threshing floor to turn the stalks over or to
the oven to remove the parboiled grains, put in a fresh
batch and rebuild the fire.

When it is time to cook the afternoon meal Shamila has her
mother-in-law do it since she cannot spare the time. She
measures out the rice and pulses needed for the meal, washes
them and gives them to her mother-in-law to cook. Her
mother-in-law sits by the oven, tending the fire and stirring
the meal as it cooks. The stalks have been threshed by now
so Shamila gathers the straw and stacks it, then collects
the grains in a basket and takes them to another part of the
courtyard to winnow. She cleans the courtyard of the
remaining grains and puts them in a basket. Now that the
sun is strong, she spreads the boiled grains in the courtyard and takes the straw and spreads it to dry in the outer
courtyard.

After she has finished cooking, her mother-in-law puts out
the fire and goes to the courtyard to chase away the
chickens from the drying grains. Sitting there she cleans
the jute leaves for the evening meal and shakes a bamboo
at the chickens when necessary. Meanwhile, Shamila goes
to the oven and puts the food in a bowl, from which she
serves the children. She winnows the threshed grains,
spreading the just winnowed grains for further drying and,
from time to time, turns over the parboiled grains that are
drying in the courtyard. Then, she picks up a broom and
pitcher, goes to turn the straw that is drying in the outer
courtyard and continues to clean the cowshed. She takes
the pitcher to the pond, fills and takes it back to the cow's
food bowl. Returning to the pond, she dips herself two or
three times, fills the pitcher and carries it home. After
changing her wet clothes, she washes her small son and
reminds her mother-in-law to go and bathe. With her son on
her hip, she checks the drying grains by testing a few grains
in her teeth and turns them to dry further. Peering beyond
the courtyard, she sees that her husband and the laborers
are bringing fresh paddy and makes room for it in the court-

yard. She sets out the mixture of rice and pulses and the
pitcher of water for their meal. Once again she turns the
straw.

The sun is no longer overhead. Shamila quickly takes her
meal with her mother-in-law and then, with a hoe, collects
both the dried parboiled grains which she puts in a basket
and the threshed, winnowed grains which she puts in a sack.
She sweeps the courtyard and goes to stack the straw and
sweep the outer courtyard. It is nearly cooking time again.
She puts rice on to boil, goes out to pluck eggplant and
green chili from the vegetable plot and puts them in the
oven to bake. She mixes and washes two kinds of pulses and
puts them on to cook, and prepares the green leafy vegetable.
She takes the water that the pulses were washed in to feed
the cows. Her child, meanwhile, is crawling around after
her and crying, but she does not have time to pick him up
and her mother-in-law is too old to carry him. Her mother-
in-law brings the goat from near the pond and closes the
chicken house after the chickens. Shamila finishes cooking
and sets out the food. She washes her son, picks him up and
suckles him while she is walking about and supervising the
others. Her mother-in-law lights the kerosene light and
puts it in the room. Shamila goes and lulls her drowsy
child to sleep.

The laborers return with the harvest and stack it in a
corner. Her husband tells her to feed the laborers, and she
serves them rice, lentils, eggplant, and greens. They eat
on the verandah. Shamila feeds the other children. When
everyone has eaten she and her mother-in-law sit and eat.
By now it is ten o'clock. She puts the cow and goat in the
cowshed, takes some *pan* and lies down to rest.

As the preceding description illustrates, the most concentrated
and busiest work for women in rice production occurs when the
rice is harvested and brought into the *bari*. The steps involved
in converting paddy to edible rice include: preparing the courtyard with a fresh layer of mud and cow dung so that sand and
dirt will not get into the rice; threshing to separate the rice
from the stalks (the role of women in this process varies); drying the straw for cattle food; winnowing and sieving several
times; parboiling, and, usually, steeping; drying; husking twice
after parboiling and once before eating (unless it is sent to a

mill(4) which eliminates the need for husking in the *bari*);
supervision of storage; and periodic redrying. The seed stock,
chosen by men, requires special processing, especially as regards
drying, and special storage procedures.

At every step of the process, women have to make decisions that
will affect the quality and quantity of rice and seed processed
from the paddy. Speed is an important factor. Storage capacity
has to be considered and the weather to be taken into account.
How much is to be stored at what stage of the processing has to
be decided both as a matter of spoilage deterrent and food
management. For example, rice that has been parboiled stores
better than rice that has not. Proper sun drying before storage
or husking is a critical factor in maximizing yield. If grains
are not dried properly, they will break in the mill or in husking
and spoil in the storage containers. Factors affecting decisions
about drying include the size of courtyard, the amount of rice
to be dried and variations in the weather. Generally women
spread the grains in the courtyard or, in some areas, on paved
roads and turn them periodically with their feet to ensure all-
round drying. Grains must be watched constantly to prevent loss
to animals and birds. Women say grains are dried properly when
a grain cracks noisily between the teeth. They say that younger
women who are not sure if it is properly dried will give it to
older more experienced women to test. Sometimes these older
women will say that it needs one more "sun" (day) or that it
needs to be taken inside and allowed to "rest" for a day or two
until it cools.(5)

---

(4) Rice husking mills exist but are not yet in widespread use
in Bangladesh. The advantages of these mills for some families
are that they save time, hard labor and the cost of laborers.
Still, women say that these mills break more rice than the *dheki*,
that there is less red (an indication of nutritional content) in
milled rice, and that it does not taste as good as home-husked
rice. An outstanding disadvantage is that they take away the
main source of employment for poor rural women.
(5) At a leading research institute in India, food scientists
who are looking for ways to process rice commercially with
minimal losses told us that drying rice is a sensitive process
because if it is not done correctly, the rice will crack at later
stages of processing. They said that they are trying to understand how drying takes place in the household so they can
replicate it.

Parboiling can also affect the amount of yield. Women have to decide whether grains should be soaked before parboiling and, if so, for how long. If they soak too long, they will sprout and the rice will be broken. Women can tell by the smell of rice, by how much it rises and how it splits, whether the parboiling is complete. Improper drying and parboiling can mean a loss in broken rice, say some women, of 10-20 pounds per 80 pounds of paddy. Proper drying and parboiling, they say, should keep the loss to two to three pounds, with an additional two pounds lost if the rice is husked in the mill rather than at home. Periodic redrying of stored grain throughout the year is necessary to prevent spoilage from dampness. Women are also in charge of this procedure.

As indicated earlier, seed requires separate, special processing. It must be processed immediately. Extra care must be taken in threshing. Seed requires longer drying time to retard spoilage and insect infestation. It requires specially prepared sealed containers to keep out moisture. Women prepare these containers - usually baskets - by coating them inside and out with a mixture of cow dung and mud. Cow dung is necessary, they say, to prevent the coating from splitting and giving access to rats. The seed is put into the containers and covered with straw, a small earthen pot or half a coconut shell. Then the mixture of cow dung is used to seal the top. Earthen jars, sacks and drums are also used. Women try to place these containers in spots least likely to attract rats, but they agree it is hard to avoid loss to rats.

In storage, rice and seed are the womens' province. They watch over them to prevent loss from dampness, insects, and rats, though they have limited means beyond human labor to help them. If there is a margin, they determine how much is needed for the family (and therefore how much can be sold), when it is to be husked or milled, how much is to be used for dishes that require special preparations of husking and grinding, how much is to be cooked each day, and how much each person gets. If there is no margin of excess, they are in charge of making it stretch and using it for as many ends as possible. Women manage rice for social and economic purposes and their decisions as to how to use it involve many variables.(6)

---

(6) An understanding of how women distribute rice informally in their *para* or *gram* might explain what happens to grain that might seem to be "lost" in storage.

Thus in relation to rice, the main crop in Bangladesh, women's skill and labor contribute to how well seed is likely to germinate, how much rice can be realised from processing paddy, how much seed and rice will survive storage, how much value is added to paddy whether for home consumption or marketing, and how the by-products will be put to use. If these factors of total rice production were measured, the percentage of rice that women are responsible for "producing", would be seen to be quite significant.(7)

We have not been able to investigate the involvement of women in wheat production which accounts for only a small percentage of crop acreage. Their traditional procedures for storage of food and seed grain should be of special interest as the Government pursues its plan to encourage the cultivation of more wheat.

Other Foods: Rice is the mainstay of the diet of rural Bengalis. But they also eat fish, meat, fruit, vegetables, lentils, poultry, eggs, spices, and milk. Women are responsible for varying amounts of labor involved in the production of all of these foods.

There are about 20 million fowl and 4 million ducks in Bangladesh of which 95% are indigenous.(8) Women are in charge of all these poultry. Most households have only a few chickens. Taking care of them involves letting them out in the morning and shutting them in at night, feeding them in the morning and at noon with broken rice and, perhaps, rice water (with bran if available), protecting vegetable gardens and other crops from their incursions, keeping them from causing damage to neighbors' property, protecting them from theft or ill-health, breeding them, providing places for the eggs to hatch, and collecting the eggs.

---

(7) At present, only a small percentage of rice acreage is under high-yielding-variety production. As Martius indicates, such production affects the work of women in a number of ways because there is an increase in the amount of paddy that comes into the compound and this paddy requires extra work at a number of steps of processing. Increased HYV production may bring with it more mills, threshers and commercial drying and storage facilities which will reduce the amount of heavy work women have to do but will take away work from thousands of women who depend on it for survival. Attention must be paid to finding alternative work for these women (Martius, 1975).
(8) Ahmed, Nafis, 1968.

Raising chickens involves *almost no expenditure*. They provide
either protein for the family in the form of eggs or, more
rarely, meat, or small amounts of cash, either on a regular basis
or to meet small emergencies. Few households have ducks, since
they eat more, including fish, make the compound dirty, require
access to ponds, and have to be led to water so they do not eat
rice growing in fields along the way.

Some women raise goats. They keep them in sheds with the cows
and bullocks, if there are any, or in the house. They take or
send them out to be grazed each day or collect leaves and other
food for them when grazing is thin. Since the feeding of goats
involves leaving the compound, women need someone else to help
them if it is important for them to maintain strict *purdah*.
They watch their health and keep track of their whereabouts, so
that they do not eat others' rice crops. Goats may be eaten on
special occasions by the family if such luxury can be afforded,
or they are sold for cash to meet needs perceived to be more
basic. Goat's milk is also a valued food. Although women do
not bring in fish, if the household acquires more than is necessary for present need, they preserve the excess for use at
another time by cutting off their heads, gutting them and drying
them in the sun. This kind of dried fish *(sutki)* is very well
liked.

The provision of milk is also the responsibility of women. They
take care that cows are let out in the morning and tied up at
night. They see to their food and make sure that they graze
properly, and are bathed and kept healthy. They milk them or
see that they are milked. Milk is usually provided first for
the family - or certain members of the family - and the surplus
is a source of small income. Although women do not usually have
much to do with the growing of lentils, an acreage crop, they
are in charge of processing and storing them and preserving the
seed. Again, women raise many of the vegetables and spices that
the family eats. They cultivate homestead land, using small
patches of land economically, prepare the soil, plant the seeds,
see to the watering, treat plants for insects,(9) pick ripe
vegetables, leave selected ones for seed stock and preserve the

---

(9) This usually involves sprinkling them with the ashes
cleaned from the stove each morning.

seed. Again almost no expenditure is involved.(10) Women may sell some for other needs, or because there is a surplus. They will process what can be preserved for another season.

Some fruit trees are planted by women and they usually decide what kinds should be planted and where. They raise them and manage the use of fruit. For example, if a storm knocks down unripe fruit they process it so that it can be used later in cooking. Or if the fruit is ripe and plentiful and there is a glut on the market, they process it for later use, by drying it or pickling it. If there are date trees, they process the syrup for home consumption or sale.

Women are responsible for food in storage, especially for re-drying it periodically to keep it from spoiling. They are also responsible for the use of the by-products that are created by their work. For example, ashes from the stove are used for washing, as an insecticide, and as a fertilizer. Cow dung, husks, and jute sticks are used for fuel. Husks may be traded to potters for pots. Straw and fruit and vegetable peelings are fed to cows. Bran is fed to poultry and cows or sold. Banana leaves are used as temporary covers for rice. The water that rice and pulses are washed in is fed to cattle or used to water plants. Summing up, the woman's labor, judgment and management provide for all the food, except rice, that the family eats *at very little expense and without waste.*

Other Kinds of Home Based Production

In the relatively small number of families that are engaged in cottage industries or family enterprises such as weaving, pottery or production of oil or syrup, women have fixed responsibilities in relation to the finished product. For example, in weavers' families, women do all the steps of manufacture prior to loom work. In potters' families, they do the lower portion of the work in pitching pots and handle the drying. There is almost no information or figures available on this more specialized type

---

(10) Attempts to introduce new foreign varieties of vegetables to households for home consumption may meet with resistance from women at first because, however "nutritious" they may be, inputs necessary for their growth - water, insecticide, imported seed - require expenditure. What women are accustomed to growing costs almost nothing and is guaranteed a local market.

of women's work. In the cultivation of jute, which is a cash crop, women in some areas are involved in processing jute for the market.

A lot of household manufacture makes use of the by-products of crops, plants and trees, thus again involving little expense and no waste. Women make hanging nets for storage, brooms, fans, winnowing baskets, fish traps, mats for drying, and many other functional items from leaves and stalks of plants and trees. No investment has to be made in most of these raw materials. The most traditional items of household manufacture by women are quilts which are the bedding for the family. Aside from being works of great beauty, they are a prime example of creation without expense on raw materials, since they are traditionally made with thread taken from worn-out saris.

Household Maintenance: Women are in charge of all daily and periodic cleaning of the house itself, and of some repair work. Cleaning on a routine basis involves sweeping out the house and courtyard twice a day, airing the bedding and cleaning the stove daily (saving the ashes and burnt coals for special uses), as well as washing women's and children's clothing frequently. For washing, women either go to a nearby tank, river, well or pump, or fetch or send for water. Cleaning and repairing on a periodic basis involve remudding and reconstructing the stove and re-plastering damaged parts of the house, especially after the monsoon or before a harvest.

Daily Sustenance: A woman keeps the family alive on a day to day basis by fetching water or having it fetched for cooking and drinking, by collecting fuel - leaves, sticks or cow dung(11) - and by cooking, serving and cleaning up. Meal preparation time involves cleaning the kitchen before and after each use, preparing the food, cooking it and cleaning the utensils. Food preparation is of two kinds. Rice must be husked several times a week, a task that involves time-consuming labor. Wheat and lentils also must be prepared in advance. Then, immediately before the meal itself, spices must be ground, vegetables chopped and other foods prepared. Households eat one to three meals a day depending on how much food there is. The first meal may require little preparation if it is left-over rice from the night before, kept in water. The second meal requires about two hours preparation time and the evening meal, if it involves left-

---

(11) If they have space, women often grow certain plants for fuel.

overs, will need less than two hours.

Childcare: Women who are married by the onset of puberty have an average six or seven live births, spaced around three years apart. They work throughout pregnancy and usually within a week or two after childbirth. They are responsible at all times for the care of children. Babies are usually suckled for one and a half to three years. Children have to be fed, cleaned and kept from danger. Their health has to be observed and tended to. If they go to school, they need special attention with regard to meal-times, clothing and supervised study. All the females of the household above seven or eight are involved in child-care.

The Value of Women's Work

It is frustrating to try to quantify the "value" of women's work. For one thing, there is not enough general information available about the rural economy, so that one does not know, for example, how much of rural production is marketed or how much of household consumption is produced at home. Then, even if one knew how much of production was marketed, one would not have a way, in most systems of economics, for recognizing the contribution of women's "housework" to the finished product. If one insists on figures to justify provision of resources to rural women as part of rural development, then women may have to wait a long time while systems of measurement are evolved or refined before attention is paid to their role and contribution. But if one keeps in mind that Bangladesh is largely subsistence economy in which 73% of the consumption of rural people is food and 14% is housing,(12) and observes, as in the preceding pages, what rural women are actually *doing*, one must see they are an integral part of the rural economy. The issue then is not whether to direct resources to women but how best to provide them with access to modern knowledge, supplies and services for the improvement of their situation and of the nation.

Class Variations in Work: The preceding section has described the kinds of work rural women do. A major variation in the kind of work women do and the benefit they derive from it is between those whose families have enough land and other income for yearly food and other necessities, and those in families with little or no land and no other adequate sources of income. These latter

---

(12) Khan, A.R., 1972.

women have less productive work in their own household because
it is hard to make something out of nothing, i.e., even non-
monetary production requires a resource base.

The woman who is resource poor will have little household work
to do that is related to rice cultivation. She is not likely
to have seeds to germinate since if there had been some rice
harvested from sharecropping or a small plot of land, it would
have been sold from the field to meet other needs, or eaten as
food grain. She will probably not cook for laborers at harvest
time; her husband and sons are likely to be laborers for others.
She will not have bullocks to care for throughout the year. At
harvest time if paddy does come into the compound, processing
and storing it will not take as much time or work as it does for
those with more land. Still, whatever paddy there is, she is in
charge of processing, storing and managing.

She may have a few chickens, though there will not be much to
feed them since, without much rice, there are not many rice by-
products. She is unlikely to have a goat to look after. She
probably does not have her own cows to attend and milk. There
are not likely to be other food or cash crops to process, nor
fruit trees to care for. There may be too little homestead land
for growing vegetables and spices. There may be no plants or
trees whose by-products can be the materials for household manufacture, nor spare old saris for making quilts.

Yet, even the resource poor woman is likely to have a small
dwelling place and a stove to clean and repair. She has to wash
clothes, air the bedding, fetch the water, collect fuel and cook
and wash the utensils. Cooking will not be as time-consuming as
it is for a woman with more resources because there will not be
food for as many meals, nor any variety in dishes. She may not
even do the husking of stored rice in preparation for cooking,
because for much if not all of the year she may have to buy
small quantities of already processed (i.e. higher-priced) rice
daily. Often, cooking depends on what (if anything) her husband
brings home that day with the wages from his labor, or what she
can get in exchange for her labor. Childcare will be a constant
responsibility as it is for all women. The children of very poor
women are not likely to go to school so there will be no question
of supervising studies. Feeding and health problems will be
managed with inadequate resources.

Some of these poor women, those with no other alternatives that
will enable them to preserve their status, will look for work in

others' houses on a casual or long-term basis, processing rice and doing the other heavy, manual tasks of women's work. Or, if they have their own *dhekis*, they may work at home processing others' rice or, with capital, on a commercial basis. They may keep cows or goats for other women on a share or *borgha* basis, make quilts for others or do other work for which others are providing the raw materials. In other words, poor women, because rural women's work is basically subsistence, have less of their own work to do than women with more resources. But if they are able to find ways to earn food or small amounts of cash, they will ultimately have more work to do, with much less return.

In only a small percentage of rural households women will not do their own heavy agricultural work or the menial aspects of cleaning and food preparation. This is usually a matter of both status and wealth.(13) In these households there may be male servants to do some of the agricultural work and some aspects of animal husbandry. There may be full-time female servants. The women of these households are by no means idle; because there are more resources, there is more work. But their own work involves fewer menial tasks and more managerial, supervisory functions.

The following are examples of the work of prosperous and poor women, as they describe it themselves. The first case is that of a prosperous farm woman of about fifty who lives in Bogra. Her family owns about 30 *bighas* or ten acres of land. Her husband is a business man too busy for farm work and so they share-crop all the land. They cultivate two crops of rice on 25 *bighas*, jute on three, potatoes on one and a half and vegetables on half a *bigha* near the house. With this production they meet the food needs of the joint family of 24 persons, of which she is the head woman. She says, in response to being asked what she does:

> "I have to supervise when crops are brought home. I have 14 grandchildren and most of them are studying in Bogra town. I have to supply rice, pulses, and vegetables from the village for their food. I also have to supervise the processing of the paddy. I myself see to the drying and boiling. Since I've done this from girlhood, I'm used to

---

(13) However, as Qadir points out, some households keep servants not for prestige but because the family has too few members to do all the work (1960).

it. Rice does not break if I do it myself with care and so
I look after it without leaving the responsibility to others.
Afterwards I have the servants husk it or I send it to the
mill. I have to decide on the amount of rice that will be
cooked every day. I even have to arrange the supply of rice
for the whole year. Besides this I also have to decide where
and when to sow seeds for onions, garlic, potatoes, gourds,
pumpkins, and various other vegetables. I also have to fix
the daily menu. I even have to serve the curry. I have to
look after washing the clothes and the house and also to
check on the cleaning and tidiness of the floors and rooms
of the house. I also look after the domestic animals - a
pair of bullocks, three milk cows, and their calves. Though
the responsibility for looking after them is handed over to
a servant, I still have to supervise regularly whether they
are brought home properly, get their food and water, etc.
Then there are three ducks and 12 chickens. Opening and
closing the doors of the chicken house and feeding them
daily have become habits. They are part of my daily life.
I even know the color of every chicken. There are six goats.
I feed them myself. I might even forget to eat, but I never
forget to feed them."

The remainder are the much shorter responses of three poor women
from Barisol, Kushtia and Jessore. A married woman of 28 from
Barisol says:

"I have to maintain my family by cooking in others' houses.
That is why I usually do not have any rest. Daily I have to
wash dishes, wash clothes, clean the house, bring water, and
grind and prepare spices for others. At the end of the day,
I come home and prepare food for my own family. During the
harvesting season my work increases."

A woman of about 40 from Kushtia, whose husband is not well, says
she does not have much work to do all day. When, at the end of
the day, her husband brings some rice or pulses, then she cooks
them. When she grinds someone else's paddy, then she has work to
do. Besides that, she weaves mats in the morning or afternoon.
When she has no work she visits neighboring houses. A woman from
Jessore says:

"When there is no food, how much work can there be? The day
when there is some income or if some crops which have been
harvested are brought home, that day I will have some work."

Role Variations in Work: As indicated earlier, an important basis for the sexual division of labor is whether the work is done inside or outside the shelter of the *bari.* Within the *bari,* in the realm of women's work, there are variations in the kind and amount of work women do that are the function of their relationship in the family. These variations exist in most families though with a wide range of deviations from the norms described below.

The daughter of the family usually does not have fixed responsibilities in the household work routine since she will be moving to another household at a fairly early age. From the age of six or seven she cares for younger siblings, carries messages, collects fuel and tends animals on a casual basis. If she goes to school she is likely to have few definite chores. If she is very poor she may go along with her mother to work in others' households. As a young girl approaches puberty, she is restricted to the *bari* and, again, helps only casually.

However, when she marries and goes to another household as daughter-in-law, she is expected to do all the heavy, menial chores of women's work, unless there are servants or hired laborers to do it. Even if there are, she still does the less prestigious, more tedious tasks of those left for the household women to do. A young woman of 15, married for four years, says:

> "I have to work a lot as daughter-in-law. In my father's house I worked as I pleased, but here I have to work whether I want to or not. I have to work out of fear. No-one knows what to expect; they can say anything at any time. There is a younger sister-in-law. But she is small and came after me. How much can she do?"

The mother-in-law of the house is in charge of women's work. She makes all the decisions about what is to be done with the resources within the compound as regards food, health, and child-care. She decides what foods are to be cooked together at a meal, who gets what share of the food and how milk is to be distributed. Her daughters-in-law carry out her orders. There is a hierarchy of tasks in the household with the less prestigious allotted to the daughters-in-law. For example, the daughter-in-law may do the husking of rice, grinding of spices, cleaning of fish, and washing of pots and pans. The mother-in-law is freed from most of the daily routine of work and when grandchildren arrive has the more prestigious responsibility of child-care. Of course, when the pressure of work requires the participation

of all the household women, she will do it, but she remains the
boss. In some families where human resources are limited and
it is important for status reasons to keep the new daughter-in-
law in *purdah*, the mother-in-law may take charge of grazing the
goat or fetching the water.

After her husband dies and she lives with her son or is supported by him, the amount of work and degree of authority of the
mother-in-law depend on her relationship with her son as well
as his resources. Generally women who have lost the status they
get from having husbands - those who are widows, divorced and
separated - do the more menial work of the household, if they
are dependent on others for support.

CHAPTER IV

·

WOMEN AND INCOME

In Bangladesh it is customary for the male to provide for and
protect the female. The obligation that he undertakes as sole
authority is that of sole provider. Bangladeshi rural women's
work, unlike that of African women, or to some extent Indonesian
women, does not involve, as a norm, *any* economic autonomy.
Women say, "if men give us food we can eat; if they give us
money, we can spend." Men say, "we provide." Perhaps that is
the reason, in addition to the universal tendency to overlook
the struggles of the very poor, why one has to look rather
closely into rural women's lives before one sees that many women
are earning small amounts of income, out of different kinds of
need.

In order to design programs that women will be willing and able
to take advantage of, one must know as much as possible about
how and why women, in contradiction to the prevailing custom,
are earning income and about what they are doing with it. One
must not accept prevalent myths about women and income such as
that women are not wage-laborers, that only destitute women are
motivated to earn income, that rural women who are not poor want
money only for frivolous purposes, and that male control of the
purse is perceived by women to be in the best interest of the
family.

These and other myths can flourish in the absence of information
about the income-oriented behavior of women, which is a subject
of great complexity. For one thing, the lack of attention in
the past to the existence of laboring women makes it hard now to

estimate the degree of unemployment there is among them as the
result of the gradual increase in the machines that replace
their labor. Women seek work as laborers when they can no longer be concerned about status. For some women, this condition
occurs abruptly through the loss of male support and resources.(1)
For others, it is an aspect of the socio-economic condition of
the whole family. The number of women who are laborers is not
known, but even if it were, it would not reflect the number who
are willing to do such work but do not find opportunities. An
additional complexity is that the number of very poor women *in
need* would not even be reflected by the numbers who would do
laborers' work if there were enough opportunities available.
Many rural families, in this situation of dwindling resources,
even those in which male members are working as laborers, will
tolerate great deprivation before suffering the loss of status
involved in allowing women to work.(2)

What is the work of laboring women? The most common way for
these women to earn food in rural areas is to sell their labor
in other households, processing rice and performing other menial
tasks of women's work. There are a variety of arrangements for
doing this work (excluding the exchange of labor among economic
equals). One arrangement is the formal contract negotiated for
specified periods of time - a few days or a few months or more.
The amount of food, clothing and money to be paid for labor will
be agreed on in advance and, of course, it will vary with season,
supply, and demand. One two-month contract involved payment of
three meals a day, clothing, 80 pounds of rice and about 25
takas. An arrangement for three days might involve payment of
three meals a day plus a pound or two of rice. Women frequently
do rice husking on a casual basis with a payment of so much rice
for so many pounds processed. A woman may spend five or six
hours husking for one *seer* (two pounds or the equivalent of
three *takas*) of rice. Women may have connections with particular households who call them when there is work. In order to

_____

(1) See Chen and Guznavy, 1977.
(2) In one village study where women's wage labor was noted, it
was found that a third of the landless families have one or more
woman working for others. More interestingly, a sixth of the
"small peasant" families have women for hire, *whereas five-sixths
of these families have men for hire* (Arens, 1975). It is not
known whether the smaller number of women working as laborers
indicates lack of opportunity or fear of risking status.

guarantee being called for this work, the poorer woman may have
to be generally available for other lighter services like
cleaning fish or milling rice.

A less common arrangement involves year-round work and residence.
In addition, women may do rice husking on a more commercial basis,
i.e. buying paddy from the market and selling it back as rice or
a more expensive variation, puffed rice. Some capital is required for this arrangement. Village women can also earn a little
by milking cows for others or as *dais* or midwives. In some
places poor women do post-harvest harvesting, gleaning what is
left in the harvested fields, processing it, and selling it.
They may collect fuel or harvest chilis for wages.

It is obvious that thousands of rural women are dependent on
rice husking and other forms of labor for some part of their
yearly food. The number of women who migrate to towns and cities
to work as domestic servants, and more recently, the number of
women who have appeared when projects have provided opportunities
to do field work or to carry earth in exchange for wheat is an
indication that opportunities for labor are inadequate for the
number of women who are willing to do this kind of work.

In some villages the arrangement between rich and poor women is
more feudal than commercial. For example, women from a number
of poor households may be at the call of a rich household for
various services as needed, often without even having to be asked.
Such work includes helping with rice husking and milling, fetching water, cooking at feasts, helping in special food preparations, being available to clear the courtyard of drying rice when
rain threatens suddenly, etc. For some of these services there
will be no immediate return; for others, some of the food being
processed or prepared. But throughout the year, sustenance and
support comes in the form of food distributed on religious
occasions like Shabi Bharat and Eidul Azzah, or because of
promises made to Allah for prayers granted or at baby-naming
ceremonies or death anniversaries, or in the form of saris and
relief goods during natural calamities or at election time. The
rich family may also provide small loans without credit or
publicity, or, in times of scarcity, a place to pawn one's
valuables for small amounts of credit; they can be "borrowed"
back for, say, a son-in-law's visit and, hopefully, at some time
reclaimed. The rich family may distribute used clothing, provide
special foods for unexpected occasions, lend furniture, pots and
pans and even ornaments for weddings and provide countless other
loans of assistance for which the labor of the poorer women is

the "payment". There may be less loss of status in such an
arrangement than in a strictly commercial one.

Whether such arrangements tend toward the commercial or the
feudal, they do not provide poor women with anything to build on
for the future. They provide her basically with something,
though rarely enough, to eat. Because they involve heavy manual
labor and violation of *purdah*, they are the least desirable ways
to earn food. There are other traditional ways for poor rural
women to earn small amounts of food or money without having to
work in others' houses. These women, within the shelter of the
bari, may earn for themselves as older widows or for their
children as heads of families. Or, contrary to the accepted
view of women, their contribution may be counted on as one of
the several sources of income a rural family depends on to survive.(3)

In certain parts of the country women with some capital buy
goats or cows which they give to poorer women to raise. The
poorer women get the first year's milk and issue from the animals and the second year return the cow or goat and its new
offspring. Both groups of women earn income this way, though
with different inputs and for different needs. This system is
called *borga*. Women with enough resources to buy a few chickens
and keep them alive and healthy(4) earn small amounts of income
from selling eggs, chicks, and chickens on a fairly regular basis
or simply keep them as an asset that can be converted to cash
when a need arises. One woman referred to chickens and goats as
"our friends in need". Though returns are very small, the inputs
are economically negligible - by-products of household food and
the time of women and children. A woman who keeps chickens may
market them and their eggs in the village, either directly or,
if she is in strict *purdah*, with the help of children or those
women who do visit from house to house.(5) Or she may sell at

---

(3) In the village Cain studied, where 83% of the households
counted on at least three sources of income, 41% of the households received some income from eggs, milk, goats and ducks,
which as indicated earlier, are women's responsibility (Cain,
1977a).
(4) Periodic epidemics of poultry diseases wipe out large
numbers of chickens, so that women cannot afford to risk investments in them. Profitable ways of raising improved varieties
have not yet been developed.
(5) Women who keep *purdah* are thus dependent on older or poorer
women who do not.

the nearest market with the help of a child or a male relative
or middleman.

Many women who keep goats also think of them not so much as
food for the family but as assets convertible to cash in time
of need. Besides the initial investment, input is quite negligible, but there must be someone, even an older woman,
available to take the goats out to graze, since otherwise this
would involve violating *purdah*. Milk, also, is a marketable
asset, either in the village or the local market. Women with
cows decide how much of the available milk will be used for the
family's food and how much is to be sold. Again, the amounts
of income possible from such transactions are quite small.
Small amounts of other foods - vegetables, fruit, date syrup,
etc. - bring in a few *takas* for women. Or women may use them
as barter, along with rice, in exchange for a variety of small
household items and trinkets that tradesmen bring directly to
the village.

Since all these food items are in women's sphere of responsibility, it is they who decide whether to eat them or sell them.
The basis for their decision will be family need, but nutrition,
in the sense of an improved or balanced diet, is not likely to
be the priority if the family is poor. It is important to
remember, because rural women consider it important, that if
women market their produce outside the *para*, they are always
dependent on others as intermediaries in the transaction. In
other words they do not automatically control the income their
work produces. Whether they do control it depends on many
factors, but especially on whether there is an intermediary and
if so, who he or she is.

Poor rural women also use their traditional skills in handiwork
to bring in small amounts of money. This kind of work can be
done in the security of *purdah*, if there are any males or
children to help out, but at the same time women have no direct
involvement in the financial transaction. Women may make fans,
baskets, or mats from available or purchased raw materials.
They may make quilts on contract for other women who provide
the raw materials. In some areas women make fishnets or spin
thread or make *bidis*, a kind of cigar, on contract to middlemen
who supply the raw materials, and in some cases the spinning
wheel. As one can imagine, returns are very meagre. They may
also make sweets to sell in the market or *pan*, for which they
need both material and human resources.

Women who have more resources or who have only liquid resources, have other, though not always more productive, ways to make money. They may keep small shops in their homes. Or they may stock rice and other commodities until the prices go up in seasons of scarcity. They may buy these commodities directly from other women in the village or through intermediaries from the market or save them from their own store. Some women lend rice for interest, asking perhaps one and a half or two times the amount of rice in return. Or they lend money for interest, sometimes investing in local businesses like weaving, sometimes against land as surety which they then cultivate through laborers or through the "owner" as tenant. In one village near a cottage weaving industry, women of all classes invest money in the weavers, getting perhaps 15 *taka* a month interest for an investment of 100 *taka*. Similarly women from weaving families may lend money to farmers in the sowing season and get rice as interest. As one woman said, whatever money they have should not be idle; it should be put to work.

Although there is not enough information to indicate how many women are engaged in which kinds of income-producing activities, there is enough to show that rural women are trying in a variety of ways to bring income into the family. It is important to emphasize that many of these small-income producing activities are being carried on out of the lime-light, so to speak. They are not secret (except in a minority of cases) but they are not something to be flaunted. Thus, unless one has the confidence of rural women, one may not see how many women are involved in earning income or interested in doing so, provided certain conditions are met.

There seem to be two reasons for this semi-secrecy. One is that the fact of women earning income for herself or the family runs counter to the custom of man as the provider, entitled to obedience because he provides the food. In village society where status accrues to those who approach the custom neither men nor women may want to publicize the fact that women are contributing to family income. Another explanation is that women have reasons for wanting access to and control over the income their work produces but men, they say, do not always want them to have control. An understanding of both these issues is very important in the development of a project that women and their families will respond to.

How do women spend the small amounts of income they control? Women in very poor families and women who are heads of households

usually spend what they earn on immediate survival - i.e. daily
food. In addition, they spend on such expenses as the following:
small household needs like oil or soap; school fees and other
educational expenses for their sons; household emergencies like
medicine; releasing land from mortgages, leasing in land, buying
land or a house; gifts for their married daughters; support for
their widowed mothers; special luxuries and treats for their
sons; and ornaments (i.e. *personal* assets) for themselves. The
nature of some of these expenses and the indications we have
from women that secrecy is sometimes necessary suggest that
something more is involved in women earning income than simply
adding to family resources managed by males.

Let us look at the issue of secrecy first. A number of rural
women with whom we have discussed income generating activities
have been so concerned with the question of marketing that they
have indicated that they were not interested in earning money if
it would have to come through the hands of male relatives. In
interviews, we have heard of specific attempts women have made
to keep income-generating activities a secret from their husbands.
Women told us usually what *other* women have done. For example,
one woman stocked rice in another woman's house so her husband
would not know she had it. Another woman had a neighbor raise
a goat for her so her husband would not know about it. Another
woman secretly sold rice from her own store. Yet another woman
has opened a *pan* business with her young son and has told him to
keep their earnings a secret from the husband. Most women say
that they hide their savings in holes in the bamboo, in the roof
or under piles of cloth.

What are the reasons for the secrecy? There seem to be several.
One is the desire to save. Women have said that if their husbands knew there was extra money around, they would spend it,
work a few days less if they were day laborers, or give women
less for expenses if they were wage earners. Some husbands, if
asked to market an item for their wives, would keep the money
for themselves and not hand it over. Women indicate that this
is a matter of the character and behavior of individual husbands,
not an accusation against all husbands. They say that if husbands are "good", women can trust them to buy and sell what the
women request. But if the husbands are not "good", women try to
sell through other women or through vendors. Some husbands, they
say, are so bad they will take whatever they can.

Having saved money, women use it for several ends. One is to
meet family emergencies if they arise and to provide for family

security in co-operation with the husband or, perhaps once in a while, in spite of him. One woman said she earned money secretly through stocking goods, told her husband the money came from her family and bought a house in her own name. She said if it were in his name, he would sell it and "eat" the proceeds. Another reason is to be able to spend money on obligations women especially feel, i.e. for their mother's or daughter's well-being, without having to ask permission from the husband. Another is to provide for their own security when it seems at risk, i.e., if divorce seems imminent or a co-wife's(6) children are getting more of the family finances. Special treats and advantages for one's sons are a way to try to ensure future security from his position and gratitude. And another is to be able to have some respect and influence on decisions in the family for having provided needed income discreetly.

---

(6) See p.76 for an explanation of the co-wife system.

CHAPTER V

REPRODUCTION AND HEALTH

The restrictions of *purdah* and the reticence and taboos related to menstruation, sex and childbirth make it convenient for rural women to rely on health services that are available in the village. To seek help, in the form of modern health care, outside the village would involve such inconvenience that women are not likely to seek it unless they see it as clearly superior to what is already within their reach. In its present form (including availability), modern health care is obviously not superior. For the most part women are dependent on each other within the *para* and on local resources in the village, with little help from outside, in dealing with the reproductive functioning and the health of their families. Let us look at some of their beliefs and practices.

Reproduction

Ideally, unmarried girls are not supposed to know about sex or menstruation before they experience them, but in fact they learn about these matters in the course of growing up from young married women in their own house or neighboring houses. They learn about sex in a joking, teasing way, not as an activity to be discussed seriously. Often teasing is related to morning bathing, since women are required by religion to bathe before prayers if they have had sex. Sex is not usually discussed between husband and wife, nor between mother and daughter. Whatever "discussion" exists will be among role peers or daughter and grandmother.

Some girls may not learn about menstruation until the onset of their first period, but others may have heard about it earlier from their sisters-in-law. They learn from them that menstruation is good for the health because it gets rid of bad or dirty blood. Absence of periods, aside from pregnancy, is an indication that something is not right. They learn how to keep clean during periods, how to avoid letting others see that they are menstruating, what bathing ritual to follow, and other such practices. In some areas there are special ceremonies for the first menstrual period, involving food and purification rituals, and a special feast and presentation of gifts, especially if it occurs after marriage. (This is called *sesser bia* or final marriage). Menstruating women are considered contaminating in various degrees. In some places they must not enter the kitchen or use the cooking utensils until they have bathed. In some places they must not milk cows during their periods.

Married women usually become pregnant within two or three years of their first period, which means in their mid-teens. They usually experience dizziness, nausea, "head-spinning", and a distaste for certain foods. They do not follow a special routine, nor are they treated in special ways, but there are a number of "guidelines" for their own safety in childbirth and that of the baby in varying degrees which affect their behavior. Since they want to avoid giving birth to a fat baby because of the difficulties of delivery, some women mention that they will not take medicines during pregnancy, while others advocate eating a lot to keep the stomach full and the baby small. Most women agree that it is dangerous to go out in the afternoon or to go near ponds or trees for fear of evil spirits in the breeze that might cause the baby to be stillborn or adversely affect the mother's health. Some women say that for ill health during pregnancy, they fetch holy water from a *moulvi*, or religious man. There is a special ceremony in the seventh month of pregnancy that involves special foods and presents for the woman - a kind of last supper, since childbirth, especially the first, is approached with some fear.

The first delivery is usually the most difficult. Twenty years after the event, women recall their first delivery in all its details. Women give birth in the in-laws' or sometimes the parental home, in a section of the main room partitioned with a screen or in a separate room built for the purpose. They are usually attended by one or two female relatives who are used to helping in childbirth; not all women feel comfortable in attendance. Only occasionally, in difficult cases, are village mid-

wives or *dai* called in. These are older, poor village women
who have a reputation for expertise in delivery. Birth position
may be kneeling or squatting or lying down. The *dai* may physically intervene in the birth process if there is difficulty by
molding the child's head or turning it. More common, when there
seems to be difficulty, are the practices of taking sweets or
water blessed by the *moulvi*, wearing a *tabij* or religious amulet,
or putting certain specially blessed flowers to open in water.

After delivery, the umbilical cord is cut with a bamboo sliver
or a blade and tied with cotton thread. To prevent infection of
the baby's navel, the women in attendance apply the warm ashes
of a cloth burned in a kerosene lamp, a hot compress of clay
from the oven wrapped in cloth, or simply the pressure of warm
thumbs. To dry up the birth canal and uterus which are considered to be raw and liable to infection, women in attendance may
apply warm dry cloth compresses or the pressure of warm hands
spread with mustard oil on the lower abdomen. Or the woman who
has given birth may squat over a ball of earth or mud heated in
the oven and covered with a piece of burlap. Dietary practices
to dry up the birth canal, prevent infection, replenish the
blood, and help lactation include temporary restriction of the
intake of meat, curry, and fat fish and emphasis on eating hot
spices with boiled rice and a spicy dish called *kalo jeera barta*.
Women are supposed to remain in the delivery room for seven days
and within the household for 40 days. All the clothing and
utensils connected with childbirth are considered contaminating
as are the mother and child for a specific period of time.

If they can, women suckle their babies for two or three years,
usually until the next baby is born. Babies get little if any
food in addition to breast milk for about six months. If breast
milk dries up early, which often happens, women may feed their
babies rice flour water or barley water with sugar. Women are
often in ill health after childbirth, suffering from infections
and complications. Infant mortality is very high. About 16%
of infants die within their first year.(1) We have heard women
tell of the loss of half or three-quarters of their pregnancies
and births. Women identify diarrhea, fever and smallpox as the
causes of their infants' deaths, but the most frequently mentioned cause is the evil spirit. Women adorn their babies with
amulets to combat ill health and evil spirits. They give names
to children who survive after a number of infant deaths, like

---

(1) *Statistical Yearbook of Bangladesh*, 1975.

"ashes" or "throw away" to keep the spirits from being tempted to take the child.

Aside from modern Western methods of family planning which have been introduced in the last ten or 15 years, village women seem to have few traditional methods of contraception, besides breast-feeding. Withdrawal may be a traditional form of contraception but we have not heard women mention it. We have heard, of course, of abortion which, while not socially approved, is attempted by women throughout Bangladesh, especially in cases of poverty, ill health, illicit pregnancies and pregnancies that come when the woman has grown-up daughters or sons, which are considered shame-ful. Sometimes husbands know and approve of abortion; at other times they are told that the loss of the fetus was caused by evil spirits. Probably most women know some methods of abortion or who to go to in the village for help. Eating raw pineapple or soap or insertion of certain herbs in the uterus are methods women can administer themselves. Local "doctors" may prescribe pills and injections. Several women from different parts of the country told us that they had taken powders made from herbs for permanent sterilization without cessation of periods and that these powders, bought from village "doctors" who will not reveal their ingredients, have been successful.

Health

Women are in charge of the health of their families. They treat health disorders in a combination of ways: with food and herbal remedies they themselves know; with magic or quasi religious spells and charms from divines (*pirs*) and fakirs; with remedies from older village women with reputations for successful cures; with remedies from *kabiraj* or *hakim*;(2) and with homeopathic, ayurvedic and allopathic diagnoses and medicines. In a typical village, access to allopathic medicine, hospitalization and surgery usually involves travel, expense, and a strange, often unpleasant environment. Homeopathy is likely to be second highest in expense, and is usually preferred to allopathy because there seem to be fewer risks and side-effects and less dislocation.

---

(2) *Kabiraj* and *hakim* are indigenous professional doctors whose approaches are familiar and acceptable to village women because their diagnoses and remedies involve a practical consideration of the patient's socio-economic situation and a "magic touch" in the food and medicine prescribed.

There are a number of criteria which women consider in determining what combination of resources they will use. One is how
serious the illness seems to be. For example coughs and colds
are usually taken for granted and treated routinely with household remedies involving food and herbs.(3) If these do not work
and the illness worsens, women will turn to other resources.
Another criterion is whether the illness is likely to be caused
by spirits or evil spells. Probably they are considered to be
involved to *some* degree in all illness. As one woman said, she
does not go to a "doctor" for ordinary illness or ailments
because she thinks that illnesses like diarrhea or dysentery
usually are caused by the evil looks of others. For this reason
she does not want to spend money uselessly on a doctor. She
gives the child holy water and other such things.

Another criterion is the question of *who* is sick. It is likely
that male children will get what is considered to be the best
medical care. Lindenbaum cites a family with four daughters and
one son, which gives health care to all the children when needed,
but "only the male child's health merits consultation" with *all*
the available practitioners.(4) Wives and daughters-in-law are
less likely to get care that requires the husbands' involvement,
because women are slow to indicate their own ill health and may
wait until someone else notices and also, frankly, because
husbands are inclined to wait a little longer before spending
money on a wife's ill health than on a male child's or a bullock's.

Other important criteria, of varying importance in different
situations, are the accessibility of health resources, their
costliness and their efficacy. Local health resources usually
include expert women, *kabiraj*, *hakim*, and fakirs who are relatively inexpensive and who can be consulted easily. For women,
seeking help at a health center, family planning clinic, or
hospital involves *purdah* considerations related to travelling

_____

(3) Village women have indigenous medicines for other common
illneses like dysentery, worms, skin diseases, boils, eczema,
urinary trouble, vomiting, eye infection, cataract, fever,
whooping cough, cuts, muscular pain, measles, rheumatism, head-
ache, indigestion and even breast or neck tumors. Food remedies
are often based on the dichotomies of hot and cold, wet and dry.
See our "Some Health Practices of Rural Bangladesh" in *Shishu
Diganta, A Child's Horizon,* Issue #2, Unicef, Dacca, 1977.
(4) Lindenbaum, 1965.

and public attention to one's problems, which, if they are connected with reproduction, may become a matter of ridicule. Seeking outside help may also be related to the question of control. Once a woman raises the issue of sickness and treatment of a family member with her husband, she is usually thinking of resources beyond her reach. The decision then lies with the male. From the woman's perspective, locally available remedies and superstitious practices have just as much likelihood of success as modern approaches which, as they are presently offered, tend to disrupt her life, use up her resources and lessen her control without improving health.

As can be seen, it is village women who make most of the decisions about curative health practices. These decisions are a function of the whole socio-economic context in which they exist. Programs to improve family health, depending, as they do, on curative procedures, can have little success unless they take this into consideration. Similarly, and more obviously, women control practices related to preventive health care, such as nutrition and sanitation. But here again women's behavior is a response to available resources according to their priorities. The extent to which their behavior may be counter-productive is not just a matter of lack of information to be corrected by education. Lack of information is only a part of the problem. Those who want to see an improvement in women's health, nutrition and sanitation decisions and practices must first of all try to see *the rural women's world through their own eyes*. Attempts to bring about change have to address and respect the total situation a woman faces.

CHAPTER VI

PURDAH

Purdah, or the veil, is a characteristic of Islam. Its practice
varies from place to place. Our concern with *purdah* in Bangladesh is not with its religious significance but with the way it
affects the behavior of rural women. The strict practice of
purdah is a social and religious *ideal* in rural Bangladesh.
Strict practice means that a woman stays within the family compound or *bari* which is usually surrounded by a wall of vegetation
and sometimes has screens of woven rushes to protect the inner
courtyard. If possible she stays within the inner courtyard.
She is never seen by any but close family males. This degree of
seclusion requires access to water for bathing within the *bari*
and the presence of servants. As one of the authors observed
in "Village Women as I Saw Them"(1):

> Male guests and visitors and even male servants are atten-
> ded by male members of the family. Not only do the women
> remain unseen, but often their voices are not heard by out-
> siders. For example, if food is being prepared for the men
> to serve male visitors the women who are cooking may
> communicate and give instructions by gesture and posture.

If a woman in strict *purdah* must go out to visit her parents
once or twice a year or for an emergency, she will wear a *burkah*,
a loose garment that covers her from crown to toe and travel in
a bullock cart with a cover over each end or in a rickshaw with
the front covered, or by boat at night. As a result it is costly

_____
(1) Abdullah, 1966.

55

for a rural family to maintain strict *purdah* for its women and only the wealthy or those males (like *moulvis* and schoolteachers, or those with a name to preserve), who make a special effort of time and energy, can afford to do so.

Only a few *baris* in a village, perhaps five or six, can maintain such strict *purdah*, but what is important to recognize is that almost all the villagers look to these houses as the most prestigious and respected, an honor to the village, and to this way of life for women as the most desirable. In fact, they do not like to see a lapse in the expected behavior of these women.(2) If, in fact, there is a lapse of *purdah* in such a prestigious family, it will take time before their prestige can be restored.

Strict *purdah* indicates to villagers a family of high social, economic and/or religious rank. Socially, it is a tribute to a male's honor which is vested in the behavior of family women and to his ability to protect and provide for them. As the sociologist Florence McCarthy points out, "The mobility of the family women out of the *bari* is indicative of the condition of their husbands' status. Their mobility is a threat to the men of the family, especially if a position is being maintained, and men are likely to experience criticism and ridicule if their wives' mobility exceeds the village standards."(3) *Purdah* is a way that a family signals its economic superiority to other villages. At the same time, *purdah* commands respect in a way that money alone does not, because of its religious connotations, since it is considered good behavior from a religious point of view. Traditional village religious figures and specially esteemed preachers, who are brought to the village from time to time, always stress the religious obligation men have to keep their women inside.

So, from whatever vantage point one looks at the issue of *purdah*, social, economic or religious, one sees that its practice is considered an asset. A village woman from Daulatkhan, answering a question about whether she keeps *purdah*, tells a lot about its significance. She says that, when she got married, her father-in-law's financial condition was not very good and the women of

----

(2) A woman from a family with a very respectable name was asked why she did not take a family planning job. Her response was: "What are you saying! If the women of this family worked in the village, what would people say?"
(3) McCarthy, 1967.

the house had to go out when necessary, but that, now, his condition has improved and so has the family name. If she does not
observe *purdah*, she says, it is an insult to the family and,
particularly, the men of the family. Besides, it would be difficult to arrange a good marriage from the family if it had a
bad name for not keeping *purdah*.

For whatever reasons, almost all village women aspire towards
observing *purdah*. Except for the very poor who have no choice
but to work in others' houses or beg or glean the fields, most
rural women practice *purdah* that strives to emulate the ideal,
yet has the flexibility to allow for the economic realities of
the family situation. These women may move discreetly within a
cluster of *baris* - usually of related families - when men are in
the fields or at night. Beyond these *baris* which they can get
to by sheltered paths, may be open fields and public roads which,
using Mernissi's terminology, are "male space".(4) Women do not
usually traverse male space except on visits to their parental
homes. They wear *burkahs* if they can afford them. If not, they
may cover their faces and bodies with a sari arranged like a
burkah and shield themselves with an umbrella. Those who cannot
afford these symbols of modesty, cover their heads and faces as
much as possible with part of the sari they are wearing.

Very poor women who have to work in others' homes are likely to
be seen by non-family males, as are women with no male intermediaries who must go out to find a way to eat, and women with
no males or children at home to help them graze goats, get water
or collect fodder for cows. Florence McCarthy points out that
villagers accept such behavior when the necessity for it is
apparent and do not make it a matter for shame. Poverty is the
result of fate, not bad behavior.(5) But still, poor women of
Bangladesh like the poor everywhere are keenly aware of the
disparity between their behavior and that which is considered
socially acceptable. Within the village such women may be
treated decently, but to protect themselves in male space where

---

(4) What Mernissi says about Morocco seems to apply to Bangladesh. She writes that sexual segregation divides all space into
male space and female space, and that the overlap is limited and
regulated by a host of rituals. She says that the street (in
rural Bangladesh, the road or field) is male space. Women have
no right to be there. Women in male space are considered to be
both provocative and offensive (1975).
(5) McCarthy, 1967.

58

they are particularly vulnerable, they may have to develop sharp
tongues, a form of behavior condemned among the "respectable".

However, there are many rural women facing real economic hardship
whose families consider the maintenance of *purdah* a more valuable
asset than the violation of *purdah* involved in going out to find
ways to earn income. Families may try to help these women in
need by giving them food, by taking some of their children to
raise or by helping them in small income-generating "respectable"
work that can be done at home. Here, the price for respectability is complete dependency. If these women are forced out of
purdah by their own perception of how desperate their situation
is, they are likely to face unpleasant comments from others,
acting as social pressure. For example, one woman from a "respectable" village family in Jessore, after losing her husband
and in-laws, had to put her two children in an orphanage and,
with her elderly mother, struggle to manage their acre of land
and find a way to hold the family together. She says that men
comment that she loses her status by going out. But, she
explains, the men do not understand that she has to maintain
herself. "If I go out, I can at least get myself organized."
Other such women say they hear others comment that their daughters will not find good marriages.(6)

It can be seen, then, why women are so dependent on men in rural
Bangladesh. Maintenance of *purdah*, the behavior society values
and enforces, means that women cannot have access to the world
that lies beyond the imposed physical boundaries of their mobility except through intermediaries - young children for small
matters, husbands, fathers, brothers and grown sons for whatever
they need that comes from outside. They do not go to the marketplace which is the center of economic, social and political
activity, not to speak of its display of clothes and food. They
do not go to the mosque, the center of religious and social
activity. They do not go to the fields, the accepted center of
agricultural activity. They do not go to school past puberty,
even if they can afford it, if it involves being with males or
walking beyond permissible boundaries. They do not have direct
access to the products of their labor nor the chance to labor
when in need. They do not go to the Union or *Thana* where

---

(6) See also Chen and Guznavy, 1977.

medical and family planning services are available.(7) They do
not have access to the courts. They cannot see the families to
whom they send their daughters in marriage.

It is a commonplace to say that women's work is complementary
or auxiliary to that of men, i.e., that women help men. But
that terminology is not useful. To understand better the
situation of women, it is important to see that women's work
does not have *direct* access to the marketplace. At every turn
it comes up against boundaries beyond which male intermediaries
are necessary if it is to find market or social value. Women
without men simply cannot get their money's worth or their
rights.(8) This is why the greatest need in a woman's life is
male support,(9) which does not mean necessarily that he earns
her food, but that he is the middleman for her production and
the defender of her rights.

No matter how much power a woman may gain in the family within
her sphere of activity, whether it is food production or health,
the limitation on *resources* over which she has control keeps her
from the best exercise of her power. Akhter Hameed Khan emphasized the significance of this dilemma when he said about rural
development in 1966, that "the main obstacle to progress, to
rapid change, to adoption of new methods of agriculture, health
or education, [is] the segregation of Muslim women ... Our real
problem is the segregation of rural women and their exclusion
from economic activities."(10)

Although this description of *purdah* has been stated in terms of
its negative aspect and as if it were unvarying to emphasize the
restrictions in the lives of rural women, it is important to know
that there are variations in women's experience of *purdah* and

------

(7) A woman from Daulatkhan says that she will not show herself
to a male doctor because she believes it is better to die than
to commit such a sin. If women want contraceptive pills, in
areas where Government workers do not visit, they have to depend
on their husbands to bring them.
(8) Village society expects that a family speaks through its
head male. The more responsibility a woman has for supporting
her family, the fewer resources she is likely to have and the
less chance to get fair value for them. (See McCarthy, 1967
and Ellickson, 1975).
(9) See Jahan, 1975.
(10) Khan, A.H., 1967.

that there is flexibility in its interpretation.(11) Within
the average rural family there are variations according to age
and role. A girl under five or six has almost as much freedom
as a boy of that age. But when she approaches puberty she is
put in more strict confinement until she is married. In very
poor families, girls may have to work in others' households with
their mothers, a risky situation for a girl at puberty. In some
influential families, girls may go to school past puberty with
appropriate arrangements for coming and going. The strictest
purdah for a woman is during the first few years in her in-laws'
house where she will be kept closely confined until she has had
a child or two to establish herself. One young woman from Bogra,
a district known for the progressiveness of its women, complains
of the abrupt change from life in her parental home where her
father was lenient about *purdah*:

> After marriage I was restricted by *purdah* in my in-laws'
> house. They call me an impudent bride if the cloth falls
> from my head in front of my in-laws or any other relatives.(12)
> To go out by the front door or back door of the house is for-
> bidden for me. I can't go to my family's house. Everyone
> else here is used to it. But to me it is intolerable because
> I was not brought up in this environment. Therefore, some-
> times the house seems to me like a jail.

When a woman goes home after marriage to visit her parents, as
she does fairly regularly during the early years, she has much
more freedom to move about among neighboring *baris* since she is
a daughter of the village. Gradually she will gain more freedom
in her in-laws' house and as she reaches her forties and becomes
a mother-in-law herself, she will have increasing mobility,
though always within the boundaries set by village standards.
She may serve laborers and deal with tutors, but still when she
speaks to elder men she will communicate through an intermediary,
perhaps a child. She must be cautious according to village standards once she has a son-in-law, because his family has a stake
in her maintaining the status of the family they have made an
alliance with. Otherwise her daughter's marriage might be at

---

(11) It is also important to realize that in spite of *purdah's*
restrictions, rural women know a great deal about what is going
on in the world as it involves their interests.
(12) Traditionally women should cover their heads in the presence
of their in-laws, elder relatives and their husbands. They are
not to speak to their husbands in the presence of others.

risk.

There are other kinds of variations in interpretation of *purdah*
besides those based on age, role in the family, and, as mentioned
earlier, class or status. Districts differ from each other in
how closely confined women are. Noakhali and Comilla are considered the most conservative about *purdah*, Bogra perhaps the
least. Villages differ from each other, sometimes because of
degrees of accessibility to towns and urban areas where women's
behavior is different; sometimes because the village is made up
of new settlers with little social pressure to conform to the
standards of traditionally prestigious families; and sometimes
because the leading families of a village have for generations
had a progressive attitute toward women. There are variations
among families, especially with regard to which males are
accepted as "fictive kin", so that women in the family can be
seen by them.

Another variation is between generations. There seems to have
been a slow, steady loosening of the restrictions of *purdah* (at
least in the memory of older women), accompanied and perhaps
influenced by the introduction of *burkhas* and more recently by
the pressure for female education as a basis for a good marriage.
Young women who have had education are taking village-based
Government or non-Government jobs and are explaining *purdah* in
ways that were not heard in the rural areas very often ten or
fifteen years ago. The following comments represent their
attitudes: "Even if we walk outside we can maintain *purdah*.
Even those who stay home can sin." or "To me mental *purdah*
[as opposed to physical confinement] is the greater *purdah*."(13)
In areas where projects offer wanted resources in acceptable
ways, village standards may modify a little to accommodate
changes in the behavior of women, or at least some women.
Comilla Women's Program, IRDP Women's Program, BRAC, Gonoshosto
Kendra and Companiganj Rural Health Centre are some of the
projects indicating modifications in *purdah* behavior of some
women.

The following are examples of the variety of ways women of
different classes and ages respond to the question, "Do you
keep *purdah*?":

---

(13) This information is based on personal communication with
Florence McCarthy.

A widow of 50 who works in others' houses said she does not maintain *purdah*. She could not get food if she did not go from door to door. Many times she has to carry news from one house to another. She did not observe *purdah* when she was just married either, except that she covered her head on the road. Now she does not even do that.

A poor woman in Rangpur said she does not maintain *purdah* because she works in others' houses. "If Allah does punish you if you don't maintain *purdah*, then why did He make our family like this?"

A poor woman in Jessore said: "I cannot observe *purdah* at all. If I have to observe *purdah* I will starve to death. Besides, I am a girl of this village so I can go everywhere."

A widow of 40 with four young sons in Mymensingh said she observes *purdah* but sometimes she has to abandon it to carry out the household responsibility. She could not go out of the house when her husband was alive and had to observe *purdah* strictly. Now if she had to maintain it, she would starve to death. In her village, she said, *purdah* means not going out of the *bari*. In this respect it is not possible for her.

A woman of 50 from Daulatkhan commented on change: "Nowadays girls do not maintain *purdah* as strictly as before. Before, if the wife of the house talked with someone from outside for any reason the people used to criticize her. But nowadays most girls talk with others by wearing *burkahs* or by keeping their heads covered. Though there is less restriction through *purdah* in the village now, still if you don't wear a *burkah* or cover the rickshaw while going out, people will criticize you. Many people observe *purdah* because they want to, but most because they are scared of being criticized."

One young girl who is a leader of a new women's co-operative and has to go to the *Thana* center said: "One day the *moulvi* said to us, 'There is flood and drought because girls walk outside and don't keep *purdah*. You are Allah's curse.'" In response she said, "We may be Allah's curse - but you're a *munshi*.(14) Why do you look at us?"

---

(14) Religious person.

The mother-in-law of a girl who goes to the *Thana* center as leader of a co-operative said: "A lot of people talk about it. We want to let our girls work but there are people who spread many rumors. They say we have let our girls go to the men in the offices and so on. Sometimes I think I won't let her go again."

A Bogra woman in her 40s said: "We have been maintaining *purdah* from our childhood, so it has become a habit. At the age of nine or ten, restrictions of maintaining *purdah* started. Mother used to say that one should not pass in front of any unrelated men or wander in the neighborhood. Since then I have worn a *burkah* to go to relatives' houses. Observing *purdah* is bred in my bones. The restriction of *purdah* was present before marriage and it did not change after marriage. But now I have become much older and the problems in the family are increasing. Thus day by day the restrictions of *purdah* have become less. Today we need help and co-operation from others in many areas. So, if I maintain *purdah* strictly, I cannot keep the family running smoothly. For the education of my grandchildren I have to meet with several teachers. Therefore I cannot maintain *purdah* as before because of my duties though I would like to."

A woman of 30 in Rangpur with eight children said "Muslim girls should keep strict *purdah* because everyone will die and you will have to give an account of your good and bad deeds. That is why one should observe *purdah*." When asked why she let her 17 year old daughter attend school, she said, "She studies in a girl's school and keeps a cloth over her head." The daughter said, "It is nonsense to say that you break *purdah* by going out. You can observe *purdah* and still go to school. In this age there should not be so much *purdah*."

More briefly, other comments have been:

"A woman can do all she needs behind *purdah*."

"I don't like it but keep it for fear of criticism from my elders."

"I keep it for society's sake."

"I keep it for religion and society."

"*Purdah* is covering your head, having a boundary around your house and not being seen by strange men."

"*Purdah* has several meanings. To some, a woman who passes several strange men without a *burkah* or without covering her head is not observing *purdah*. To others the same situation is *purdah* if the woman's behavior and inner thoughts in passing these men are correct."

"Muslim village women should maintain *purdah* in fear of religion and society. In the *town*, where there is no problem of criticism, maintaining *purdah* is not necessary."

There are probably two main points about this complex institution of *purdah* that those involved in projects to bring about change in the behavior of rural women should keep in mind. One, of course, is that *purdah* allows for flexibility and can be variously interpreted to accommodate access to valued new resources. It can never be a reason for failure to initiate projects. But another is that because *purdah* is status-related, all those who aspire to status, which usually means all those who do not have it or are not secure in it, will strive toward observing *purdah*. Poor village women who are able to survive only by violating *purdah* are likely to want to marry their daughters into *purdah*. Projects involving women must look for ways to involve not just poor women whose behavior has no influence on others, but in addition the women of families who set the standards for the village. Resistance to such involvement is likely to be strong. Social pressure in the form of gossip, rumor, and unpleasant encounters can, if a village is united, effectively exclude these women from such projects. But there is evidence that many villages are not united on this issue and change that will have a lasting effect may be possible, if resources *and* long-range committment are in the service of such change.

CHAPTER VII

STATUS

From the point of view of project work intended to initiate
change in the conditions of women in villages, status or prestige is a concept one must grapple with, since the social ideology of status or prestige, set by the more powerful, controls
the behavior of almost all women in the village. If one is
seeking to extend resources to poor women to enable them to
improve their economic condition, one must first understand how
the ideology of status limits the ways in which they can afford
to respond when new opportunities are offered. The guidelines
a project evolves to initiate action toward long-range objectives must take into account the perspective that rural women
have on their own situation.

Definitions of economic categories in Bangladesh are usually
based on land ownership or control over land; they distinguish
four groups - the landless, the small farmer, the middle farmer,
and the rich farmer. The landless have no more than a homestead,
sometimes rented. Small farmers own up to about two and a half
acres, middle farmers up to four or five, and rich farmers above
that. Landless and small farmers comprise about 50% of rural
families; they cannot feed their families from the land.

What we have found throughout the project is that such categorization of rural women does not fully explain variations in
their behavior in response to resources as efficiently as does
the concept of *status*. Many of the women in the 50% of rural
families that are poor would be unable to act to improve their
situation, if opportunities were made available, because of
status considerations. One questions the categorization of

65

middle and rich rural women according to the amount of land
owned by the series of men they depend on (father, husband, son,
brother), since they frequently do not share in the fruits of
these resources (see the chapter on "Life Crises"), and are
liable to very sudden shifts in resources because they are
women.(1) The following examples illustrate the dilemma in
using land as an indicator of a woman's access to resources:

> Roushan's father was landless, but earned income as a jute
> trader. He married her to a farmer in a nearby village who
> owned land and a house with a tin roof. However, while
> keeping her as his wife, her husband squandered the land on
> a series of wives in addition to her. Roushan gave birth
> to three daughters and one son. Her husband died when the
> eldest was eleven. She returned "home", but her father had
> died, her brothers had left, and there was only her elderly
> mother. Roushan is trying to support herself and her chil-
> dren by working in others' houses, selling puffed rice and
> sewing quilts. Her eldest daughter is also working in
> others' houses.

> Fazletunessa was married to a tailor with land. When he
> wanted to take another wife he sent her home without divor-
> cing her. He kept their three sons and she has their young
> daughter. She does not receive any support from him. At
> "home" are her elderly mother, her sister who was abandoned
> with three children and her own daughter. These three women
> and four children have three acres of land - a substantial
> amount if there were family males to manage it, but halved
> in productivity because it must be sharecropped. There are
> of course no alternative means of income.

Village women use such terms as "Garib" or "poor" to describe
certain economic conditions. They are those who live from day
to day: "with what they get each day, they eat." But this
definition does not enable project staff to explain why some
"poor" women will take advantage of certain economic opportunities and resources and other "poor" women will not. The cultural
distinction in understanding the behavior of rural women in
response to resources seems to be how a woman and her family feel
about their status.

---

(1) See Chen and Guznavy's study for striking examples of such
shifts.

Status in rural society is not entirely separate from land
ownership in the history of the family, but it can remain operative in controlling behavior for some time after land has been
lost. Status in rural society is frequently a basis for power
and influence. It is usually accompanied by land ownership and
financial means, but it may also substitute for them when a
family's economic condition has deteriorated, or is recuperating.
A family that is newly rich may try to increase status by marriage alliance with a poorer family that has prestige, usually
between a boy with money and a girl with status. Status is a
viable socio-economic asset in that it is a basis for good
marriage alliances that will sustain or improve a family's
position, and for maintaining power, influence and control over
resources. Thus, a land-poor family will seek to hold on to
status as long as it can.

One traditional sign of status in rural Bangladesh is the behavior of the women in a family. Appropriate behavior for high-
status women includes strict *purdah*, strict sexual division of
labor and relative freedom from menial work. Only families in
good economic condition can afford to support such behavior,
but because it is the symbol of a family with influence and
power, most families aspire to come as close to it as possible.
The image of relative idleness among its women is projected by
families that want to indicate their status.(2) On a trip to
Rangpur, project staff spoke separately to the men and women of
a prosperous, conservative farm family. The women, in response
to questions about what they did, spoke about their chickens,
vegetables, rice processing, etc. The men, in response to the
same question about their women, said that "they cook and sew
quilts."

The image of shelter for widows and other dependent women is
also projected as a mark of status. As indicated earlier, even
when women are in real need, determination to maintain status
will keep them from revealing that need by violating *purdah* or

---

(2) See our paper "Finding Ways to Learn About Village Women -
Experiments in a Project in Bangladesh", Ford Foundation, Dacca,
1976 for a discussion of the problems created for those seeking
information about the *work* village women do, by such an index
for status. The contradiction is very ironic; women work hard
and are in fact valued as brides for their ability to do hard
work but their *families* gain status from pretending that they
do nothing.

doing certain kinds of work for money. Women themselves usually
recognize the value of preserving status, especially for the
future of their children, but sometimes their need is so great
that what the family gives them in return for limiting their
possible responses to need is not enough. Several women have
spoken of this dilemma. One woman whose economic condition had
deteriorated said, in response to the question "Why don't you
work?": "How can I? We were in a good position for so long.
Now, how can I do any work?" The interviewer asked, "You can
do handiwork, can't you?" "Yes, I can, but for that capital is
needed. Where would I get the money?" The interviewer said:
"You can grind others' paddy." The woman responded: "It isn't
possible. We might starve to death but we have to maintain our
status. Otherwise the neighbors will speak ill of us."

Another woman who is 25 years old, divorced, with one son and
living at home with her "respectable" brothers (who are seeking
another marriage for her), told the interviewer that her hope
was to raise her son to be a "real person". But she has no
money for food or clothing. She helps her mother in their own
domestic work, but she wants to take a loan through the co-
operative so that she can husk paddy commercially, since she
knows how to do it. She says that she will have to do it
secretly because the relatives and neighbors will criticize her.
"Sometimes" she says, "one may know how to do work, but not be
able to take advantage of it."

There are, of course, variations in how families and even whole
villages will enforce this indication of family status through
social pressure. But there is no doubt that it remains one of
the dominant values of rural society. If one assumes that
women in about 50% of rural families are poor by class definitions and one adds to that those who are poor and dependent
because of the loss of husbands through death, divorce, separation, and abandonment, one might expect the numbers of women
who would respond to any new economic resources to be very high.
But when one recognizes that most of these women and their
families are concerned with protecting status *as an economic
asset*, one understands the complex problem a project faces when
it seeks to direct resources toward rural women.

Among poor women (excluding for the moment those who have *no-one*
but themselves to depend on), we have experienced some basic
differences in response to resources that seem to have to do
with the differences in their status aspirations. A basic
question for a woman and her family seems to be: what do they

have to lose by behaving as if she had no aspirations to status?
Our experience indicates that women who have been without status
for a generation or two will act as if they have less to lose
than women whose families have been "respectable" in this or the
last generation. They will be more likely to loosen *purdah* to
take advantage of economic opportunities, to accept the opportunity to work, and to do *any* kind of work, than women who may
be equally in need but are restricted by status considerations.
Poor women from families that have declined quite recently,
though they may be widows, divorced, or mothers of hungry and
uneducated children and unable to get their basic needs met
from their families on whom they are totally dependent, are
likely to be reluctant to break *purdah* or to do work that is
associated with non-status women, i.e. heavy menial work, for
pay, (though they may do it as dependents on the relatives they
live with). They may be unwilling or unable to take advantage
of training unless it is given in the village, or to earn
money in ways for which there are ready markets like making mats
or processing rice. As one woman said, "We are not the kind for
making mats or selling puffed rice. Our prestige would go." In
many cases it is not just that a woman will not do this kind of
work for fear of losing status; it may be that she does not know
how to do it because of the economic condition of her family.
Rice-processing for example, requires great skill passed on
traditionally and cannot be quickly learned. Because she is
also unlikely to have been given education which might now suit
her for work which has some status, she is in a helpless position.

Some of these poor women will earn small amounts of income within the shelter of *purdah* in "respectable" ways such as making
fans, quilts, baskets, and even fishnets for commercial marketing. Ironically, they are more likely to be exploited by
family and middlemen because of the restrictions on their behavior, their lack of experience with making money, and their
dependence on others, than are the women without concern for
status who, while they may be exploited by society at large,
at least within the limits of the world of women's work, know
how to negotiate business-like arrangements for their own self-
interest. They can do anything and go anywhere where opportunities are offered, to the city to be a servant, to "food for
work" projects, or to special training programs if they are
offered. But of course, as soon as they get on their feet, they
will work to re-establish their status.

However, no matter how hard these women work and how well they do, no one in rural society will emulate their path or consider it respectable, though other poor women may see it as a way back to respectability and shelter. Any project that is concerned with the integration of women in rural development must, therefore, deal head-on with the issue of status. It is not something to be lost sight of in efforts to reach the "poorest of the poor". Nor are the needs of these women who value status to be rejected because they offend the work ethic of planners and critics. Project administrators must recognize that rural programs for women have to be concerned with changing social values related to women, not just patching up failures in the system. They must try to find ways to substitute work for idleness as a status symbol and they cannot do so by addressing the poor alone. They must address the more complex problem of how to enable status-bound women to maintain and even raise their status through regular income-producing work. It is not easy, but it is the only viable way. It means that the long-range policy of a program for women must be to find ways for all women in need to *be able* to work, not just those who are now the poorest. If one wishes to move in that direction the policy of the present generation must be to find varying kinds of work for women under varying social pressures and with varying skills.

CHAPTER VIII

LIFE CRISES

For a rural woman born twenty or thirty years ago, a picture of
the good life might reveal the following features. Born into
a landholding household without need, she is suckled for two or
three years, cared for and carried around by an older sister
until she is able to manage for herself. At the age of seven
or eight she begins to take on casual tasks at her elders'
bidding - watching a younger child, collecting leaves for the
goat, or carrying messages for her mother who does not go out.
She attends early morning classes at the religious school nearby
where she learns to read the Koran in Arabic and to say prayers.
For two or three years she attends primary school, but as
puberty approaches she is withdrawn from school to stay inside
the *bari*. Her mother begins to teach her how to look pretty and
dress nicely. She helps with the cooking and does needlework,
but there is no real pressure of routine tasks.(1) By the time
she is twelve an acceptable marriage offer comes from a good
farm family in the next village, they pay a good bride price and
do not expect anything beyond token gifts from the bride's
family.

Her in-laws and husband are happy to receive her because she is
a healthy farm girl with a religious education who is modest,
obedient and hard-working. In fact, she has to work very hard
in her in-law's house; she is rigorously confined to the compound;

----

(1) One mother says she does not ask her daughter to work because
the whole life of women is working. Soon she will be exhausted
by work in her mother-in-law's house, "just as I was".

71

she has to please everyone. But she learns quickly, shows skill
in her work and is appreciated by her in-laws. They recognize
her need as a young girl to enjoy the freedom and familiarity of
her parents' home, so they allow her to go home from time to
time for the first few years to make the adjustment smooth.(2)
Within three years she has produced a healthy son whom she
suckles with abundant milk. She regains her strength, continues
to work hard and contributes to the running of the household to
everyone's satisfaction. Her husband continues to appreciate
her. She has another son and a daughter over the next seven or
eight years and is able to manage well.

Her father-in-law dies and her husband, with a share of the land,
separates his kitchen from the other brothers. They have to work
very hard in agriculture, he in the fields, she in the compound,
with the burden on just the two of them for several years because
their five children are in school. Her thrifty ways and good
judgment enable them to manage to educate their sons. One of the
sons gets a service job and another takes more responsibility for
the land, finding ways to increase the yield. Her respectable
behavior has enhanced the status of the family so that their
daughters, educated to class four or five in a religious school,
make good marriages which bring important alliances, and her
sons bring in good, respectable, hard-working, obedient daughters-in-law. Land which they have had to mortgage to relatives
during the pressing years of educational and marriage expenses,
they are able to buy back. Her husband is hard-working, treats
her well, expects obedience but respects her judgment. Her sons
appreciate her sacrifices. At 45, she becomes a widow. Her
sons rely on her for her knowledge of farming and her thrift,
and they and their wives support her with respect through old
age to a peaceful death.

When one meets this rural woman at any stage of her fulfilling
life, there is no mistaking her look - she is handsome and
radiant. But such women are rare. There are too many things

---

(2) These visits to the parental home are important occasions
in a woman's life and continue for many years. After the period
of adaptation when they may be frequent, she will usually go home
once or twice a year. These visits are occasions for relaxation,
relative freedom, a chance to eat at whim, and to keep ties
strong.

that can go wrong at every stage of her life,(3) some as a
result of changes in the rural condition because of pressure on
the land causing transitional attempts for new ways to deploy
family resources, and some that are inherent in this socio-
cultural context.

The following are some of the obstacles to the good life (which
is her view of the good *family* life) that the rural woman faces
and tries, through various strategies, to cope with. We will
look first at the woman with enough resources so that need,
though it may be present, has not reduced her to abandoning the
status that comes from keeping *purdah* and on which she can base
some hope for a better economic future. Later we will look at
the situation for rural women who are outside that category.

We are not suggesting that women, like all people, do not experience poverty as the primary obstacle to the good life. This
aspect of rural life is well-documented in most literature on
Bangladesh. Scarcity of resources is the dominant reality. But
the point we want to stress is that females face possibilities
of economic and psychological impoverishment independent of the
fate of the family, that affect their behavior and *will determine
their priorities of action in response to new resources.* To go
back to girlhood, then, the hardships a girl faces in her
parental home before marriage because she is female may be mostly
the result of scarcity of resources and goods. The fact that the
infant mortality rate for girls is higher than that for boys is
the result, in a situation of scarcity, of giving more food and
better medical attention to boys than girls because boys are the
most important investment for the future.(4) Girls learn early
that patience and sacrifice are the way to please.(5)

Marriage, which is universal, is the really critical event in a
girl's life. She has no say in who her husband or in-laws will
be, but relies on the judgment of elders, mostly but not

---

(3) Jean Ellickson reports that 28% of 277 women over 15 years
old in the Rajshahi village she studied were without husbands:
52 widows, 15 not yet married, eight divorced and three abandoned. Of these women, 31 are heads of households, only four
with enough land to support them. These 31 are 16% of all
householders (1975).
(4) For children aged one to four, the mortality rate for
females is at least 35% higher than for males (Lindenbaum, 1975).
(5) Jahan, 1975.

exclusively, male elders and on luck.(6) She meets her husband
on the day of marriage, unless he is a relative she played with
when she was very young.

The first two or three years in her in-laws' house, when she is
about 12 or 13 to 15 or 16, are critical ones when a number of
things can go wrong which will set her back considerably, though
probably not, at such a young age, irretrievably. She may find
her husband totally unacceptable perhaps because he is too old,
unpleasant or cruel or because she learns that he already has
another wife who lives in her parental home. Or he may find her
not to his liking, perhaps because he was interested in someone
else. He may physically abuse her. She may find the mother-in-
law unbearably cruel, giving her too much work, scolding her
constantly and torturing her by not allowing her to eat enough
or at appropriate times. If the husband favors the bride and is
attentive to her, his mother may complain to him about the girl's
behavior, placing him in a situation of great conflict which
usually, if he is dependent on his parents, will adversely
affect his behavior toward his wife. The girl's family may have
promised gifts to the groom's family which they are late in sending. This exposes the girl to continuing abuse from the mother-
in-law and others in the family.(7) Or, having pleased and been
found satisfactory by everyone, she may find at the end of two
or three years that she is not pregnant.

What happens to a young girl in response to these situations?
The cruelty of her mother-in-law or her husband may make her
flee to her parents' home. At first her parents are likely to
smooth over the situation with the in-laws, perhaps coax or
threaten to beat the girl, and send her back. If at some point
they feel their family honor is offended by this behavior toward

---

(6) Marriages are sometimes arranged with the help of middlemen.
Most members of both families, especially the elders, have a say
in the marriage. Men, since they alone have contact with the
outside world, handle the arrangements and have the ultimate
authority. Males from the groom's side, often including the
groom, come to look at the prospective bride. The prospective
groom may reject the girl, but she rarely is given the right to
reject him.
(7) Aziz reports 12 divorces in 12 years in the village he
studied as a result of the dowry not being paid. He says that
parents who cannot afford a good groom may marry their daughters
to older widowers (1976).

their daughter, they may prevail on the husband to grant a divorce and they will take her back and seek to marry her again. However, it may cost more to find a good second marriage since divorce is frowned on (though practised) in prestigious families, the more so as a family tries to use respectability as its basis for status, and the expense and risks of having a non-productive young woman at home may be a burden. Therefore, the family with few resources and precarious social position may find it very difficult to extricate their daughter from her uncomfortable situation in the in-laws' house. She is totally dependent on the decisions of others which in turn are affected by socio-economic factors. She has no alternative, if her parents cannot take her back, but to bear the situation.(8)

Sometimes in these situations, the husband may divorce(9) the girl or leave her at her parents' house and not bring her

---

(8) Suicides among young women in Bangladesh seem to result from such "hopeless" situations. The specific cases we have heard about were said to be caused by beatings by the husband, a flare-up by the father-in-law, and conflict between in-laws and parents over whether the daughter should be divorced or returned to her husband.

(9) In a Kushtia village, there were 59 divorces among 211 marriages. 26 men had 36 divorces. 20 women had 23 divorces. Of those who had been divorced two men and 13 women were not re-married, (Arens, 1975). In a village in Comilla, 16.5% of all marriages ended in divorce, (Ellickson, 1972). Divorces occur among all classes, though more frequently and with less stigma among the poor. Because of the stigma, those who are concerned with preserving high status would in most cases choose permanent separation rather than divorce. In response to questions about their attitude toward divorce, middle class rural women have said: "Divorce is extinct from the rich and middle class, though it exists among the poor."; "We don't hear about divorce nowadays."; "There is no divorce in our own family."; "Divorce brings a bad name to the family and the woman and her children become a burden if she can't get married again."; "I hate and despise divorce from the heart."; "Only the poor get divorced. Well-established families consider it a vice."

back.(10) Or if the wife is not fertile, husbands may in these
situations, often with pressure from the mother-in-law, bring
in another wife.(11) Having a co-wife is rarely pleasant for
the wife who is being replaced, especially if she is handicapped
in the competition for attention by low fertility. In general,
though with exceptions, divorce is preferred by the poor and
separation and polygamy by those with a better economic condition
as the way of replacing an unsatisfactory wife.

During these first few years when a girl is so dependent and
insecure, with no power base at all in her new home and little
claim on the assets of her parents' home, her strategies are
limited. One young daughter-in-law sums up the situation
realistically:

-----

(10) These "separations" are not counted in most statistics about
marriage, yet we have encountered such situations all over the
country involving women of all ages and all classes. There are
several causes for these separations. If the husband wants a
second wife but does not want to keep the first one, she may
return to her parental home rather than be divorced. Or a husband may refuse to give a divorce because he would be expected
to pay *mehr*, or the amount fixed in the marriage contract to be
paid to the wife if he dissolves the marriage. Or a husband may
simply desert his wife. In almost all cases these women are
dependent on their parental families.
(11) Under Islamic law, a man may not have more than four wives.
Few rural men have four wives. Once it may have been considered
a status symbol to be able to maintain and control so many women
in one *bari*, but now it is usually beyond the reach of even the
wealthier village men. In one village Ellickson studied, 6% of
the marriages were polygamous, out of 358 (1972). In two
villages Aziz refers to, 19 out of 1681 and 14 out of 280 families had more than one wife - about 1% and 5% respectively
(1976). There are several kinds of motivations for taking
second or third wives. One has primarily an economic base. For
example, families for whom weaving is a traditional home-based
industry may practice polygamy because wives have the additional
work burdens involved with weaving and one wife cannot manage
the whole burden. Taking a co-wife because the first wife is
not able to bear children, or *male* children, is also economically
motivated but this situation more obviously involves a failure
of the first wife to be of value.

"If I don't obey my husband or father-in-law, they will give divorce without further question. They threaten that they will send me to my father's place. If I go there my father will marry me again. They won't let me stay there forever. So I have to listen to all that they say."(12)

Her best strategy is to have a son, but that is out of her control. She turns to charms and prayers to help her, and probably finds family planning advocates totally incomprehensible. Beyond that, she can only practise the virtues of patience and sacrifice taught her from childhood as the role of women.

Assuming she makes a reasonable adjustment during these early years and has, say, three children in ten years, whether she stays in a joint family or sets up a separate kitchen, her dependency increases. With young children the likelihood of her remarrying or finding adequate shelter with her parents or brothers becomes more remote. The dangers now are loss of her husband through death or alienation of her husband through divorce, separation or polygamy. Widowhood is inevitable for most rural women(13) but when it comes early, with young

---

(12) The traditional village code of behavior for a woman suggests the strategy most likely to avoid conflict: she should be soft-spoken, sweet and polite in speech, never quarrelsome; she should say her prayers, keep *purdah*. A bad girl is one who quarrels, talks in a rude way, and spreads bad feelings. Even women blame the woman in a failed marriage. They praise a woman who accepts her fate and comes through, as opposed to one who protests and acts against her fate. This code of passivity, in some ways the only practical strategy when alternatives are non-existent, does not work all that well for young women. Women's mortality rate during the years 15-39 is higher than that of men. Shirley Lindenbaum suggests that this is a time when there is added pressure for women to give birth to sons but as yet little cultural protection for the new mother (1975).
(13) According to 1961 figures, 41% of women between 40 and 59 and 82% of women over 60 were widows (Aziz, 1976). Rounaq Jahan points out that the Master Survey of Agriculture indicates a sharp increase in the number of widowed females after the age of 34 with no such corresponding increase in the number of widowed males. It is at about this age that women have a number of dependent children and would find it difficult to remarry (Jahan, 1975).

children, a woman is in a very difficult situation. She is not likely to be able to remarry so her alternatives are dependence on her in-laws(14), her brothers, for whom, having lost status, she will do the menial work of the household, or, worst of all, herself.(15) Divorce may be less likely at this stage of a woman's life than earlier but she regards it as a threat and considers obedience to the husband, including hard work and hot meals served on time, essential contributions to her security.(16) The introduction of a co-wife now is a serious threat especially since her children, who are her main future security, might get less favored treatment and less education. A woman from Jessore describes what many women fear:

> My husband used to love me. Now, after marrying again, he cannot tolerate me at all. There is no relationship between us. If I tell the co-wife something regarding work, she tells my husband and as a result he beats me. If I didn't have three children I would go to my father's place. My children go to school, but my father-in-law bears the expense, and my husband does not look after my children at all. He is busy with his second wife's son. I want to educate my children because they are my only hope. I have as much value as a servant.

Although it is the elder's interest to keep a joint family together, it is in the younger woman's interest to separate from a joint family; perhaps that is why such break-ups are conventionally attributed to quarrelling among the wives. Living as daughter-in-law within a joint family, she has no control of the

---

(14) If a woman is living in a joint family and her husband dies before her father-in-law, her children will not inherit anything when the father-in-law dies unless he has made a special provision in a will. See especially the study by Salma Sobhan on the legal rights of women in Bangladesh (1978).
(15) In the village Ellen Sattar studied, seven out of 60 household heads were widows. Of these, four had less than half an acre (1974).
(16) Women tell us that, basically, they have to obey the word of their husbands. One says, "My husband does everything according to his parents' wishes and I have to obey his word." Another says: "The wife bears all types of sufferings from her husband because after marriage he is the head and God and heaven are under his feet. Women cannot oppose what their husbands say because they will have to suffer many difficulties and sorrows."

distribution of resources to members of her family, nor much influence on her husband who is her basic resource. Once out of the joint family, her influence is likely to increase.

When the time comes to arrange a marriage for her daughter that is likely to keep her secure, the rural woman has to worry not only about the risks brides faced in her generation, but also about the new question of education as leverage for a good marriage. Should she, if she can afford it, educate her daughter past the fourth or fifth class in the hopes of making an alliance with an educated boy who may find respectable employment off the land? There are several risks.

If she gives her daughter more education and ultimately has to marry her into a traditional rural family, the adjustment problems with an uneducated mother-in-law are likely to be severe. Several young women in such situations have told us that their mothers-in-law have abused them for wearing petticoats, blouses, clean or colored saris, and using soap - all "modern" ways - and criticized them for not knowing farm work. If her daughter continues past the fifth class and suitable offers do not come in, the family may have to bear the expense and social criticism for keeping a daughter in school longer than intended in order to avoid the embarrassment of having an unmarried daughter at home. However, the more education her daughter gets, the more dowry she will have to pay to get an appropriately educated husband. The family may ultimately have to promise more dowry than it can afford to get the daughter married. Families that can do so, sell land to pay these dowries, but if promises cannot be kept, the daughter is likely to be abused in her in-laws' house or sent home. It is the now ageing mother who faces the economic implications of married daughters, with or without children, returning to the parental home, the higher cost of a second marriage, and her own impending dependency on her sons compounded by the possibilities of the daughter's dependency. It is no wonder that women tend to be a conservative force in the raising of daughters.

When a woman's sons are grown and her husband has died, she faces a number of obstacles to a peaceful, respectable widowhood. Her sons may have too little land to support her well. If educated, they may be both unable to get jobs and unable to manage the farm. Possibly they will neglect her, though traditional rural society strongly censures such behavior.(17) At any rate she will be in competition with her daughter-in-law whom she may try to keep insecure in her relationship with her new husband, so that her own influence will last. Gradually, however, the daughter-in-law is bound to gain in influence and during her last years the old woman may be treated with less than ideal respect and gratitude for all the sacrifices she has made.(18)

The situation for the very poor woman reveals some important differences, the main ones being a lifetime of extreme scarcity and dependence for survival on what one can get each day. We are not referring here to those poor women, such as wives of marginal farmers, widows, and divorced or abandoned women in families with some resources, who must find ways to cope with poverty without losing status. Rather we are looking at women who have been poor for long enough that status is not an issue. There, food, not social pressure with its rewards and restrictions, is the controlling issue. These women have more options in domestic crises, but they face other problems that result from extreme poverty.

Childhood for the very poor girl is a struggle for survival against malnutrition and disease. She has no education, either religious or Bengali. If her mother works in others' houses, she may go along to help out and earn her food. She is likely to be married quite young. Her parents are not likely to be able to take as much care in the choice of a husband as those families with more of a margin of resources. Marriage is not as costly nor is divorce much of a stigma. During the early years of marriage a very poor girl may face similar domestic problems to those described above. But she is much more likely than the status-bound woman to resolve her problem with divorce and quick remarriage. The increased independence is, of course, a matter of economics. The very poor girl is not likely to be

---

(17) According to Islam "a woman's heaven is under the feet of her husband; a man's heaven is under the feet of his mother." (18) Shirley Lindenbaum points out that a mother's investment in her son gives her about ten years protection in widowhood. At the ages 50-59 the mortality rate for males is higher than that of women. From 60-69 women die at a higher rate than men. As she points out, these are the years when the daughter-in-law, perhaps now married ten years, has several children of her own and has growing status and attention from her husband (1975).

a burden at home because she can earn her own food and, therefore, she can abandon an unsatisfactory marriage. However, the
situation has its negative side. Poor husbands are more likely
to divorce or abandon their wives, which at first may not be a
problem since the woman can remarry easily; but with young
children it is a disastrous situation.

A very poor woman is dependent on having children to keep a
husband and to provide future security. Raising them does not
involve much expense and the hope is that by the age of ten
they will be bringing in money. Because she depends for survival
on her economic autonomy as well as on a man, a very poor woman
faces some of the same risks as a very poor man - lack of jobs,
ill health and lack of children in old age.(19) But of course,
her struggle is hampered by her physical weakness during child
bearing years, the presence of dependent children and the per-
vasiveness of male domination of public space which puts her at
a disadvantage if she seeks employment other than that which is
strictly traditional for women in rural areas.

Poor women separate from joint families fairly early. They have
more influence *vis-a-vis* mothers-in-law and husbands than status-
bound women. They can expect their husbands to share some of
their work and to pay some attention to them in decision making
because they have a degree of economic autonomy. They have the
freedom to take advantage of work opportunities and to travel
to where such work is offered and some adeptness at protecting
their self-interest in economic situations. But there is no
doubt that these women, if they were to better themselves, would
want the security of *purdah* and male protection for their daughters or granddaughters. Their economic autonomy and independence
make them outcasts according to the social values of the rural
community.

The following are fairly typical examples of the *real*, as
opposed to the good or ideal life, that rural women are coping
with.

---

(19) We have encountered situations of extraordinarily high
infant mortality among the very poor - in one case, only two
children survived from 16 pregnancies.

Malika from Mymensingh is about 45. She has one son and little land. She supports herself and her son by supervising the cultivation of the land and by making and selling brooms and other such household items. She tried to educate her son but he played truant and she was unable to control him.

Asufa from Mymensingh has seven children. She has a house but no land. Her husband used to grind oil from mustard seed. She supports herself and her family in the same way. Her daughter does the cooking and a son sells for her.

Mehrunnessa from Rangpur is about 35 and has five children. She supports herself by working in others' houses and begging. One son is married and lives separately. Another lives with his in-laws.

Kamrunnessa has two sons and three daughters. They have almost no land. The eldest son is educated but does not have a job. With money from the land she started a kerosene shop with her youngest son. There is not enough money to support five people. As she says, "If we get rice we don't get curry; if we get salt, we don't get oil." Her daughter is 15, but it costs too much to marry her. Her son is unable to find a job.

Another woman has a daughter of about 12. She sold the land she inherited from her husband and went to her brother's place. Her brother took the money, saying he would buy her land, but he hasn't. Eventually she was able to get a tiny piece of land from her brother and has a house on it. She and her daughter husk rice in others' houses.

Zarina is 47, has two sons and one daughter. Her daughter is married, as is one son. The other son, 14 years old, helps his brother. She has been widowed for six years. She says: "In the time of my father-in-law and my husband I was very happy. My father-in-law used to ask me before doing anything; my husband also. My elder son, even now, does not do anything without asking me. My husband left me eight *bighas* (two and two-thirds acres) in my name after his death so that I don't have to suffer. But now I have to tolerate the abuse of my daughter-in-law who is beautiful and from a prosperous family. She does not love me or care about my

food. She even scolds me sometimes. I take care of four
grandchildren all day, but if there is any fault she starts
scolding indirectly. Instead she behaves as if she loves
me. I cannot tell my son because he would think, since he
has never seen his wife behave in this way, that I was
telling lies."

Divorce, Polygamy and Abuse

One woman, the daughter of a fisherman, was married to a
man in the same village who had some land and a shop. She
lived with him for 14 years and bore 11 children of whom
three survived - two sons and a daughter who is lame. He
divorced her while she was pregnant. "The village people
said that divorce could not be given while I was pregnant
but still it happened." She explains, "My husband drove out
his first wife for some reason and then married me. After
my first child he brought the first wife back home again
and after that I lived with a co-wife. Sometimes I had to
go to my father's place because of the co-wife's plotting.
But for the sake of the children I again returned to my
husband's family. Coming and going this way, I gave birth
to children at the beginning and the end of the year and in
this way I had 11 children. At last because of the conspir-
acy of the co-wife and my mother-in-law, my husband divorced
me while I was pregnant." She does not blame her husband;
she says the fault was the co-wife's. Now she supports
herself by working in others' houses. Her children stay
with her during the day, but eat and sleep at their father's.

Another woman was married to a tailor who had two acres of
land. He was an only child. She bore three boys and one
girl. When the youngest was two, the wife had a fever for
three months. The in-laws did not try to take care of her.
They sent word to her mother to bring her home but when no-
one came she was sent home with her son. After one year
her husband married again. The three sons live with their
father but visit their mother now and then. The husband
does not give her or their daughter anything. The village
women put the blame on the mother-in-law. They say that
since she could not get seven daughters-in-law from seven
sons, she would get them all from one son.

Shireen is married to a man with two and a half acres of
land. She is about 40. They have four daughters and two

sons, the oldest 15 and the youngest four. She says that
the day she gave birth to her youngest child her husband
went to another village saying he was going to buy straw
for the cow. Others in the village said he'd gone to get
married but he denied it. However, a few days later he
brought back his new wife. She does not know why he took
a second wife - there was no trouble between them. It came
as a complete surprise. The new wife is about 16. She has
borne two children. The first wife is worried about how
she can educate and feed her own children. She says there
is conflict between the two women. They keep separate
kitchens.

Another says that she was married to a man who had a first
wife. Within a year her husband divorced the first wife
saying she was too dark-skinned. He used to beat her without cause. When she could not bear any more she objected
and as the relationship between them was broken he divorced
her. She died a year after the divorce.

Asufa says she was married to a man who had another wife.
The first wife could not stand her and said things about
her to the husband who used to beat her. She thought of
divorce, but remembering the children, she bore all the
hardship.

Problems of Young Women

One woman tells of her daughter who committed suicide because of the violence of her husband. The interviewer
commented: "There is a system of divorce in our society.
A little girl cannot tolerate such violence. You could
have set her free." The mother replied: "Yes, many people
told me that. But there has never been divorce in this
well-known family."

A girl of 16 explains that she is not yet married. There
are 11 people living together, her parents, six children
and three others. They don't get enough food from the land
to feed them for a year. Her father is a clerk. She has
passed high school and wants to study more, but there is no
money. She says, "Due to my mother's illness and my father's
economic condition, I am not yet married."

Another girl has passed high school and wants to go to

college. Her father cannot afford it and has had her
married to a man with a B.A. But the groom's side has not
yet taken the bride home. She says she cannot study and
cannot lead a married life.

A young married woman of 19 tells the following story:
"Since I am the oldest daughter-in-law of the house, I have
more or less to ingratiate myself with all the members of
the family so no-one can find fault with the bride. I have
to flatter my father and mother-in-law, sister and brother-
in-law, and even the servants and neighbors so that they
will always praise me. Otherwise they will make a mountain
out of a mole-hill. The faults of the daughter are no
faults but in the case of the daughter-in-law a small fault
becomes a dangerous one." She was educated through high
school in her parents' house. "After the result of my
examination, preparation for my marriage started. Getting
a good proposal from a good family and boy, my mother ignored my wish to study in college. I was told that my in-
laws would let me continue with my education after marriage.
But after marriage I did not get any chance to study there.
My sisters-in-law are not good at study so they used to say
that there was no need for further study for the bride. I
used to think that I would be married to a service-holding
boy in town, that there would be no connection with the
village, that I would visit the village once or more a year,
and that everybody would love me and take care of me. But
there is no hope of that now." She has been married six
years without a child. "There is no question of divorce.
My husband might get married for a second time because I
don't have a child yet - I have tried many things but there
is no hope for the future. Other people in the house do
not look at me in the same way as before. My in-laws have
decided to give their son in marriage again. My husband
does not say anything openly but they have his consent. So
I have decided that if my husband marries again, I will go
to my father's house and spend the rest of my life there.
This will not exactly be divorce, but we will be separated."

The pretty young daughter of a very poor man was given in
marriage to an old man who asked for her and who paid her
father half an acre of land. This man had been married
four times before. His first wife was quickly divorced at
her own wish. The second fled twice, and bore two daughters.
The third bore a daughter and a son. The fourth got a
divorce. The fifth, this young poor girl, says she is happy

to marry into a rich household.

Another poor woman was married before she lost her first teeth to a man of 30. The arrangement was that the in-laws would raise her for five years before the marriage be consummated. She says if she went there in the morning, she fled in the evening; if she went in the evening, she fled in the morning. Her mother-in-law considered her a maidservant and would not give her enough food. She was always hungry. She came home to stay with her mother for a while. Her husband took another wife, so she got divorced and in three months was married again. She bore her second husband two children, both of whom died. She has left him to work in the city as a domestic and with her savings is buying land in the village which her brother and mother are cultivating.

Of course not every woman experiences directly the misfortunes related in these examples, but enough women in *all* villages do for them to influence every woman's behavior. In the absence of new resources, the risks women face may reinforce their dependent behavior. But even when new resources become available, women and their families must weigh carefully whether they are substantial enough to rely on.

CHAPTER IX

FAMILY STRATEGY AND FEMALE STRATEGY

When projects for women are introduced into rural society, they must, if they are to be accepted, be perceived both by women and their families as advantageous in terms of their main objectives. Families will not permit their women to participate if they do not see advantages in terms of their strategies for survival and security. Women, even if allowed or urged to participate by their families, will not make good use of new resources, unless they find them suitable for their own strategies, which, though they may have the same objectives, sometimes involve different tactics. Let us look first at some family strategies for women and then at women's own strategies to get a sense of what they are and how they may differ.

Family Strategy

Traditionally rural people seek to gain and control resources through the family. The contribution of its members to the social and economic strength of the family is the only available basis for security. Whether functioning as a joint family (i.e. returning all gains to the head of the family to redistribute) or separated into more nuclear units, family members in Bangladesh are interdependent in most matters. Family strategies involve the deployment of each member, not for his or her own ends as individuals, but for the better survival of the whole group. Opinions about the behavior or options to be chosen by individuals are taken from the whole family and are usually valued according to the age and position of the members.

How do rural Bangladeshi families tend to "use" their women?
In very poor families, the best strategies are perceived as
early marriage to relieve the financial burden on the parental
family, direct economic contribution to the woman's own support
and perhaps that of the children through labor in others' houses,
and high enough fertility to increase earning power and group
strength. In families that are trying to maintain or increase
status, the strategic uses of women may be different. Marriage
is still the most important strategy, with the hope being that
a good alliance will give a daughter a secure, permanent home
and the family an extension or increase of social influence and
economic benefit.(1) To make it possible for the daughter to
gain those advantages, they will have tried to give her a religious education, some vernacular education, and training in
respectable behavior. A new strategy for families seeking to
make alliances with families that have position and influence
in the non-rural sector is education beyond puberty. What the
girl's in-laws' family hopes to gain from her is status from
her behavior, economic benefit from her hard work, and security
from her fertility. Failure to perform well in these areas
reduces her value to the family quite drastically.

When a woman loses her husband through death, divorce, separation, or abandonment and is economically dependent on her in-
laws, her children or, once again on her parental family, their
strategies for her include remarriage when appropriate, menial
service to the family or perhaps some discreet means of earning
income. On the one hand, status accrues to a family for shel-
tering dependent women, but on the other, acute scarcity of
resources make her dependency a drain that they may be looking
to eliminate. These families may be the first to avail themselves of new strategies if they are offered in respectable

---

(1) With few exceptions, marriages are arranged, since in rural
society they function as an economic and social alliance between
two families more than as a romantic relationship between two
individuals. Since fathers and mothers depend for survival on
the support of their sons, a daughter-in-law must not deflect
his attention from their needs. Even more, her behavior should
serve to enable one whole family to adjust to another whole
family. This is more likely when she comes from a background
similar to her husband's family and is familiar with their ways.
"Love" marriages, in which partners choose each other, contra-
dict the primary functions a marriage is expected to perform.
Most love marriages we have encountered have not been happy.

ways.(2) Once accepted within the village, these strategies
may provide sanction for new behavior in many families.

It should be apparent then, that when projects for women enter
a rural community offering new resources in the form of employment, commercial enterprise, training, or health services,
families have to evaluate the risks and advantages, compared to
traditional strategies for their women, that would be involved
if they let them participate.

Female Strategy

As indicated earlier, the greatest threat to a rural woman is
to be without a male guardian, whether father, husband, son or
brother. Whatever the quality of that support, even if the
husband is cruel or lazy, or the son is negligent, or the
brother exacts menial work, the support and protection of males
are the basis of a tolerable life for rural women. Male support
is not only or always a matter of provision of food; it is a
matter of acting for women in "male space", the public world
they are not supposed to enter.

Since they are familiar, from examples in every village, with
the consequences to women and their children of the loss of male
support, rural women practise strategies for survival that are
distinct from family strategies. Much of rural women's behavior
is an effort, first, to hold on to her support and, second, to
gain some control. Since Bangladeshi men can divorce women by
saying "I divorce you" three times or can take co-wives (legally
only with the first wife's consent, but since she has no choice
because he might divorce her if she says no, that law does not
really mean much), obedience to her husband - "listening to his
talk" - is the foremost rule of her life, whether the obedience
is slavish or a formality. In practical terms, obedience
usually involves having meals ready on time, efficient farm
work and respectable behavior.

Since her mother-in-law has a strong hold on her husband's
emotions and can be a strong influence on his behavior, a woman
will also be obedient to her mother-in-law, especially during
the early years of marriage. It is important to avoid conflict
with the mother-in-law that might put a strain on the husband's

---

(2) See McCarthy, 1967.

90

loyalties, since the mother-in-law is likely to have more power.
Mother-in-law and daughter-in-law are rivals for the support of
the same man at a time when both women, one a young mother, and
the other an ageing woman, are especially helpless and dependent.
The balance of power over the male will shift to the weight
of each woman's claim.

Sacrifice to her son is another basic rule of a woman's behavior
since he is her future support. That is why mothers give their
sons more than their daughters and always take less for themselves to give their sons more. Since the head woman has control
over the food and can express favoritism through distribution of
choice foods, it is important for a daughter-in-law in a joint
family to get free of the mother-in-law so that she can be the
distributor of food. With whatever she has to give, the mother
sacrifices throughout her life for her son. She makes him, if
she can, her secret ally; she pampers him with treats; she
dresses him as smartly as she can; she tries to pay for his
education.

A woman's behavior in relation to her legal rights suggests how
important male protection is to her.(3) By Islamic law, she
inherits a proportion of her father's property. However, with
few exceptions women do not claim this inheritance since de-
priving their brothers of this source of income might antagonize
them. Since she may, as a widow, or divorced or separated woman,
have to depend on the protection of her brothers, she does not
keep the property for herself but relies on the shelter they owe
her for sharing her inheritance with them. Similarly, though
she has a right to claim the money pledged to her by the groom
in the marriage contract if he divorces her, she may forego it
for fear that prospective grooms and their families might find
such behavior unacceptable and that therefore she would be left
without a husband. All women, however, claim their share of
their husband's property when he dies.

Given the structure of rural society as it affects women, the
strategies of obedience, self-sacrifice and submission, which
we have referred to earlier, seem the most likely to provide
women with some guarantee of security. They do not always work,
but there are no obvious alternatives. These, of course, are
the strategies that are operating at the surface. At the same
time, beneath the surface, each woman tries first to loosen the

(3) See works by Sobhan (1978) and Alamgir (1977).

mother-in-law's hold on her husband and thereby gain control
over the women's sphere, and then, to strengthen her position
in her relationship with her husband and sons so that her future
is provided for. A lot of women's strategies at this level are
semi-secret, involving the distribution of resources under their
control including money where possible and, in situations where
resources are not available or do not help, such as lack of
fertility, ill-health and the threat of abandonment, recourse
to magic and spells. It should be obvious that though some of
their patterns of behavior are of necessity passive, rural
women are by no means passive by nature. Mernissi quotes a
woman who was very unjustly treated by her mother-in-law as
saying that she had no alternative but to accept the injustice:
"To protest, you have to have someone's support" (1975).

Rural women are very practical in gauging and attempting to get
what is necessary for their security. But the fact that they
so often fail to get what they need indicates that their resources are not adequate. Nevertheless, rural women look carefully at projects that offer them new resources to calculate
what they must risk for what possible gain. Like most rural
people they will look to minimize risks rather than maximize
profits.(4) Project designers must be constantly looking for
ways to *enable* rural women to take advantages of resources that
will increase their range of strategies and make them more
likely to succeed in gaining control over their lives, and thus
ensure survival and security.

---

(4) Some foreigners who had set up a project for women were
surprised and disappointed when a widowed participant who was
earning income quit the project, leaving her child with her
mother, to marry a man known to be a wife-beater. Similarly,
very poor Harijan women in Bihar sometimes choose to earn less
money by secluding themselves in the household rather than
working outside in the hope that this will lead to a more advantageous marriage. It should be obvious that at present *no* chance
of security for a rural woman seems more realistic than a husband.

CHAPTER X

CO-OPERATION AND CONFLICT

Rural women spend their days in a women's world, with little
direct or prolonged communication with adult males. In the
world of women there are, aside from individual attractions or
antipathies, general areas of co-operation and conflict. Let
us look first at areas of conflict.

As we have seen there is liable to be a current of tension between mother-in-law and daughter-in-law caused by their rivalry
for the same critical resource - the son/husband. Similarly,
daughters-in-law in a joint family are likely to feel some re-
sentment toward the mother-in-law and rivalry over the distribution of resources to husbands and children. Daughters and
daughters-in-law in the same household may experience conflict
because the daughter is likely to be much more favored. She
does not have to do much work or keep strict *purdah* or eat at
another's pleasure. There is, of course, frequently conflict
between co-wives who live in the same household.

These tensions within the family are rarely expressed openly.
Families valuing status condemn quarrelsome behavior so that a
lot of the tension is expressed indirectly. The belief that
ill-health or mishaps have been caused by spells cast by rival
women and the frequently voiced concern to avoid jealousy in
new groupings of women like co-operatives through equitable
distribution of resources suggest that rivalry and jealousy are
experienced as disruptive forces by women. When conflict is
expressed openly, it is usually the result of outbursts over
the distribution of food or the uncontrolled behavior of children, chickens, goats, and cows.

Although there may be tension and rivalry among women, it does
not often disrupt the co-operation, or mutual help, that exists
among women in all spheres of activity. In some aspects of
their lives, such as work, the give and take among strata of
women like rich and poor or mother-in-law and daughter-in-law
may be hierarchical; in others, such as health, it may be a
mutual exchange based on the common concerns as women of all
those past puberty. What are some of the ways women help each
other? They share the household work of routine or special food
preparation. They share the cooking for family or village
feasts. They help each other carry out small-scale buying and
selling within the village, with women who can move about a
little helping those who cannot. They give small loans of rice
or money without interest. They assist in childbirth and in
problems of health. They help each other in the management of
spells and charms prescribed by *pirs*.(1) They help a poor woman
marry her daughter or feed her children.

Often these exchanges of help are among the few occasions when
women beyond the immediate household are able to be together,
since meeting for no purpose but to talk is not socially acceptable, nor do women have much free time. For example, if one
woman is at the *dheki*, another woman who has no special chore
at the time may come to help without being called, and use the
time for a chance to talk and share news. Or women may get
together to help someone make noodles or puffed rice and talk
and eat as they work. They say they adjust the amount they eat
while working to the amount that is available. If women bathe
and wash clothes in the river, as in some parts of Bangladesh,
they combine these talks with the exchange of news and talk. In
other parts of Bangladesh, where there are more likely to be
tanks within most *baris*, women still get together but not from
as many families. In the monsoon, especially in parts of Bangladesh that are regularly flooded, women become isolated from
all but *bari* women. Women keep each other informed of the relevant news and appreciate in each other a willingness to chat.
Although one cannot say that women as a group have much social
influence, they can exert pressure against misbehavior by
talking about it.

This combination of conflict and co-operation among village
women exists in a society where there are scarce resources, a
strict sexual division of labor, a relative seclusion of women

---

(1) Saints

from each other and a strict exclusion of women from access to
outside resources except through males over whom they are forced
to compete. Without the introduction of change, it is difficult
for women in these circumstances to develop effective group
power or leadership. With new projects there is at least as
much potential for co-operation as there may be tendencies
toward jealousy and vindictive behavior.(2) But project administrators must be realistic about how women will respond. For
example, in the project described in Part Two, which brings
women together for opportunities to save, take loans, receive
training and have access to service and supplies, one should
not, just because these groups are called "co-operatives",
expect members to engage in joint economic efforts. Rather,
given the specific structure of this rural society, one would
expect them to avail themselves of resources for their own
families.(3)

Preliminary indications from the project suggest that more
information about patterns and groupings of co-operation among
rural women will better explain the interactions of the rural
community. It is likely to show that women are responsible for
distributing food to others in the neighborhood and village
during periods of scarcity or famine. It is also likely to
show that women control the extent to which conflict among men
is allowed to threaten family or community cohesiveness. It
may add an important dimension to understanding dependencies
between those with more and less, since women who keep *purdah*
are dependent on the services of women who move around. It may
show the role that daughters, and not just sons, play in helping their widowed mothers.

---

(2) Interestingly, only the latter tendencies are mentioned by
males when they question the feasibility of projects involving
women.
(3) Those who criticise this kind of behavior because it does
not conform to their notion of "co-operative behavior" are
probably imposing foreign conceptions on rural Bangladeshi
culture and failing to see clearly that development efforts
must have a cultural base.

CHAPTER XI

CHANGE

In almost all our interviews with rural women over thirty, they
offered unsolicited comments on changes they had experienced in
their own lifetimes. Mostly these changes were related to age
of marriage, practice of *purdah*, education for girls, and the
dowry system. These are some points of direct impact on rural
women's lives of larger forces that are working in the economy -
rapidly growing population, increased fragmentation and alienation of landholdings, and diversification of income generation
to other sources besides land. As Dr. Senaratne carefully
describes, changes in the rural resource base produce changes in
social practice to take advantage of it; belief systems are
concomitantly revised to support the practices of those who control most resources.(1) Thus new patterns in education, marriage
and *purdah* should, if they seem to be successful strategies for
deployment of women, produce shifts in belief systems, mainly
the criteria for status and prestige connected with behavior
of women.

In relation to the age of marriage,(2) most older women recalled
having been married one or two or even more years before the
onset of menstruation. They say that such early marriage was
then considered conducive to a good adjustment in that the new

---

(1) Senaratne, 1975.
(2) The consensus seems to be that average age of marriage has
been going up. Cain writes it is about 14 in the village he is
studying (1976). Aziz suggests that it is between 15-19 in the
area he is writing about (Aziz, 1976).

daughter-in-law had not yet had time to develop her own person-
ality and was still malleable. Besides, it was considered a
waste of money to keep a daughter in the parental home where she
would require food and clothing, but do little or no work. Now,
they say, the appropriate age for marriage is the onset of puberty, 12 or 13. However, they also indicate that there are a
number of girls in the village past that age who are still unmarried and they consider this a recent social problem. It is
obvious that there is no strong rural belief system to justify
later marriages since relatives of unmarried girls who are
obviously 16 or 17 will consistently report the ages of these
girls as 12 or 13. These young women are a social embarrassment;
there is no appropriate role for them. If they go to school,
their families will justify their being unmarried in the name of
education, but in most cases will take them out of school if a
good marriage offer comes along. Their families would probably
welcome new strategies that would relieve the embarrassment
connected with later marriage and give them some positive justification for having their daughters still at home.(3)

Another change that women indicate is the relaxation of *purdah*.(4)
Women from prestigious families recall that *purdah*, especially
for travel outside the *bari* was very complicated and stringent,
to prevent any chance of their being seen by strange men. They
continue to emphasize the importance of *purdah* but recognize that
it is being interpreted in new ways, which some condemn and some
support, depending, no doubt, on whether they experience advantage from the old or new ways. Some prosperous older women who
have had to relax *purdah* to manage their households efficiently,
say that they have done it "for the sake of work". Parents and
husbands of girls past puberty who are going to secondary school
or who have taken some of the new jobs being offered in rural
areas that involve contact with men, are talking about "inner

---

(3) One such justification used often to explain involvement of
women, both married and unmarried, in co-operatives or jobs is
"for the sake of the village" or "for the sake of the country,"
when the primary motivation, unexpressed, is obviously economic.
(4) Probably the most important change in the recent past was
the introduction of the *burkah* about 40 years ago which allowed
women from respectable families to leave their *baris* when
necessary (Abdullah 1966). Now the availability of the *burkah*
makes possible new kinds of ventures. These days, some women,
especially younger ones, who can afford a *burkah*, are not using
it.

purdah" being as valid as seclusion or the *burkah*. In the past
higher education for most girls was said to be not possible
because it would "hamper *purdah*"; now the *definition* of *purdah*
is being changed. Although strict interpretation of *purdah* is
still the operative norm in most villages, the reasons for these
deviations among respectable families indicate that *purdah* might
be relaxed for more women if the "trade-off" were really advantageous.

Poor women have always had to relax *purdah* in order to eat, but
their behavior has no influence on the social system of beliefs
and values. If young women from families that are perceived as
respectable relax *purdah* restrictions to take advantage of resources that are perceived as valuable, they may set a standard
in the village for the interpretation of *purdah* that will influence others. The fact that dependent women from well-off urban
families have in recent years taken secretarial training and
become secretaries has given that job status, so that other
women who are more in need but concerned with respectability
can also do that work. However, as indicated in the section on
purdah, this aspect of women's behavior is controlled by male
social pressure because it is related so closely to male honor
and prestige in the community. History indicates that change is
possible but one must be very sensitive to *how* it is possible if
one wants to work toward further relaxation of *purdah* restrictions.

Another significant change reported by rural women is the education of daughters. Secular education as a strategy for rural
Muslim males is a fairly recent phenomenon, perhaps a matter of
the last 30 years.(5) Primary education (up to Class 5) as a
desirable standard (not necessarily an attainment) for rural
girls seems to be a matter of the last ten or 15 years. There
are indications that secondary education for rural girls is on
the increase though still very negligible, with higher numbers
enrolled where there are girls' rather than only co-ed high
schools in the area. Such girls' schools are, however, very

---

(5) There is a great need for statistics in this area. According to Khatun (1977), the total enrolment of boys and girls in
primary school in 1947-48 was 2,661,629. Of these, a quarter
were girls. The total enrolment of boys and girls in primary
schools at present is 7,793,529. Of these one third are girls.
See forthcoming second volume of *Women for Women* for more information about the education of girls.

rare.

Only few of the women over 35 whom we interviewed had more than
a year or two of primary school. Most were illiterate. They
gave a variety of explanations for their lack of schooling.
Basically, they said, it was not customary to educate girls in
those days. Their fathers and mothers believed that educated
girls would not obey their husbands, that their characters would
be spoiled, and that they would not adjust well in marriage.
Their job was not to learn Bengali, but to learn Allah's *kalam*
(words or sayings). That would serve them in the next world.
If they made their husbands happy and maintained the family,
they would reach paradise.

All of these women report that they have given some education to
their daughters or have wanted to but could not afford it. Even
those few who say they do not believe in it say they have done
it out of social pressure. In these cases, some education for
daughters seems to have become a form of behavior associated
with status. This seems to be a situation where the advantages
of new behavior are so widely accepted among those who set rural
standards that the old belief system that education for girls is
bad has been almost completely undermined. It is likely therefore that the main obstacle now to some primary education for
more rural girls is lack of resources, both in the family and
the national budget, and not social sanction.(6)

Here are a few examples that are typical of most of the responses:

> An illiterate woman of 45 with five children says that
> education for daughters was not customary in her day. It
> was thought they would go bad. But with her own children
> she is not making mistakes - she is educating them.

> Another illiterate woman who has two daughters and one son
> says she was not allowed to study. "Now", she says, "I am
> being careful about my children's education. They are all
> studying in school."

> An illiterate woman of 50 had five sons and two daughters.
> She says she really does not see the value of education for
> girls. "It makes their minds different." But still she
> put her daughters in school for several years, though she

---

(6) See Sattar, 1977.

did not want to, "because all the girls go to school today."

Another woman with four daughters and one son who does not
have extra resources says she is struggling to educate her
daughters "because it is hard to give girls in marriage unless they have some education." (It is important to keep
in mind that they are talking about only a *few* years of
school attendance.)

It would seem that education past puberty is still rare,(7)
though the numbers are increasing. It seems as if parents who
see it as a possible strategy for their daughter's secure future
are often unwilling to risk it because it may not have the
desired results despite all the expense involved. For example,
one illiterate widow from a surplus household is sending her
daughter to secondary school which is co-ed because there is no
separate girls' school. She wonders how long she will be able
to let her daughter study in a "boys'" school. Many people are
talking, she says. In the end, her daughter's chances for
marriage may suffer. "I have the will but no way. Honor and
respect come first, then education," she says. To risk the loss
of the requisite status for a good marriage by violating *purdah*
standards and spending money to send their daughters to secondary
school in the hopes of a better marriage is too dangerous for
many families that might, however, be interested if there were
segregated schools.(8) The mark of respectability has already
been given to this approach by urban high status families and
some rural high status families,(9) but those who might be more
in *need* of this new avenue to resources are, because of their
need, in too precarious a position to risk social criticism.

What are the reasons for the change in attitude about girls'
education that has led to an increase in their enrolment? The
reasons are still related to the strategic deployment of

---

(7) Many rural female staff of the project described in Part
Two report that they are the only girl in their village or one
of two or three with high school or intermediate college degrees.
(8) This is not to suggest that segregated schools or higher
education for all rural girls now is an appropriate strategy for
Bangladesh, since it is a predominantly rural nation and its
resources are limited.
(9) See Jahan, 1975, and McCarthy, 1967. It seems to be becoming
a status symbol for husbands to marry wives with secondary
education.

daughters. Just as rejection of education was seen as a strategy to ensure a good adjustment and lasting marriage, so pursuit of education is seen as a means to ally the girl and the family with an educated boy (i.e. someone who has what is perceived to be an advantage when land is so scarce and is getting scarcer), and to enable her to adjust well in the marriage.(10) Since primary education for daughters is a resource with the full sanction of respectability, rural practices have changed.(11) Secondary education however runs counter to the time-tested resource of status which involves keeping girls under *purdah* restrictions at puberty and, therefore, cannot be accepted so rapidly by those who are not fully confident of their status.

The change that elicits most concern among women from families concerned with status is the shift from bride price to dowry. Most older women mentioned that in their day the groom gave to the bride's family, who gave little in return. The typical comment was: "In our time the bride's father did not have to give a compulsory present in the marriage. Whatever he gave of his own free will was enough. Fathers in those days did not have to suffer in giving daughters in marriage. Nowadays you have to give a dowry to the boy - a cycle, watch, transistor, etc. But in our time the groom's side needed to give lots of gold ornaments to the girl." Probably the dowry system is not yet an issue for those who do not care about educated husbands for their daughters or for those few families whose status is enough of a dowry. As Shirley Lindenbaum has pointed out, the new emphasis on dowry rather than bride price is the response to a shift away from land as the primary basis of status to the accumulation of money as an alternate or concomitant basis.(12)

Many marital dislocations are being blamed on this problem of dowry. Brides of 14 and 15 are being divorced or not even

---

(10) In Abdullah's study (1966), the reasons given by women were: to get an educated husband, have more understanding, practise religion better and be able to get a job.

(11) In her unpublished study of women in a village in Kushtia, Jeneke Arens points out that among the poor and middle peasant children in primary school, there are more girls than boys, with the ratio of girls to boys larger among the poor children (18:8) than among the middle class (17:15). There were no children from landless families in school. Among the surplus farmers the ratio was 32:33 (1975).

(12) Lindenbaum, 1975.

claimed from their parents home because promised dowries have
not been paid. Girls married to older or already married men
are having difficult times adjusting to their marriage. Educated
girls who marry into rural households are being especially abused
by their mothers-in-law. Daughters are likely to be considered
more of a burden under these circumstances, i.e. more costly when
resources are scarcer, then when they were married young and
valued for their ability to do farm work. Families facing these
dilemmas might be ready for alternate strategies.

A Look Ahead

From all indicators, this is a time of change in Bangladesh that
is likely to affect the situation of women. Population growth,
war and inflation have created a strong awareness among rural
people of the dwindling of traditional resources and a search
for new ones. The burden of dependent women on family resources
is becoming heavier. Shifting strategies to attempt to deploy
women more advantageously with regard to new resources may be
increasing the number of dependent women in status conscious
families as well as the number of partially educated women who
are stranded in transition between rural and modern life. The
number of families who are both status-conscious and in need are
increasing. Certainly the number of unemployed poor women is
increasing with the mechanization of the heavy work of rice
processing.

Change in the social situation of rural women could be very rapid.
Both the high-status families who control village values and the
heads of families who control family behavior have fewer resources to offer in return for the dependent, secluded position of
women. Women's eyes have been opened by the atrocities of the
recent Liberation War to an awareness of how insecure their
situation really is. Once belief systems begin to shift, the
change over the next generations will be very rapid because the
numbers of young people will so outweigh the numbers of elderly.

These changes that rural women have cited as important in their
lives have occurred without policy intervention. In a sense,
population growth has loosened traditional social controls because
they are no longer efficient for those who most benefit from
them; there is a transition to new social controls. If change
continues without significant intervention, one can predict what
will happen to rural women. Very poor women will take advantage
of any opportunities that are available, whether it be projects

like earth-lifting in exchange for food, brick-smashing to build
roads, or migration to the cities. Elite women will get status
from higher education as they do in the cities(13) and certain
kinds of jobs for those who remain in rural areas will not only
be acceptable but will have some status attached. The response
reported by most projects involving rural women is that after
initial hesitation there was little problem in hiring women
(usually under 30) for a variety of jobs, all of which provide
income.(14) As in every culture, white-collar work is more
respectable than blue-collar. Education and jobs will increasingly become respectable family strategies for rural girls and
the job market will be quickly exhausted.(15) The majority of
rural women will be unable to take advantage of this new standard for prestige, again set by a small elite, and will be left
still without resources, without an alternative to traditional
behavior and with even less perceived social value than before
when farm work was considered important.

A Vision

Planned change would involve intervention in a social system
already loosened by economic forces to make possible changes in
women's behavior that will be realistically in line with national
goals. The resources rural leaders now ask for, and women and
urban leaders respond to, because they are from the same class,
are more schools, "white-collar" jobs, sewing machines and handicraft work. These are, for many reasons, unrealistic development
approaches for a population of 75 million in a largely

---

(13) Upper-class city women have been taking jobs for several
years and even achieving status for doing so (see Islam, 1975),
so that rural families that have been "progressive" enough to
educate their daughters see a respectable precedent for allowing
them to take certain kinds of jobs. Several project staff from
rural areas were influenced to seek jobs by family members in
the city.
(14) This has been the experience of Companiganj Model Health
Project, Gonoshosto Kendra, BRAC, IRDP, and the Social Welfare
Department. One project that involves several hundred rural
women collecting information for 100 *taka* a month reports that
in recent years the workers are increasingly young women, rather
than as formerly, elderly women.
(15) Applications for jobs for educated women in Dacca far out-
number the jobs available.

unmechanized, largely rural nation, where women are doing so much of the work of food production. Everyone would agree that education is important but education should not be confused with schools for a few that are seen by parents as a way to get a husband and/or a modern job. The elite will get their schools with or without the help of Government, but they will not mean much to the majority of rural women nor will they bring about desired changes in women's behavior. Schooling *is* necessary for rural women, but it must go hand in hand with other changes, and not be expected, in isolation, to produce those changes.

As we see it, Government must intervene to create alternatives - alternatives that will benefit the country as a whole - for the masses of rural women who are in need but who are controlled by status considerations. Such intervention would aim at changing belief systems that now control women's behavior so that they are *able* to engage in work that is beneficial to the nation and provides social rewards that they want and their families appreciate. Only in this way will women gain control over their lives. To change systems of belief, we think, involves offering new chances for resources to women in the growing number of families that are experiencing need, chances which are more valuable than the ones women and their families get from the traditional system.

To give this approach a fair chance, one must have first, an IDEOLOGY, a recognition that rural women are economically and socially valuable citizens whose work should be economically and socially rewarded - i.e. by money and respect; second, a COMMIT-MENT to involve women fully in national development plans; third, a POLICY, one that is geared to society as it is now and sensitive to the needs of rural women and their families, especially as regards social pressure; and fourth, INVESTMENT (the true sign of commitment) of time, creativity, training and money. Those who have worked with rural women, even in projects with limited resources and in isolation from larger processes, have seen the changes in their lives that these resources make possible and know what the prospects for such an approach can be.

PART TWO

THE PROJECT

CHAPTER I

DESCRIPTION OF THE PROJECT

In the preceding pages we have presented a picture of rural
women which serves as an hypothesis on the basis of which resources can be directed to them with some degree of realism.
As indicated earlier, what we consider important about the focus
of the picture is that it has been dictated by the need for a
project concerned with extending resources to rural women to
understand how they perceive their own situation. The following
pages provide a detailed look at that project, describing it
with great specificity from its beginnings to the present, four
years later.

The format of this section is a case study of the early stages
of a project for rural women, when a project's primary concern
is to organize itself to address the basic priorities as perceived by those women. It records how the project started, how
it organized itself, especially in terms of staff, how it
entered the village, how it organized rural women, how it initiated the first phase of its services, and how women responded
to it. We think that such a case study of *project implementation* highlights issues that will probably arise wherever programs
for rural women are centrally undertaken. It is important, we
feel, that problems which those who implement projects confront
should be shared with the planners and donors so that the
communication among these groups may be more fruitful. Although
these pages record only the first phase of an on-going, evolving
program, they suggest a basic formula for translating objectives
into action, which is the function of a project. This formula
includes the following elements: isolating the first step towards
a given goal (e.g. co-operation starts as the formation of a

group, economic opportunity may start as a particular credit
system, etc.); introducing that step to the village and village
women; observing and attempting to understand the nature of their
response to it (distinguishing, for example, to what extent the
response is created by institutional deficiencies, by inappropriate guidelines, by aspects of the social system that a project
cannot address, and distinguishing between patterns and random
behavior in responses to new resources); and, finally, appraising
all these issues as a basis for taking the second step. We think
this is an important formula for understanding project work so
that it will not be misinterpreted, but can be supported in its
efforts as an essential link in the process of development or
guided change.

Context

Before looking at the institutional context, which to a great
extent determines the approach of a project, it is helpful to
review those aspects of the situation of rural women that are
particularly relevant and the priorities of Government that need
to be addressed. Both of these elements contribute to the ideology and objectives of a project.

As we have seen, rural women of Bangladesh do not form an homogeneous group. They are divided among classes that have markedly
different degrees of control over resources. At the same time,
within these classes, they do not usually have the same amount
of control over resources as males. Across class lines, women
have interests in common. As members of a neighborhood or
community, they participate in various forms of co-operation,
depending on needs and relationships. The behavior of women of
all classes in village society is governed by the social ideology
of the village which operates primarily through the mechanism
of status. Basically, it dictates that a woman should not be
visible and should not have to work. In the conditions of economic need that exist in the villages, this social ideology affects women of all classes adversely. It degrades the labor of
the poorest women, it denies women in economic need, in families
other than the poorest, the possibilies of "self-help", and it
denies direct access to resources and services to all women.
In addition to (and to some extent because of) the social ideology, lack of employment opportunity and lack of education and
training prevent women in need from improving their own economic
situation and that of their families.

PLATE I A woman turning rice with her feet to dry
it evenly. On the line behind her is the household
bedding, hung out to absorb warmth.

PLATE II Two women are husking rice with traditional technology. One woman pedals; the other
stirs and checks what is being husked.

PLATE III Taking care of livestock is women's
responsibility. Women often control the distribution of milk for household consumption and market.

PLATE IV A woman is drying dung for fuel, perhaps for the next day's cooking.

PLATE V These dung cakes and sticks of dung have
been collected, arranged and dried by women. They
are used as fuel.

PLATE VI A woman is repairing the door step with
a mixture of mud and cow dung. Such repair is
women's responsibility.

PLATE VII   Women make fishnets.

PLATE VIII Women make mats for regular household use as bedding and for drying rice.

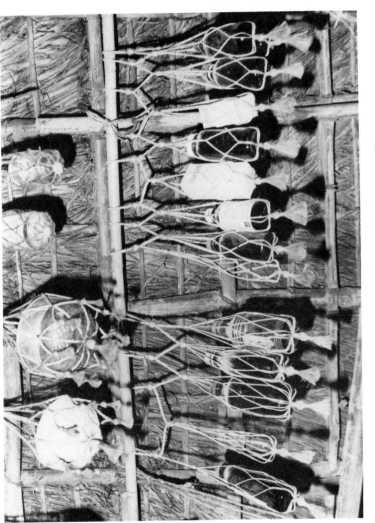

PLATE IX Women are in charge of storage. They make the hanging containers to keep food and other precious things where there is air and away from rodents.

PLATE X A traditional skill of women is making
fans for special and household use.

Women in this situation are coping to the best of their ability. They and their families seek to manipulate the ideology, in whatever way they can, in order to survive. They are not likely to risk what they already get from dependency on males or on families with resources (though this dependency affects them harshly), since there are no other options that guarantee survival. There are indications, borne out by the project, that the social ideology of the village is now in conflict with the economic reality of rural life. The village cannot support increasing numbers of dependent women as its ideology demands. Without planned introduction of change, the social ideology is changing to accommodate new options for women who have had education and for families who can afford to educate their daughters. But there are no options available to the large majority of rural women in poor agricultural families that would enable them to improve their conditions.

As we have seen, rural women in all classes work with skill and knowledge in aspects of food production that are exclusively their domain and are of critical importance to the rural economy. In addition, they control or at least influence decisions about health, nutrition, and reproduction. The mobilization and participation of rural women in national development could directly affect major goals of rural development - increased food production, increased family income, increased rural savings, more equitable distribution, improved infant and child health and lower fertility. The guidelines of the project are an attempt to align both the needs of rural women and their families and the priorities of Government.

Institutional Framework

Beginnings: The IRDP Pilot Project in Population Planning and Rural Women's Co-operatives, referred to in these pages as the Women's Program for the sake of brevity, began in 1974 as a component of the Bangladesh Population Planning Project funded by the World Bank. The Bangladesh Population Planning Project introduced projects designed to lower fertility into a number of ministries *other* than the one directly involved with family planning. Three of these projects were addressed specifically to women, two through the Ministry of Social Welfare and one through the Ministry of Land Administration, Local Government, Rural Development and Co-operatives. It is the latter which is described and analysed in the following pages.(1)

The original project papers, though they had to be revised for
reasons indicated below, were ahead of their time in project
development, we think, because they addressed the economic needs
of rural women as an element of their fertility behavior. When
the original project papers were drawn up, very little had been
written about the rural women of Bangladesh beyond what came
out of the Women's Program of the Academy for Rural Development
at Comilla, the only precedent for this project.(2) There was
almost no other written information about their work, their
culture, or their socio-economic situation. The original scheme
did not take into account the extent to which the project would
have to be a process both of learning about rural women and
finding ways to reach them effectively. The following analysis
of the shortcomings of the original design is not meant as a
criticism of those who drew it up, since they were well ahead
of their time in directing resources to rural women and operating in uncharted territory, but as constructive advice for those
who may be involved in such planning in the future.

The original papers described a program for women that included
functional education in home development, family planning, and
unspecified income-generating "trades". The timetable for the

_____

(1) For more detail on most of the issues discussed in the
following pages, see especially papers and reports of Bangladesh
Population Planning Project and IRDP Population Planning and
Rural Women's Co-operative. Actually, the project in the rural
development ministry has two parts, one addressed to rural women
and the other to population education and education of rural
males. The same staff administer both parts of the project.
This study is concerned with the part of the project directed
toward rural women.
(2) The Comilla Women's Program started at the Academy for Rural
Development at Comilla in 1962. Operating in 42 villages of one
Thana of Comilla District, which is one of the more conservative
areas of Bangladesh, it proved that rural women could be organized in terms of their interests at the village level and that
an important program interest of rural women is opportunity for
economic gain. In her M.A. thesis, "Bengali Village Women:
Mediators Between Tradition and Change" (1967) Florence McCarthy
analyzes the socio-economic characteristics of key women in the
program. See also, for description and analysis, the reports
of the Comilla Womens Program listed in the References.

pilot project was three and a half years. It allowed for two weeks training of rural staff to administer the project in rural areas and two administrative posts at headquarters for supervising the nationwide project. The expected results were to be 20,000 women trained in income generating trades able to show other women "the possibilities of improving their status and increased earning". A quarter of these women were expected to be family planning acceptors.

The main shortcomings of the project arose, it seems, from an implicit assumption that a viable program for rural women had already been evolved and simply had to be set in place, whereas, the truth was that this pilot project had, with guidelines from the Comilla Women's Program to be sure, to *create* a program. The Headquarters staff had to address itself to collecting information about rural women and experimenting with and evaluating new approaches. It had to face the questions of whether rural staff could be recruited, who they would be, how they should be trained, how well they could supervise program work when it involved frequent travel to villages. Though there was no doubt that economic gain was a basic need of rural women and their families, the project had to face the complex questions of what *kind* of economic program rural women would want and would be allowed to take advantage of, how it must evolve to appeal to increasing numbers of rural women and how it could address the priorities of the rural development ministry. It had to face issues related to training rural women: who would train them, what methods would be most suitable, and what training could women use to best advantage. It had to face the problems of providing appropriate equipment in rural areas in ways that would neither promote corruption nor support a "relief mentality" nor simply waste resources. The timetable, budget allocation, and objectives of the project did not fully support this kind of effort. Its design seemed to reflect confusion as to whether the project was to be a pipeline for family planning services with little development content or a program to develop rural Bangladesh through the direct support of the contribution of women.

An economic project for rural women that has a population objective must be based on the clear assumption that rural women are reasonable people whose contraceptive behavior is part of their total response to their culture. The major effort of the project therefore has to be to explore ways to bring about changes in their culture so that contraception would be an acceptable choice and women would be in a position to make it. The design of the

project, its timetable and budget have to support that effort.
To concentrate from the beginning on encouraging acceptance of
family planning is counter-productive, and produces a distorted
perception of the program in the eyes of rural women, village
leaders, staff and Government, that is bound to affect their
response. This does not mean that full family planning services
are not an essential part of an economic project for rural women
from the very beginning, since many women are already seeking
ways to gain control over their reproductive life. It means
that a distinction has to be made between immediate and long-
range population goals and that the design and allocation of
resources must be realistic in terms of these goals.

From an administrative point of view, a project for rural women
has to address the national priorities for rural development *as
they are allocated to different ministries.* To focus prematurely
or with disproportionate resources on family planning in a project under the rural development ministry leaves less chance to
find ways to address the development priorities of that ministry.
Donor institutions, we know, have to answer the hard questions of
cost/benefit with regard to the expenditure of their resources.
Similarly a nation's development institutions have to account for
their expenditures. A rural development institution will have a
hard time justifying the use of its limited resources on projects
that seem to have only family planning features. If the emphasis
is not on what rural women *do* with their new resources and opportunities but only on whether they accept contraception, then the
project will be considered more appropriate under the family
planning ministry than the rural development ministry.

The Integrated Rural Development Program (IRDP) is a major
institution of the Ministry of Land Administration, Local Government, Rural Development and Co-operatives. The Women's Program
operates as a pilot project within this institution, under its
administration and following its approach to rural development.
It is important therefore, to have some understanding of the
IRDP. The institution came into existence in 1970 as an instrument of rural development through organizing farmers at the
village level in co-operatives, which are affiliated to a central
co-operative at the *Thana* level and managed by a committee of
elected co-operative leaders working with Government officers.
One objective of these co-operatives is to provide a number of
facilities in support of increasing farm productivity and income.
They especially promote the cultivation of high yielding variety
rice, a priority of rural development, through loans, extension
services, access to improved seeds, fertilizer and pesticide and

irrigation facilities. The leaders of each co-operative are
expected to attend weekly training and discussion of modern
information conducted by Government extension officers who sit
at the *Thana* center, and to convey this information to the
village co-operative at weekly meetings. The IRDP program is
administered at the *Thana* level by a Project Officer, at the
District level by a Project Director and at the national level
by a Director-General and five Directors. The staff and
participants are by and large male.

The institution which was four years old in 1974, when the
Women's Program started, has organized, as of June 1976, 18,800
village co-operators in about 150 *Thanas* with 522,000 members,
share capital of 12,792,000 *taka* and deposits of 18,488,000 *taka*.
It has given 181,237,000 *taka* in short and medium term loans and
has realized 119,039,000 of that amount.(3) The IRDP is often
under criticism and is modifying its structure to meet some of
the criticisms, but it remains the only rural development institution with an infrastructure in the villages.

Rural Women's Co-operatives

The Women's Program, as we have seen, was established as part of
the Bangladesh Population Planning Project and is administered
under IRDP, following its co-operative approach. Its incorporation in a rural development institution, as opposed to isolation
as a separate women's institution, is critical as to its ability
to function. However, because it is directed to women, it has
its own character which is expressed in its objectives and the
major emphasis of its approach.

Objectives: The long-range vision of the Women's Program is the
full participation of rural women in the process of national
development. In pursuit of this vision, it is striving for several objectives. One is to enable women in need, of whatever
class, to work for monetary gain. This emphasis on the economic
participation of women is based on certain assumptions about the
benefits of social rewards for work. One is that women will
become able to act in meeting their own needs and that of their
families and will have alternatives to dependency on males or
feudal relationships. Another is that women who contribute income to the family will have increased authority to make

_____
(3) IRDP Monthly Report, June 1976.

decisions, and increased access to resources enabling them to act on those decisions in the aspects of life and work which are already their sphere of responsibility. A further assumption is that the nation will benefit through an increase in needed production from shifting rural women's work from domestic to commercial production, as well as from increased family income and savings. Given these assumptions, major emphases of the project must be on finding realistic ways to make work for women socially acceptable and to provide training and resources to enable women to create or find work based on their skills and knowledge. Another objective is to enable women to have direct access to the resources and services they need as women and a direct voice in determining the kind and quality of these resources and services. The emphasis in achieving this objective is on a village-based institution that provides an opportunity for group strength and leadership to evolve.

The specific aims of the project as spelled out in the project papers are: to provide training and resources for economically gainful activities and to create an atmosphere in which women can pursue them, to provide women with resources and training in family planning and health care that will enable them to act on their decisions in these areas, to provide literacy training, to develop leadership among rural women, and to learn more about the lives and problems of rural women. These goals cannot be achieved in three and a half or four years. Rather, the pilot project is a vehicle for exploring ways to bring about these goals and provide bases for continuing action.

Approach: As an integral part of IRDP, the project seeks to initiate change in the direction of the goals stated above, through *a village-based institution* for women, referred to as a "co-operative" (but different from western-originated co-operatives in fundamental ways). This village-based institution offers its members supervised credit, training in modern techniques and skills and direct access to the variety of existing services relevant to women. As an institution accepted in the village, it provides sanctions to members to use new resources in ways appropriate to their individual situations and the group strength women need to participate in solving individual and community problems.

Emphasis is given, in all aspects of the project, to ways to get feedback about the responses of women to various approaches. Major emphasis is also given to staff training, since the rural staff are responsible for administering the project and have more contact with rural women than the headquarters staff. They translate the guidelines into action and are in a position to observe how rural women respond and what directions their responses point to.(4)

_____

(4) See Appendix B for a description of the Basic Program.

CHAPTER II

STAFF

Continuous, appropriate training for rural staff(1) is the backbone of the project. As indicated earlier, a project is a process of initiating and monitoring change. The success of this process depends on the project staff. It is they who work directly with rural women and are in a position to observe and build on their responses to the resources offered by the project. It is essential that the staff have the opportunity for training to enable them to carry out their responsibilities and that channels be kept open to enable them to communicate what they know to those who make policy. A careful examination of some issues involved in past training should throw light on the key role of staff in the functioning of a project.

Roles

Headquarters staff, most of whom are, of necessity, inexperienced in projects for rural women, have received much of their training on the job. Their responsibilities include developing policy, organizing and providing staff training, administering the

---

(1) "Staff", "project staff", and "rural staff" are the terms used throughout the study for those who are *paid employees* of the project, whether working at Headquarters in Dacca or in the rural areas. Co-operative leaders, though they receive travel allowance from the project budget, are *not* employees of the project but are village women who have joined the co-operative and been selected by other members of the co-operative to represent them.

project, keeping contact through tours as well as reports, mediating between the project and relevant Government offices. They are given as many opportunities as are feasible to participate in relevant training and in aspects of the project outside their immediate area of responsibility, with the hope that they will gradually have first-hand experience of the totality of the project. Rural experience through the project is as important for their work as advanced information or skills training.

Rural staff participate in more formal training. Before examining the training process, it is important to understand who the trainees are and what they are being trained for. Rural staff at each *Thana* include one Deputy Project Officer and two Inspectors. The responsibility of the Deputy Project Officer is over-all supervision of the Women's Program at the *Thana* level. She is assisted by the Inspectors in motivating women to organize in co-operatives, helping them with Government procedures involved in organizing, providing continued guidance to co-operative members, organizing and supervising training for rural women at the *Thana* center, co-ordinating services in the *Thana* and channelling them to co-operatives, and collecting information for reports. All three staff members are expected to visit village co-operatives, though it is the *regular* duty of the Inspectors. The Deputy Project Officer is supervised by the IRDP *Thana* Project Officer in co-ordinating and carrying out Women's Program policy through IRDP procedures.

Qualifications of Rural Staff: The Deputy Project Officers are recruited and appointed centrally. They must be college graduates under 35. Preference is expressed for married women, already residents of the areas where they will work. Their male counterparts must have Bachelor's degrees, at least 2nd class, may come from anywhere since they are not posted to their home *Thana*, and may be married or unmarried. The difference in educational qualification for female staff is based on the assumption that there will be few if any women with 2nd class degrees living in rural areas. The difference in marital and residential preferences is based on the assumptions that unmarried women will move away, when they marry, to their husband's place of residence, that they may have special difficulties with both male colleagues and rural women that married women will not encounter and that secure accommodation in *Thanas* where unmarried women have no family may be difficult to provide. All of these assumptions are being tested and may be modified. The Inspectors are recruited and hired locally. Male or female, they must be high school graduates. Again, the preference is for married women.(2)

The characteristics of the first batch of Deputy Project Officers (D.P.O.'s) and Inspectors are as follows. The 18 D.P.O.'s range in age from 21 to 32, with the majority under 25. Three have Masters degrees and the rest Bachelors. 12 are married and six unmarried. The majority of the married women have one or two children. One has four children, two have three. Eight have had previous work experience. Of these, three had been in the Women's Program as Inspectors and co-operative members. The rest were college and school teachers, traditional, more sheltered positions for women. The large majority of D.P.O.'s are Moslems. Nine are not from the areas where they are working. Among 28 Inspectors, the age range is 18 to 30. However, all but two or three are under 24. Thirteen have I.A. degrees (high school and two years of college) and 15 have high school diplomas. Eighteen are married, eight unmarried, one divorced and one widowed. The large majority of married women have one or two children. Of the first 12 Inspectors, four had had prior work experience.

From a socio-economic point of view, the fact that all these women were educated indicates that they come from unusual rural families, with status, though not necessarily large resources.

---

(2) Prior to initial recruitment of IRDP female staff, there were very few educated women working in the rural areas from whom experience could be gained to guide recruitment policy. Among the unanticipated changes in the rural area is the presence of unmarried educated girls seeking jobs that involve working side by side with men, travelling on the road for village visits and discussion of family planning and other matters related to reproduction. Until very recently, such behavior would have been considered a damaging violation of the stricter *purdah* that is enforced before marriage and is considered necessary to indicate the bride's propriety and virtue. 82 women from 19 districts of Bangladesh applied for 19 Deputy Project Officer posts. They included unmarried women in their late twenties and women with M.A.'s, M.Sc.'s and M.A.-M.Ed. degrees. Since the recruitment for Inspectors is local, it is hard to know how many applicants there were for each job. Because the salary is quite low and the job requires regular village visits and because there is not the same status attached as there is to the D.P.O.'s post, there are problems in some *Thanas* in filling these posts. We have been told in several places that it might be easier to recruit unmarried than married women.

At present, one-third of them, those without husbands, are dependent on parental families at an age, at which traditionally, even 10 years ago, all would have been married. There may, in these cases, be social and/or economic pressure to have occupations outside the home. Among the married women, there seems to be economic need, either, in a few cases, for special reasons like unemployed husbands or extreme problems with mothers-in-law which make separation necessary, or, for the most part, because husbands are wage earners with little or no income from land. Since thousands of women in rural areas are in a similar situation, what makes these women special is not so much their social or economic need for jobs, but the fact that they are qualified by education for the few jobs that are being offered. The counterpart jobs are considered highly desirable for men, so that the jobs are already seen as indicating status; what is new is that families are allowing their women to take them. The characteristics that are most significant in planning training are that these are rural or town women who are young, educated and relatively inexperienced in the work world.

The following are the case studies of four staff members, two Deputy Project Officers and two Inspectors from four different *Thanas*. We are presenting them as part of the text rather than relegating them to an appendix because they contain material directly related to key issues of our study. For one thing, they provide information about families and women who form a tiny minority of rural society. These are families that have initiated change in the options of their daughters through higher education and, even more important, through permission to take new jobs being offered to women in rural society. If they and the other families who observe them find these new options advantageous, rural girls from more varied backgrounds are likely to be educated as a way to get jobs. The case studies tell us something about these "pioneer" families and their range of socio-economic background. Another reason for presenting these case studies in the text is to give concreteness to the issue of how project staff will work with rural women who do not have their options. In reading evaluations of projects for rural women in other countries, we have noticed frequent references to implementation problems that result from inadequate attention to the kind of responsibility that field staff are expected to assume. There has been an attempt in this project to guide the potential of field staff which has been based to some extent on an understanding of the ways in which they are like and unlike other rural women.

Case I: Nasim was born in 1957. Her father is a farmer who was educated to Class Eight. Her mother studied to Class Five and reads the Koran. Her maternal grandmother came from India and now lives with her. Her maternal aunt is living in India caring for the land. Nasim has one sister studying in Class Ten and two brothers studying in Classes Eight and Three. Also living with them are a paternal aunt, living apart from her husband who has a co-wife, and one child. They live one mile from the *Thana*. They have about seven acres of land on which they cultivate rice, jute and pulses. They have two bullocks, one cow and two calves. They keep a contract laborer and cowherd. All their basic needs except for kerosene, salt and cloth are provided by the farm.

Nasim went to primary school in the village and then to a girls high school in the *Thana*, to which she used to walk. She is about to appear for her B.A. exam. She was always a good student and especially good at sports. She is the first person in her family to reach such an educational level. She is the only college-educated girl in her *para*. Her family encouraged her to take this job. She would have applied for a job with the family planning office except that she was visiting relatives when applications were being accepted. She was the only girl in the union qualified for that job. When the IRDP job of Inspector was advertised, she applied and was accepted. Her father's neighbors teased him that he couldn't maintain his own family and had to send his daughter out to earn money. Her mother said, "Let them talk. My daughter has education and should use it."

She was married at 19. Her husband is 30. He failed his B.A. and works for a mill in another district. His parents' home is several miles from hers. They have eight acres of land. He has five brothers and three sisters. Three of the brothers have jobs, while the sisters are studying. Nasim is not living with her in-laws yet, because she is preparing for her B.A. Her husband approves of her job. He says, "It's easy to leave a job but hard to get one." He earns 500 *takas* per month whilst she earns 236. She pays her own college fees and transport and gives the rest of the money to her father for the expenses of the younger children. Her husband sends her saris, but does not maintain her. He sends his salary to his parents.

Case II: Saleha is 24. Her father who died three years ago was a schoolmaster, though he was not a high school graduate. He owned two thirds of an acre. Her mother studied to Class Eight. Her two brothers both have M.A.'s. She has one sister who is 15 and studying in Class Ten. When her father was dying he drew up a will and left property to his wife and two daughters who now jointly own almost two-thirds of an acre. Saleha studied to Class Eight at the village school and then went to a hostel until she completed high school in 1969. She married the same year.

Her husband has an I.A. degree and has worked for ten years as a telephone operator. His father has one and a third acres of land and is in the jute business. There are six sons (four of whom have jobs, two of whom are studying) and three daughters. Five family members live at his father's house. They are able to sell some rice. Saleha lives in a nuclear family with her husband, two sons, her sister, and alternately her mother and grandmother. She keeps a married couple to look after the house. Her sons are six and five and are studying in Classes Two and One. She uses contraception. She and her mother supervise laborers on the land her father left them. This provides enough food for her mother and grandmother and some rice and pulses for her. They are able to sell brown sugar - five *maunds*(4) this year for 1200 *taka*, and rice - eight *maunds* this year for 100 *taka*. With this money she bought land for a house and took the mortgage on a relative's land which he now sharecrops for her. She provides the seeds and fertilizer.

She has had two jobs before this present one as IRDP Inspector. She took the first job after she was married, before she had children. She was then living in her father's house because her husband was posted out, and her father encouraged her to work. When she heard of an available job she took it because she knew that since her father-in-law had nine children, her husband would not inherit much property. There were no family objections to her working; her mother's cousin's sisters were working women. Her husband appreciates her working because they have a lot of expenses and four dependent females.

---

(4) A *maund* is about 80 pounds.

At first she was criticized by women neighbors who mocked her for working outside. "We don't work," they said, "and we still get food. What your husband earns is enough. Why do you want more?" They criticized her husband as someone who could not maintain his wife. He was getting depressed and feeling insulted. Now, some of these same women, the ones who are qualified, are working for the family planning office.

Case III: *Roushan's* father comes from another district. He is a railway station master, educated to B.A. pass level. He has lost contact with his home district and no longer gets produce from his father's land. Her mother studied to Class Nine. Her maternal uncles are all educated. Her grandfather was a homeopathic doctor. Her cousins are all studying. She has three brothers and two sisters. One sister has a B.A., and one has an I.A. and is married; one brother is studying for a B.A. with honours and two are in Classes Nine and Seven. They have eight acres of land, and lease out the land that is far from home, paying laborers to cultivate the rest. They get nine months to a year's worth of food for the family, but don't sell any. They keep one male servant.

Roushan studied to Class Eight near home and then went to a girls' school in the *Thana*. Her father encouraged her studies. She is the first girl to matriculate in her area; there are not many boy matriculates either. Her father bought her a rickshaw so she could travel to college where she studied for her I.A. and B.A. Neighbors teased her father saying it was time to marry his daughter. "When pumpkins are in the market, people like to buy young ones," they said. He replied, "Those who know the value of a mature one, they will take my daughter." She is 23 and not married.

A class friend told her IRDP was recruiting for a female Inspector. Although her father had not wanted her to take an available job in a primary school, he allowed her to apply for this one. She was selected out of 16 applicants. She has since been promoted to Deputy Project Officer. She spends her money on her brothers' and sisters' educational expenses and clothes for her nieces and nephews. She gives some money to her father and mother.

Case IV: Farida's father, a railway office auditor, has a
B.A. at pass level; his sister has a B.Ed. His first wife,
Farida's mother, studied to Class Eight. Farida is the
eldest of her mother's two daughters and three sons. Her
mother died in childbirth and her father remarried. With
his second wife he had a son and a daughter. This wife has
recently died. Farida has B.A. and B.Ed. degrees. She had
a job as headmistress in a girls' school for 150 *taka* per
month until she got married at the age of 26. Her in-laws,
who were farmers, are dead. Her husband, who is 33, is the
youngest of three surviving children out of ten. He was
raised by his brother who is a college professor with an
M.A. He has a B.Sc. but lost his job because of new age
qualifications. They have one child, a daughter. Her
brother-in-law supported them while her husband looked for
a job. He applied for male Deputy Project Officer but
failed the exam. He heard IRDP was recruiting for female
D.P.O.'s and told his wife, "I've failed the test, but there
is another way. You apply." There was no opposition. She
supports her husband, her daughter and her brother.

Training

The functioning of the project depends on the ability of the
rural staff both to administer the project and to provide
accurate feedback about the responses of rural women to policy
guidelines. As we have seen, the rural staff are by and large
young, educated, and inexperienced rural and town women who are
among the first to work in development in rural areas. Therefore, the training of this staff has to include, *in addition* to
appropriate skills and information, the development of appropriate attitudes to the rural situation, to the project, to
family planning, and even to working life. Training takes a
variety of forms: intensive pre-service training both in class
and on the job, regular in-service seminars, and visits from
headquarters staff. Such seminars and visits need to be frequent
and regular for many reasons, including the opportunity to reinforce new ideas about working with rural women that do not find
support from other quarters. Orientation and involvement of male
staff in training opportunities have greatly increased their
understanding and support for the project.

Training methods include lectures, discussion groups, field trips
and research assignments. As the project expands and the staff
increase, training will have to be farmed out to a number of

national institutions. It is important that attitude development remain a part of training and that ways be found to ensure
its inclusion when, for efficiency, training becomes more rou-
tinized. For this reason we include, in some detail, the
experiences with the first groups of staff.

Attitudes Toward Rural Life: The fact that the rural staff are
educated through high school, college and, to some extent,
graduate school has had a strong influence on their thinking
with regard to a number of issues that are relevant to their
project work. For one thing, they have been taught almost without exception by the lecture/note-taking method and, naturally,
this is their only model for communication of information. For
another, they have been encouraged, through the prevalent system
of education to value the deductive more than the inductive
approach to knowledge - i.e. they tend *not* to value sensory
observation as a basis for the evolution of theory. More insid-
ious, perhaps, is the polarization that develops as the result
of education in their thinking about rural and modern life.
Modern life is to be valued as advanced; rural life is to be
rejected as backward. There is almost nothing in their education
that teaches them about rural Bangladesh, how it is administered
and what its economic and social realities are. What their
education teaches them to value, a more modern, urban, scientific view of life, leads them to ignore or reject rural ways
without understanding the basis for rural behavior.

As indicated earlier, the fact that they are educated means that
they are from socially elite, though not necessarily economically
well-off, families. As a result they are liable to share attitudes toward poorer rural women that some of the educated elite
have developed, either as a reflection of their own cultural
values or as a result of the absorption of foreign ideas about
assistance for women. For example, they may not acknowledge the
economic motivation of rural women other than laborers, since
their culture does not foster that perception. They may support
programs for "needy" women that offer relief or an opportunity
for genteel, but not commercial, undertakings by such women that
either exploit or undervalue their labor. The goal of such work
is usually to help these women, whom circumstances have forced
outside the pale, to get back into the system rather than to
change it substantively. They may have a "relief" or "savior"
attitude toward these women - i.e. "they" are poor, "we" must
uplift them. Or they may support "home development" programs
that emphasize better cooking habits, sanitation, thriftiness,
home management, and handicrafts and sewing for home use, but

that have little to do with the real problems of rural women.

Though they themselves are working women very much concerned
about their salaries, they may not readily acknowledge the value
of social rewards for the *traditional* work of rural women, but
tend to see education as the solution for most of their problems.
To some extent, their culture is beginning to accept women working in government jobs as respectable behavior. The only other
"jobs" for women that the culture has accepted are laboring for
food or work as domestic servants, neither of which is considered
respectable, but merely necessary. It is difficult for the young
rural staff to understand a project approach for rural women that
is based on the participation of women in socially rewarded work
(though they themselves are doing it), because the nature of the
work has not been culturally or socially valued. Between education and white-collar jobs on the one hand (a recent development
for women), and social welfare for destitute women on the other
(leaving out the traditional laboring class altogether), there
has been no development approach for the mass of rural women.

Early in their formal training, the rural staff were given
assignments that revealed their attitudes toward rural women.
Some, though not all the staff, characterized rural women as
ignorant and superstitious. They described the problems of
rural women as   lack of education, child marriage, polygamy
and poverty. The solutions, they indicated, would be nutrition
education, family planning, health education, and handicraft or
needlework training. In other words they judged the behavior
of rural women by comparison with modern knowledge, rather than
as responses to their culture and resources, and then they looked
for solutions that had no relation to the *real* problems.

One written assignment was especially interesting in revealing
the split in the apparent thinking of these women between experience and "knowledge". They were asked to describe the *situation*
of a rural woman they knew "who had a problem", and then to list
the problems of rural women. The short case studies they wrote
included: a poor girl divorced by two husbands, then married to
an older man with two wives, unable to have a child; a poor girl
married because of her beauty to a rich man and then cast off;
a poor woman divorced once, remarried and then widowed; a poor
girl married to a good family, unable to conceive a child and
therefore threatened with divorce; and a woman divorced while
she was pregnant whose step-mother would not accept her in her
parental home. These were the situations the staff thought of
when asked to describe real problems they were familiar with.

VWB - J

It is not surprising that their analysis of these problems was often sentimental rather than economic or socio-cultural. One staff member wrote that a young rejected wife from a poor family wanted to remain in her husband's house, though he took a second wife, because she loved him, not because there was no security for her outside his house.

As young, favored women, relatively in control of their own lives (both because they are not very poor *and* because they are earning incomes), and, like most people, relatively unconscious of the workings of their own culture, they could not be expected to analyze the forces operating on these women. Romantic love and cruel mothers-in-law played more of a role in their stories than economic bases for alliances and separations. This was not at all surprising. What was surprising was that their characterization of these basic problems of rural women over which they have little control was "ignorance and superstition." Perhaps this was only an indication that they had never analyzed the experiences closest to them.

Training classes introduced an emphasis and approach that was new for the trainees. Basically the staff were encouraged to admit their own ignorance about rural life, though they were from rural areas themselves, and to recognize that solutions to the problems of rural women could not be developed until their *real* problems were understood. They were encouraged to recognize that there were reasonable bases for rural behavior which they characterized negatively, perhaps because they did not understand what rural women understood. They were encouraged to think of rural women as the experts about their own lives. For example, they were asked to think about *why* rural women's clothes are often dirty, why animals are kept inside the house, and why women do not want latrines in their compounds. The only answer they had heard before, that these women were ignorant, was challenged by other explanations grounded in the reality of rural life. For some of them, perhaps those with more rural experience, these new ideas quickly challenged the facile ones.

They were stimulated to look at the economic reality of rural women's lives. One written assignment, to calculate the economic loss to a rural family of the death of an old man, a baby, a young man, and a young mother, was especially revealing. All of them felt the death of the young mother was a significant economic loss, when in fact she is the least expensive to replace. It is natural that the staff, most of whom are young mothers, had never looked at rural marriage in economic terms or analyzed

familiar behavior in economic rather than sentimental terms.
They were encouraged to think of the project as promoting real
economic opportunities for women, regular income, work as a
social value and rural women's work as significant, ideas they
had probably never heard from any quarter before and which found
no theoretical reinforcement in their homes or in their offices.
These ideas were introduced and reinforced in a number of ways.
They were raised in the classroom where facile interpretations
of rural behavior were constantly challenged and sound knowledge
recognized. They were reinforced on visits to rural areas by
the behavior and approach of Headquarters staff in contacts with
rural women. They were promoted in homework and field assignments and, above all, they were encouraged and supported on the
job.

The results to date are varied. That is, the attitudes and
behavior of most staff have obviously changed and of a few have
not. There is little we can find to explain the differences
except that those three who have changed least are, in one case,
among the most highly educated with the best grades, and in the
other two cases, women with the greatest social distance from
rural women. Another explanation is that there is so little
support for these new attitudes away from training. On the one
hand, some staff are still talking of literacy and handicrafts
as the solution to women's problems, defining the problems as
child marriage and polygamy and characterizing women as ignorant
and superstitious. But a growing number are developing rapidly
in their ability to look at rural life and listen to rural
people as if there were something important to learn from them
in developing projects and creating policy.

It is worth noting here the new kinds of analysis offered by
some of the staff in their field assignments, which came after
six week in the classroom and a minimum of three months on the
job. They wrote about the problems of women in new terms. They
wrote about women having to be obedient to husbands and in-laws
because of the threat of divorce. They wrote about women suffering from poverty, with repeated pregnancies, liable to deser-
tion, yet unable to act on their own behalf because of the
status value to them and their families of the *purdah* system.
They looked at the obstacles women faced if they wanted to find
ways to support themselves. They analyzed the village power
structure that control women's behavior. One staff member described the process by which machines were taking away the work
of poor women without any new sector being created to use their
labor. She looked at the situation of slightly better-off women

whose economic importance was diminishing and the reflection of their lowered value in the gradual substitution of dowry for bride price. She pointed out that those women who do not work are appreciated for their ability to make men's lives more enjoyable and she called that condition "slavery". She pointed out that the liberation of women would create the same problems for men as the liberation of the poor would create for the rich. Significant social change, she indicated, is a long way off, but efforts can be made now to support the economic work of women, especially their valuable work in livestock raising and vegetable growing. Such changes in attitude over so short a period of time are very encouraging, but the lapses, as well as the absence of support away from training, indicate the *continued* need for opportunities for reinforcement.

But what about behavior, which is an expression of attitude, and is very important in working with rural women who will immediately reject or cleverly manipulate those who set up a social distance in the way they talk or act? Those whose behavior seems the most effective are, not coincidentally, in *Thanas* where the attitude of the whole staff toward the rural people is most egalitarian. Without that model from one's immediate superiors, it is hard to avoid setting up the barriers offered by one's position and education. Still, luckily, most of the female staff, because of the cultural support for egalitarian behavior among rural women, are predisposed to act in ways that encourage confidence and trust. Providing new models for behavior seems the most effective training in this respect.

Learning to Collect Information: Because this project started at a time when there was little available information about the lives of rural women and great difficulty in collecting such information, it was necessary to use the project and the available project staff to increase information rapidly.(5) Among the basic questions that needed at least general answers when the project began were:
> what do rural women *do* in the rural economy?
> what are the bases for co-operation and conflict among rural women?
> what health, nutrition and family planning practices do women follow?
> what is the balance of power between men and women? and

---

(5) See our "Finding Ways to Learn About Rural Women: Experiences from a Pilot Project in Bangladesh."

to what extent are women engaged in money-making activities?

As fundamental as these questions are, there was no doubt in our minds that the project should begin on the basis of what was already known rather than wait until information was gathered, because the project provided the most likely possibility, through the contact of rural staff with rural women in situations that were conducive to trust and mutuality, of collecting information that was of practical value. What was necessary was to develop new attitudes toward information in rural staff and to help them develop their skills in collecting it.

The general change in their attitude toward rural life and rural women, the realization that there was something to be learned rather than taught, that rural people were knowledgeable, and that what they knew and contributed was of great significance, was the first step. The next step was to help the staff realize that what was part of their everyday observation or part of their unconscious knowledge or readily available if they observed or questioned those around them, was, in fact, valuable information. Especially the farm work of rural women must have seemed to them so commonplace and so negligible that it took a long time before they were able to observe and report it in any detail.

Emphasis in all staff learning situations was placed on the importance of information about the lives of rural women and men. Assignments were set to develop skills and change attitudes. Lectures in elementary rural sociology were included in their training. Part of their learning included how to interview, including how to pursue responses that indicated differences between norms and practice. In class they practised by taking each other's case histories. Other assignments involved their going in small groups to villages or projects to interview people for information relevant to topics that were being discussed theoretically in class. For example, when the function and purpose of women's co-operatives were being discussed in class, they were sent to a rural *Thana* where women's co-operatives were already in operation to find out what women had to say about them. The difference between what was said in class and what the rural women said was illuminating in substance as well as good practice in developing basic research skills. The staff responded enthusiastically to this emphasis on practical research. It was a way of learning they had never experienced in their education. It was interesting, given this fact, how quickly they were able to frame good questions, develop a sympathetic style that evoked frank responses, and report without embellishment.

A major pre-service training assignment, on the basis of which their appointment was determined, involved three months combined research and actual work on the job. The research included in-depth interviews of at least ten rural women of varied ages, classes and familial roles, a modest village study, and a des-cription of projects for both men and women. One purpose of this assignment was to encourage the staff to get a sense of the background out of which specific problems emerge, and to see the inter-relation of seemingly different problems revealed by project work. Another was to encourage them to visit women of lower status than their own, a practice not followed in rural society, to enable them to learn about differences in problems of women from different backgrounds. A further purpose was to give them practice in observation and in learning how to gain the confidence of rural women. Yet another was to stress the importance of knowing about the rural and administrative context of which women's lives form a part.

The results were excellent. This aspect of training has run into almost no obstacles. Headquarters has been able to request information on specific topics and rely on the responses.(6) There are limitations, of course, to the kind and amount of information that can be collected this way, related to the workload and research sophistication of the staff, but the channels for communication of information have great potential. One indication that a period of work service combined with this kind of training emphasis produces the intended results - respect for, and, hence, the ability to observe certain aspects of rural life - has come from a brief "test" given to new and old staff, (including two males, one new, one old). They were asked to describe the work of rural women and their problems. Those who had been in the project longest gave the most detailed descrip-tions. Many of the new female staff gave perfunctory, inaccur-ate descriptions but the two males both summarized women's work as, in effect, serving their husbands and taking care of children and animals.

Learning to provide feedback: In addition to basic information about rural women, the project depends for its efficacy on feed-back about the responses of rural women to the guidelines of

---

(6) The agricultural case study on pp.180-2 is an example of staff work.

the project. There are two reasons for this need, both of which will continue for the life of the project. One is the lack of precedent for the kinds of activities the project is introducing in rural areas. It is important to know how women are taking advantage of new resources, which women are responding, which directions for commercial enterprises are better than others, how the village is reacting to new behavior on the part of women, and so forth. Even when the project is older, it will continue to have this kind of need for feedback since it will, if it is vital, continue to evolve in new directions, creating change on the basis of which it must develop new policy. The second reason for the ongoing need for feedback is the "ideology" of the project. The project does not offer a set program to rural women. It offers guidelines, based on Government structure, procedures, and resources in line with the national priority goals it hopes to achieve. But the actual program itself will be determined by rural women whose response to these resources will point the way toward activities for which further investment, training, technology, and support will be useful. Their responses will also indicate what needs (e.g. health care and labor-saving technology) are prerequisites for further development. The project is based on a committment to the development of leadership among rural women while, at the same time, it must continually attempt to align women's responses and Government priorities. Accurate and continuing feedback is therefore essential.

Such feedback can only come from the rural staff. They are in contact with rural women and in a position, if appropriately trained and motivated, to observe and report their responses. Based on their information, policy can then be modified. The problem is that they are also responsible for administering the project. It is their job, as we have seen, to organize cooperatives, supervise their development, set up training programs, and in general, carry out policy as issued from the Headquarters office, which in turn is supervised by two ministries. Targets fixed by Headquarters for numbers of societies to be formed, membership to be enrolled and loans to be given and collected, in line with its timetable and budgetary allocations, are passed on to rural staff to carry out. In addition, there are strong pressures from the top for records of increasing numbers of family planning acceptors, with the implication that failure to perform well in this area would call the whole project in question. Attempting to meet these targets in a project without precedent in their areas requires great effort of the rural staff in the face of great obstacles. The temptation to report the kind of progress for which rewards are traditionally given is also great.

The problem then is to help the staff see that "failure", if
honestly achieved (i.e. after genuine effort), if accurately
observed and, if possible, explained, is as important as success.
In other words, what one can learn from a project is one aspect
of its achievement. The staff have to be trained to see themselves as the authorities about what will work, what will not,
and why, on whom others depend for development of policy.
Training involves a delicate balance between rigorous demands
for performance and genuine respect for analysis of problems and
failures and suggestions for change. Staff must be able to
trust that they are valued both for carrying out policies in
line with targets and for spotting problems and failures that
indicate that the framework and targets may have to be modified.
They must be respected, rewarded and promoted for this kind of
performance.

So far, this approach is showing signs of success. Its most
important vehicle is the three or four day in-service training
session held several times a year. At first these sessions were
dominated by instructions and guidelines from Headquarters.
Gradually, however, they have become discussions among staff,
assembled from all over the country, about what problems they
are facing in carrying out these guidelines and how they are
attempting to solve them.

It is not easy for the staff to admit to their "superiors" some
of the realities of the project, for example, that village
meetings are not taking place as they should, that training
classes are often ineffective, or that some women who take loans
may be lying about how they are using the money. But with encouragement, they not only express some of the difficulties or
failures or imperfections in their work, but attempt to understand how to deal with each kind of problem. Their judgment
and self-confidence are increasing and their value as the channel
of communication from rural areas to Headquarters and back is
being realized. These in-service training sessions are the best
sources for feedback to Headquarters staff about the progress of
the project, on the basis of which policy is being evolved. Unless this channel of communication is kept open and functioning,
policy objectives and project reality will quickly diverge.

This approach requires adequate Headquarters staff to run in-
service training sessions and to make site visits, since direct
knowledge of the individual situation each rural staff member

is facing - the kinds of villages she is working in and the
quality of the project in which she has been placed - makes it
possible to understand special problems she may have that she
herself is not aware of. These visits also give project staff
more status in the eyes of other *Thana* officers and in the eyes
of village people, which makes their work less difficult.
Unfortunately even if training staff were available, so that
regular visits and in-service sessions could always be assured,
the whole approach would be undermined by the traditionally
hierarchal pay-scale and the value system it reflects. The
reality is that the staff who are closest to rural people, who
administer the project, who are potentially the best source of
information about it, who live with the least amenities and face
the most hardships in carrying out their work *are the least
rewarded.* The social rewards for the kind of performance that
is being asked of this staff are so meagre that one cannot
realistically expect their unusually fine response to be sustained for long.

Learning to discuss family planning: The rural staff are responsible for the family planning activities of the project. Specifically, they organize family planning classes for the village
co-operative leaders which are usually taught by officers and
staff of the family planning department and supplemented by
discussion and explanation from the project staff. Also, in
attendance at weekly village meetings, they supplement the work
of the co-operative leaders in giving information, answering
questions, providing supplies and keeping records. In general,
these rural staff act as a liaison between the *Thana* family
planning office and the male and female co-operators participating in the IRDP program. Through close contact with co-
operative leaders and co-operative members, they are in a position to provide family planning support and follow-up information at the village level. It is essential, therefore, that
they understand not only what services are offered by the family
planning department and where supplies may be procured, but, to
the extent possible without medical training, how the reproductive system functions and how different methods of contraception
act on the body in preventing conception. This is important
because, with so few sources of information in rural areas that
women can turn to if surprised by an unexpected reaction,
information becomes a key resource.

Communicating such information to the rural staff is not in itself difficult, although there is a scarcity of appropriate
materials, even in English, for this kind of training. It was

anticipated that there might be difficulty in overcoming the attitude toward what is culturally acceptable behavior for young married and unmarried women with regard to knowledge and talk about sex and family planning. Although talking about family planning is not exactly the same thing as talking about sex, to understand thoroughly how conception and therefore contraception take place, sex is an implicit, and sometimes explicit, part of the material.

Fortunately, there was no real difficulty in bringing about change in the behavior of rural staff in relation to their family planning work. They were advised that unless *they* were convinced about family planning, others would not be either. They were reminded that sex was universal and natural, that family planning was a national priority, and that shyness, embarrassment, blushing, and giggling in learning and carrying out their family planning work was totally inappropriate. Probably not because of this advice but because there were sanctions and rewards throughout the system in which they were working for this new behavior, their behavior changed rapidly. From misinformation or ignorance to knowledge, from joking or hiding any interest they had about these matters to openly discussing them seriously (for possibly the first time in their lives), took only a matter of days. It is an important indication of how fast change can come when the circumstances are right.

The information content of this part of training focused on reproduction, menstruation, conception and contraception. The methods and materials included lectures, discussions, field trips, flip charts, films, and pamphlets. The interest level was always at a peak, probably because the staff were learning first of all about themselves and how to control their reproductive lives when they were already highly motivated to do so. The results were evident in many ways. Comparison of their knowledge about contraception before and after training indicates that they have moved from misinformation to knowledge. Comparison of their own contraceptive practice before and after training indicates that what they learned had first of all a personal application. Several women indicated that though they knew about contraception earlier in their married lives, they could not get the kind of information that would make them feel secure in using contraception. They are now using pills and condoms and taking advantage of menstrual regulation to control family size. On the project, these women speak freely to older women and age mates about contraceptive problems and how to solve them. Most of them are looked to as trustworthy sources of

information by rural women in the project. The rapid and
dramatic results of this aspect of training convince us of how
important it is to provide thorough information about conception
and contraception to educated people in rural areas where reliable sources of modern information are so limited, so that they
can act on it in their own lives and become additional resources
for those men and women in villages who are even more isolated
from and dependent on reliable information.

Learning attitudes toward work life: Many of the rural staff
are working for the first time and are in fact pioneers in this
kind of work for women in rural areas where the whole culture
emphasizes women's responsibilities in the home and men's
provision for women as the appropriate relationship between the
sexes. Almost all of them are working for the first time in
relatively "unsheltered" situations - in offices with men and
on the roads to and from villages - in a culture that gives
respect to women to the extent they remain out of sight. Part
of their training, therefore, has to deal with the development
of appropriate attitudes toward work life in the face of inevitable discomfort arising from the fact that they are working.

They have to deal with comments from family, neighbors and
villagers. One staff member's mother-in-law tells others not to
talk to her: "It is a sin to talk to her because she works; she
is not a woman." Neighbors tell another staff member that the
money she earns is *haram*, i.e. prohibited by religion, as pork
is. Another is told every day by her mother-in-law in whose
house she lives that she should quit. Many are teased on the
road with family planning jingles and allusions. Some, especially the unmarried, are victims of rumors about their behavior
with men. Most say that urbanized, educated men, often male
staff of the same rank or lower are much more troublesome than
village people.

Travel to the villages is one of their main problems on the job,
and their most important responsibility. Sometimes it is a
matter of expense. Their travel expenses might be tolerable if
they were free to walk much of the time. But in some conservative areas, walking is out of the question and staff must
spend much of their travel allowance on cycle-rickshaws. Unlike
men, they feel they must travel in pairs which slows down
considerably how much they can accomplish with the same amount
of effort. Some trips involve up to four hours of travelling
each way, difficult for all kinds of reasons, including the
psychological strain of being in male space. Sometimes the very

transportation system works against them. One woman had to walk
three miles each way to a village and back on muddy roads because
the public bus only carries women if they are going on long
journeys.

There are no culturally adequate facilities for many of them
where they work, no separate rooms for women, no bathroom facilities for women. At training institutions, unaccustomed to
accommodating women, either facilities are inadequate because of
the special requirements for the shelter of women or because the
attitudes of those who run the facilities are unco-operative in
solving some of the problems women may have to cope with when
they are pregnant or nursing. In many of these cases women are
staying away from their homes overnight for the first time.
Training opportunities for women are often curtailed either
because field visits, casually arranged for men (e.g. "go to a
co-operative meeting and observe the proceedings"), have to be
specially arranged for women, or because those who convene on-
the-job staff meetings, where the institution staff discuss
practical issues, think these meetings might be disrupted by
the presence of women. Instead of addressing the problems working women have because of their culture, there is a tendency to
blame and penalize them for having the problems.

Recognizing that rural female staff would face innumerable
problems *through being female*, in addition to the other very
real difficulties of the job, training had to provide strength
to cope with these problems as well as the possibility of amel-
iorating them through discussion. In training, the staff were
given advice about the problems they might face. As far as
work performance was concerned, they were reminded that they
were pioneers, that their behavior would affect those who came
after them, and that they should be careful not to reinforce the
widely-held prejudices against women workers. They were advised
to take care of their health, to plan ahead to meet their family
responsibilities, and to take few holidays. They were told that
in spite of all the pressures to the contrary, their first
responsibility was to the job and that they must find ways,
without neglecting basic family needs, to meet that responsibility. They were told that whatever personal problems might
arise among female staff, they must present a united front.
They were advised to find a way to deal with male staff that
would prevent rumors on the one hand and accusations of non-co-
operation on the other. They were instructed never to cry on
the job, though occasions were bound to arise when they felt
like it.

These ideas communicated in classrooms and on visits to project areas were, like some of the expectations with regard to family planning behavior, being heard by staff probably for the first time in their lives. Unlike the attitudes about family planning they are not being reinforced anywhere else, in most cases, besides training. This makes chances for the rural staff as a group to share problems and provide support for each other, as well as chances for Headquarters staff to reinforce appropriate behavior, very important.

Given the pressures which these young women face, the results have been very encouraging; most of them because of the strength of these women, fostered by their culture, to deal with diffi-cult situations uncomplainingly. The role of training has been to support and channel this strength. Evidence of the capacity and determination of these women was there from the start and is epitomized in the staff member who came to the first long training session in her ninth month of pregnancy, bringing along provisions for the new baby, gave birth during the session, and was back in class after a few days. Staff have found ways to get to all the training sessions. They have found appropriate ways to get along with male staff and village males. Their performance varies for all kinds of reasons including support from family and male staff, but, with few exceptions, they have all shown the strength and courage of good pioneers.

In summary, then, training of staff on a project such as this must be on-going and vital. Not the mechanics of the project but its *life* is communicated through training on the job and in regular conferences. As one thinks about expansion and future development of the project, one must find ways to ensure that such training will continue as Headquarters staff changes and new institutions and trainees are involved in staff training. As we see it, there are three major needs to guarantee the kind of training that is necessary for such a project. One is the development of training materials that will enable new training staff to carry on appropriate training. A second is increased Headquarters staff to supervise far-flung training, modify it as necessary, and make visits to rural staff on the job. And a third is adequate social rewards in the form of salary,

accommodation and recognition for women who work in the rural
areas.(7)

(7) Several rural staff have been sent abroad to conferences
about rural women. Some have presented research they have done
about rural women's lives at a conference in Dacca. Other
avenues are being explored to publicize their expertise and to
give them the credit for their work that urban officers can
often get more easily.

CHAPTER III

CO-OPERATIVES

The preceding section focused on the staff who administer the
project for rural women in rural areas. In this section we look
with some care at the participation of rural women in the project, through its basic institution, the co-operative. It is
important, in understanding the co-operatives in this project,
not to be misled by preconceptions based on an understanding of
that institution as it evolved in the West, or for that matter
as it evolved in South Asia. It may be better for our purposes
to think of the co-operative primarily as a village or community
based organisation of women, which enables them to have access
to social and economic resources, in return for disciplined
committment on their part,(1) so that those resources are likely
to be used to achieve desired national goals. As a community-
based institution it provides group strength to women who
already have a sense of responsibility to each other.

Orientation of the Community

During the period of time in which women's co-operatives were
being formed in *Thanas* selected for the pilot project, Headquarters staff paid one to three day visits to each of these
Thanas for the purpose of orienting male leaders of the area,
assembled village women and *Thana* officers to the nature of the

---

(1) The IRDP rural co-operative is registered with the Co-
operatives Department and must adhere to the rules and regulations evolved by that Department.

new project.(2) Since there had been no such project for women
in these areas before, orientation usually involved challenging
conventional ideas about "outside" help for women and explaining
the economic base of the new approach.

In almost every orientation session, the same expectations about
a women's program were expressed, perhaps in a perfunctory way,
perhaps to communicate the status of the speaker, or to respect
that of others. For instance, there was a tendency on the part
of male staff and male leaders to discuss the project as "home
development", a term and approach connected with a home economics
type of foreign assistance to women that was the basis for anything done for women in the 60s, except for the Comilla Women's
Program. This approach focused on improvement of the home,
(nutrition, health, sanitation), rather than commercial economic
ventures; training in skills like sewing or handicrafts was
intended more for enhancing the home and saving money than for
bringing in regular income. Training in improved vegetable
growing was intended to produce more for home consumption. Such
a program is in many ways irrelevant to the lives of most rural
women including those in higher-status families. But it is
acceptable if not useful to status-conscious families because it
does not violate the basic ideals of men as providers and women
as protected and sheltered. Thus a request that one heard in
these orientation sessions from men or a certain class of women
in response to the question, "What do you want from a woman's
program?", was invariably, "a sewing machine". This would have
primarily status rather than commercial value in an area where
tailors are men and professional sewing training is not available. Such a request may also have been connected with the
fact that in response to the distress of women after the War, an
international agency distributed sewing machines along with a
lot of free cloth. Items made of the cloth were then sold,
helping women by way of relief rather than commercially.

In their initial thinking about the ways women could acceptably
make money, both women and men thought of exhibitions, bazaars

---

(2) Orientation sessions were also held at Headquarters during
the period for *Thana* IRDP officers and co-operative leaders of
the men's program to solicit their opinions and request their
co-operation. This was especially necessary since their *Thanas*
were selected by *Headquarters* for a Women's Program. Now that
the project is well underway, requests are coming *from the*
Thanas to be included in the Women's Program.

or showrooms for the sale of small handicraft items made by
women. This was an acceptable way in which poor but status-
conscious women had been helped in recent years by better-off
women, who often bought up the handiwork at low prices. At most
of the orientation sessions with rural women, one found tables
with displays of such work, almost none of it of commercial
value, and little of it likely to produce any kind of regular
income. Part of all orientation sessions, therefore, dealt with
these issues and frankly pointed out that most home-made decor-
ative goods simply would not sell, that sewing machines were not
practical for economic gain, and that old approaches, such as
relief, exhibitions and prizes, formal health and literacy
classes, and processions of women making demands, did not
realistically address the issues that were of importance to *most*
rural women.

The explanation of the focus of the Project directly challenged
the ideal of the adequately sheltered woman in a way that talk
of home development, sewing machines and handicraft bazaars did
not. In general, the rural audience was not averse to discussing the new approach and, in fact, to hearing ideas about women
that had probably not been discussed in these terms before.
The project was described as having as its major concern
exploring ways for rural women to earn real income through work
on a regular basis. Women were going to be encouraged to direct
skills and knowledge they already had in their subsistence farm
work to market-oriented production, whose emphasis would be
profit, not just a few *takas* now and then from special bazaars,
but an income derived from providing commercially acceptable
products to satisfy real needs. Rural women, especially from
more elite families for whom the idea was unheard of, were
advised that they should raise their daughters to recognize two
responsibilities, family and work.

The co-operative was described as the specific and necessary
approach to the exploration of economic opportunities. It was
explained that it provided group strength in finding solutions
to problems and in making demands on Government for necessary
services. The women were interested in what benefit they could
get through the co-operative. They were advised to begin to
think of economic projects for which loans would be profitable,
projects based on what they already knew how to do, and producing
goods which everyone would want to buy. When asked, "What work
do you know?", most women replied, "None". They had to be
encouraged to think of what they did (and were highly skilled in)
every day in food preparation, food production, and cottage craft

VWB - K

142

as work with potential commercial value. The tendency was to think of economic projects as involving something *other* than the work they were already proficient at, which has value in the rural economy but is not socially recognized and, at a market level, is usually out of women's control.(3) But finally they were told to concentrate on what would sell.

Groups of women responded publicly in different ways. Those in most obvious need were most openly responsive to the discussion of increased economic benefit through their work. Those with status to protect continued to speak of sewing machines for home use or "foreign" poultry as possible commercial enterprises. Privately or away from men some of these women would say what they could not say in public: "If men give us food we can eat. If they give us money, we can spend. We want something of our own. If we work, we can achieve this." Groups of men tended to be consistent from place to place in their polite skepticism. Sometimes, if their rhetoric about women got too far away from reality, they had to be reminded that if women were not helped in some way they would beg, a religious obligation these men would have to deal with. In general both men and women responded and participated in the discussions as if *real* issues were being brought up, even though solutions were not easy to find. However skeptical some might have felt about the new project for women, most seemed pleased with the basic recognition of rural women as hard-working and productive on which the project was founded.

It should be remembered, of course, that such orientation is mostly a chance for Headquarters to present its ideas to rural leaders and request implicitly that they be accepted or at least tolerated. It is also a chance for others to listen.

What is said in these gatherings, where people are projecting images they feel the need to protect, is often out of obligation. What is actually happening in rural areas occurs at another level and can be understood by what in fact happens on the project.

----

(3) In the thinking about economic programs for rural women there is a tendency to consider their present work as non-productive and to look for other ways women can produce income, rather than to consider how increased market production of their work will benefit the total rural economy.

Formation of Co-operatives

When the project started in the fiscal year 1973-74, instructions
were sent to IRDP staff in ten separate *Thanas*, where the IRDP
was already operating a program for male farmers, advising them
each to begin to organize ten women's co-operatives. Although
there were a handful of women in IRDP farmers' co-operatives,
there were no separate women's co-operatives in the IRDP up to
this time. With the help of IRDP male staff, female staff as
they were appointed, and leaders and members of men's co-
operatives, women's co-operatives began to be formed in the
selected *Thanas*. They were promoted in general terms as offering resources to women for home development and economic advancement through loans, without spelling out a specific program.
Though all the women's co-operatives were formed through an
already established male organization working at the village
level, without whose sanction and sponsorship they could not
have gained entry, they got their start in a variety of ways,
most of which indicate that there was a ready constituency for
the project.

One way was that women, who already had mobility and were coming
to the *Thana* Center as family planning agents for the family
planning office, heard about the new program, organized women in
their village and invited IRDP staff to talk to them. One such
woman convinced 25 other women to listen to the IRDP staff by
stressing the loan possibilities of the project. She pointed
out that they were currently paying back four *maunds* of rice for
two borrowed and that IRDP loans would have much lower interest.
16 of the women who came to hear more agreed to join. Another
such woman concentrated her efforts on encouraging women, who
were interested but hesitant to spend money to join, to save in
extra ways by selling pumpkins or growing chilis for sale or
sending handicrafts to a local exhibition. 20 women attended
the orientation meeting she organized out of whom three "fled"
when they heard about compulsory savings. When the co-operative
was officially formed, 32 women joined by making initial deposits. In other cases it was this type of woman that the project
staff or leaders of a male co-operative in the village approached
to try to form a women's co-operative since she already had the
mobility outside the village and access to homes inside the
village. Or male co-operative members, who wanted a women's
co-operative involving their relatives (which was only sometimes
the case), would encourage wives or other close relatives to
organize.

In a number of cases, women's co-operatives were formed from already existing women's groups started by other institutions such as *Swarnivar*, a self-reliance movement sponsored by the Agriculture Ministry, or an adult literacy program initiated by the Education officer. In one rare case, women withdrew from membership in a male co-operative to form their own group. In other cases, project staff went to villages uninvited by women, but supported by members of a male co-operative in the village, and did the organizing work themselves. These, of course, were the most difficult to organize. The easiest were usually those which were initiated after village men came to the staff at the *Thana* center and asked them to come speak to the women.

Although there had to be some support from village men for the project to enter the village at all, organizers met with resistance in a variety of forms. Certain kinds of adverse comment were heard in every village:

> "What is a co-operative; what will it do for us? What use will it be? We've heard a lot about co-operatives but have they ever benefitted anyone? It's better for women to be at home than organizing co-operatives and roaming around without *purdah*." (The village where these comments were heard now has a co-operative of 32 members).

> "Women should take care of children and their husbands. Let men join co-operatives."

> "How can women do the work of the family if they have to go out?"

> "Such behavior is against religion; it will ruin the village."

> "What profit is there in joining a co-operative?"

> "Women join only for a chance to gossip. If they use this time in household work, it would be more beneficial."

Such comments usually did not prevent the formation of co-operatives and gradually lessened, according to members, as the co-operative began to give loans. One co-operative of 40 members that has not received loans yet because of registration delays, reports that husbands are annoyed that their wives are involved outside the home, and that other village women not in the co-operative remain critical.

In a few cases, more serious resistance was felt. For example, project staff went to one village to organize and found the men resistant. Some women were interested, but they were afraid their husbands might not agree. The women saved some money to buy shares and sent it to the *Thana* with the man who was manager of the male co-operative in the village. They found out later that he deposited only half the money and kept the rest for himself. The project staff then agreed that the women could come to training without having bought shares, but the husbands refused to let them go and there was no longer any possibility of forming a women's co-operative in that village.

In another village the whole problem seemed to lie in the refusal of one village influential to let his wife become involved in a co-operative. When the project staff went to the village the men told them that their wives would not be willing to join. Eventually, male project staff persuaded the men to consider a co-operative, but even then the women hid when a female staff member came to collect share money. Finally they told the staff member, "We can organize, but we won't go unless the 'member's' wife goes, or there will be criticism." The male staff spent a lot of time explaining the advantages of the co-operative to the men: women would be able to get loans for economic ventures without having to leave the village. The men agreed to all of this but only after a lot of persuasion would they allow their wives to go to the *Thana* for training. Now, five women attend training even though the "member's" wife does not go out. These women told the project staff later that they had been in readiness for quite a while and had even borrowed special clothes for going out from their neighbors in anticipation of being allowed to go.

No doubt much of the resistance to forming a co-operative has to do with women leaving the village for training. There is gossip that women become involved with men: "People say many evil things when women go to training. Men do not want women losing their shyness, and getting to know the outside world. They say they have no money to buy tea, so they send their wives and daughters outside." One poor woman who goes to weekly training reports: "When I used to go to work in others' houses without *purdah* then nobody used to say anything. But now that I come to training, they criticize me." Although the women's co-operatives are setting themselves against a very strong tradition by insisting that women leave the village for training, so far, the resistance is largely perfunctory, no doubt because of the benefits perceived in the project by enough villagers.

Other quite minor forms of initial resistance to the co-operatives from women involved are having to pay to join, having to save, and having low limits on available loans, but they did not seem significant in delaying or preventing the formation of co-operatives.

Since each of the original *Thanas* was able to form ten women's co-operatives within six months, whatever resistance there might have been cannot be considered the dominant response to this new program for rural women. And, in fact, this has been borne out by the subsequent response in or near areas where the program is already well under way. Some of the original project *Thanas* have requested to go beyond the ten co-operatives specified at first. They were given permission to expand once membership in these co-operatives had reached a certain number. Now they include, in some cases, twenty villages and are under pressure to expand even more. One *Thana* just admitted to the project organized co-operatives in 25 villages within a shorter space of time than the original *Thanas* had spent to organize ten. At one *Thana* not yet admitted to the project, officers have organized 17 co-operatives and are seeking to be admitted. If this trend continues it would seem to indicate that villages were ready for a change involving the behavior of rural women that has only become apparent through the actual introduction of an *opportunity* for change.

Co-operative Leaders

The women who are members of the co-operative and follow co-operative discipline are entitled to training, credit and a variety of services that Government offers rural people. For both cultural and administrative reasons, it is not feasible for those who represent Government to go to the villages to give training and credit to co-operative members nor for the whole co-operative to come to Government offices at the *Thana* to claim services. Rather, the co-operative is represented by five women who come each week to the *Thana* center, where extension agents from various Ministries and Departments of Government sit, for training, services and supplies which they then transmit to co-operative members at weekly meetings in the village. It is intended that these five women from each co-operative act as liaison between Government and the co-operative membership. The viability of the co-operative depends to a great extent on their leadership and management abilities.

Role: The role of co-operative leader has both advantages and disadvantages. These women are likely to experience pressure from the rest of the co-operative to provide good information and services and from the project staff to adhere to Government regulations and project guidelines. As village women who leave their homes to travel to the *Thana* center, they are likely to experience some criticism of their behavior. At the same time they have the advantage of increased access to resources that come from a sanctioned trip out of the village. They receive a weekly allowance for travel to and from the *Thana* much of which can be saved by walking or sharing transport. And they may gain status from their acquaintance with Government officers whom perhaps the men in their family or village have not been able to meet.

Travelling to the *Thana* Center for training as leaders of a women's co-operative is a new kind of behavior for village women. A few of the women who become co-operative leaders had already been travelling to the *Thana* Center as family planning agents employed by the family planning department, but most of them, though they may have had *relative* freedom in the village because of age and financial or marital circumstance, have not been able to travel beyond the village except to visit relatives. One may call this new experience an extension or accommodation of *purdah*, since most of the women travel in *burkahs*. But the new behavior required of these women in the classroom and in contacts with Government officials is so different from traditional village *purdah* that these women, in travelling a few physical miles from the village, are travelling an unlimited psychological distance. They have transgressed a psychological barrier on the other side of which many aspects of their lives are different. The changes in these women (as in those involved in the Comilla Women's Program ten years earlier) have been rapid and dramatic.

Another less obvious but very important change has occurred in the attitudes of male village leaders who have permitted this departure from traditional behavior on the part of village women. They are taking an important step away from the cherished cultural ideal of men providing for women in allowing income-oriented behavior on the part of women, which the co-operative fosters, to become completely overt rather than the "open secret" or exception it was before.

Who they are: It is important to know what kinds of women are becoming co-operative leaders. Their situation differs considerably from that of male co-operative leaders who are often

people of power and status in the village. The fact that women
co-operative leaders *have to travel* makes it unlikely that they
will come from families with status and power, since as we have
seen earlier, such families tend to maximize the seclusion of
their women. As co-operative leaders, with direct access to
Government resources, on whom other co-operative members depend,
they may gain a kind of power they did not have before. Whether
this will be acceptable to the traditional power structure or
whether there will be a change in the kind of women acting as
leaders remains to be seen.

The co-operative leaders are selected by the members. Certain
prerequisites are favored in selection. It is better if they
are literate since that will increase their access to information and enable them to keep records. It is better if they have
relative freedom from work so that they can spend the necessary
time each week. It is better if they have some independence and
need not worry about getting permission all the time. And it is
essential that they are free to travel. Sometimes there is a
problem in finding any women willing to travel. In one village
no women were allowed to go because the wife of the most influential man in the village was not permitted to go. Eventually,
some husbands were persuaded by male project staff to let their
wives travel even though the leader himself could not be convinced. In other villages, there is active vying for these
positions. In one case, five women from each of two *baris*
wanted to go but eventually a compromise was reached involving
four *baris*. In another village two factions formed vying over
who would be Manager.(4) In some co-operatives, all five
leaders are close relatives or neighbors while in others they
are unrelated and from different *paras* or neighborhoods.
Selection is often in favor of those who on their own initiative
or encouraged by male or female project staff initially organized women into a co-operative. The traits women say are valued
in co-operative leaders are ability to do the work, strength to
cope with opposition, enthusiasm, independence, honesty, and
co-operation.

We have collected some tentative information from a sampling
of co-operative leaders in the first two years of women's co-

---

(4) The Manager is the leader of the group of five women. She
is in charge of organization, collection of shares and savings,
and distribution of loan money (according to the group plan).
The other four women have other responsibilities.

149

operatives:

Table 1 gives the marital status of a random sampling of
64 co-operative leaders.

TABLE 1   Marital Status of Co-operative Leaders

	Number	Percentage
Married	38	59
Widowed	7	11
Divorced/Separated	9	14
Unmarried*	10	16
Total	64	100

* Most of the unmarried women were under 20.

Table 2 gives the educational status of a sampling of
38 co-operative leaders that was biased towards literacy.
This information is not particularly useful in telling us
about individual co-operatives since female education
varies considerably between *Thanas* and between villages.
There are co-operatives in which all the co-operative
leaders are literate. There is one in which the highest
qualification is Class Five. There are some in which none
are literate. Out of one group of 50 co-operative leaders
from ten villages only six were educated above Class Eight.
Out of another such group there were four. What should be
of interest is a comparison of the performance of co-
operatives whose leaders are educated with those whose
leaders are not.

Table 3 indicates the ages of a random sampling of 39
co-operative leaders.

Table 4 indicates the landholding status of a random sampling of 28 co-operative leaders. It is hard to rely on
answers to questions about landholding since women may
inflate or deflate the amount for reasons of prestige or
fear. In addition, the amount of land one owns in one part
of the country will be less valuable than the same amount
in another part where cropping is more intensive.

150

TABLE 2   Educational Status of Co-operative Leaders

Educational Level	Number	Percentage
Illiterate	12	32
Some Secondary School Education	19	50
High School Graduate	4	10
I.A.	1	3
B.A.	2	5
Total	38	100

TABLE 3   Age of Co-operative Leaders

Age	Number	Percentage
Under 20	9	23
20 - 40	16	41
Over 40	14	36
Total	39	100

Table 4   Landholding Status of Co-operative Leaders

Acreage	Number	Percentage
0 - 2	19	68
2.5 - 5	6	21
5+	3	11
Total	28	100

Table 5 indicates the "profession" of the male guardians of a random sampling of 41 co-operative leaders.

TABLE 5 Profession of Male Guardians of Co-operative
          Leaders

Male Profession	Number	Percentage
Men of Influence in Village	6	15
Farmers	9	22
School Teachers	3	7
Petty Jobs requiring Education	7	17
Low Status Jobs	9	22
Laborers	7	17
Total	41	100

While this information tells us that co-operative leaders
include elements of village society as a whole, with neither
the rich nor very poor predominating, it does not tell us who
these women are in relation to their particular village. Since
villages vary so much, a series of small studies may be needed
to indicate whether a pattern can be discerned in the selection
of co-operative leaders, perhaps with more emphasis on the
Manager who at the initial stages may be the more powerful of
the five and the one on whom the strength of the co-operative
depends. Comparison with the findings of Florence McCarthy in
her study of women in analogous positions in the Comilla Women's
Program more than ten years ago should also be revealing.(5)

_____

(5) In her study of 24 women in somewhat analogous positions to
these co-operative leaders, McCarthy noted three types among
them. (All the women were married, two had no children, all were
in their late twenties and older). One type included educated
women of higher prestige than the others. Their husbands had
high prestige jobs or village standing. The women had low centrality in their families. A second type was made up of women in
families with prestige who, for a variety of reasons, had high
centrality in their families. Their economic position was not
as good as that of the first group. A third group was made up
of poor, uneducated women with high centrality. Of the ten in
this group, six were widows, one was separated and two had
husbands who were unemployed (1967).

When one hypothesizes about the socio-economic backgrounds that would be most desirable in co-operative leaders, one wishes, of course, for some women from the village families with more resources. One is not naive about the problems that may arise when women from families with more resources are in control: they may deny poor women loans as bad risks, or they may behave as if they were doing good for poor women by running the co-operative *for* them while exploiting them in other ways, or they may themselves be under the control of their families. On the other hand, if one assumes that women from poor but status-conscious families will have more options for improving their economic conditions *because* they belong to a group that sanctions new forms of behavior for women, the involvement of women from families with more resources makes sense because they bring along the social sanction which is so important in the village as a regulator of women's behavior. The women from better-off fam-ilies who do join are usually those in some kind of need. If these women are active not only in serving others but also in *openly* making use of co-operative resources for economic gain, their example will enable poorer women to join and improve the condition of their families. It may also serve as a model to the next generation of women and their families of the value of work and the flexibility of *purdah*. One hopes also that co-operatives will attract idealistic young girls with new ideas and a readiness for change along with older women whose age gives them influence. This combination seems likely to lead to the social acceptance of new options for women in the future.

Since the ideology or social sanction of the village exerts so much control over women's behavior and is the creation of those with more power and influence, one must always be concerned with ways of "stretching" that ideology to allow women in need more options for helping themselves and their families. These are, of course, hypotheses underlying the approach of the project. To test their feasibility, it is most important to watch for variations in the vitality of co-operatives from one village to another, in order to understand what promotes co-operative rather than exploitative behavior on the part of co-operative leaders and, if exploitation occurs, what conditions enable co-operative members to develop strength to act against such be-havior. Case studies of co-operatives will be very useful in this respect.

Travel: Since, in traditional rural society, travel by women beyond the village is strictly controlled, it is interesting to look at this aspect of the experience of co-operative leaders.

In order to go to the *Thana* Center for training once a week, those women must, of course, have the permission of their male guardians. Usually the five women travel in a group. They travel from one to ten miles each way, through fields, on dirt roads, across rivers, and along tarred roads. They usually walk at least part of the way. One group travels two or three hours by bullock cart. A second travels three hours by boat, then walks for half an hour. Another group sets out in boats the night before training day and returns the following night. Some of them mention problems they face in travelling, usually not seen as serious enough to be considered obstacles. Comments and criticism are made by people on the road as they travel. Young men may tease them with family planning jingles. One group was teased that as women travelling they were like a certain kind of bad-tasting fish. They replied, "Cooked with the right spices such fish tastes very good."

Others hear accusations that they have "given up *purdah* for five rupees a week" (their travel allowance) or, more seriously, that they are respectable women losing status by going out. Women have not been stopped by these comments. Attendance at training is 70-90%. Some say criticism lessens after a while. Some make sure they spend some of their travel allowance on small gifts to family members who might tease them or on their husbands whose permission they require.

As mentioned earlier, women receive a travel allowance of six to ten *takas* a week to cover their travel expenses. To the extent they can save it, this is a meaningful amount of steady income for most women. Women have told us that they spend this money principally on food, ducks, chickens, goats, cloth, and tuition and school books for children. In addition to earning money which belongs to them and which they can spend as they choose, they benefit from the chance to have more direct access to markets, or at least market information, outside the village. It is obvious, therefore, that it is very much in the interests of these women to travel to the *Thana* Center as long as the criticism and objections to their travel are perfunctory and do not seriously threaten whatever they perceive to be of more value to them.

Purpose of Training: Co-operative leaders come to the *Thana* Center once a week for training, spending up to three hours in three or four different classes. There are several purposes for this training. One is to communicate to co-operative members via co-operative leaders information that is relevant and useful

to them and that is available at the *Thana* Center, and to provide channels to the villages for relevant supplies and services.
For example, livestock officers at the *Thana* Center can communicate modern information about raising cows and bullocks and provide access to medicines and other care required for the health
of livestock. Or family planning officers can explain contraception to co-operative leaders and provide supplies of pills or
condoms as requested. Another purpose of training is to develop
leadership among these rural women not only in responsible communication, management, and administration of the co-operatives,
but as representatives of the members, bringing to the attention
of Government the *real* needs of rural women for information and
service and making demands for meeting those needs.

The potential of such training is enormous. This is probably
the first time that many of the extension agents located at the
Thana Center have had access to such numbers of village women,
who are, in fact, the appropriate audience for much of their
expertise.(6) As we have seen, all the poultry in Bangladesh
are raised, a handful per household, by village women who keep
them not only for family food but as a way to earn small amounts
of cash. Poultry have never thrived in village households,
partly because they are seasonally decimated by epidemics. There
are vaccines for these diseases but they are not available on
time, there are no facilities for storing them, and there are not
enough people trained to vaccinate poultry. This is not surprising since there has never been much demand for these improvements,
because those who would be interested have never had a voice.
Past efforts to address the poultry question have involved foreign birds, complex technology and men, and for a number of
reasons have failed. This training offers the possibility for
women to demand the services and supplies that would make their
investment in poultry-raising profitable. In other words,

---

(6) Extension agents at the *Thana* Center - the Livestock Officer,
Horticulture Officer, Fisheries Officer, Education Officer, Co-
operative Officer, Family Planning Officer and others - are
responsible for communicating information to about 170,000 people
or 24,000 families. In some cases they are assisted by employees
at the Union level (there are about ten unions in a *Thana*), but
even then that means too many families per officer, when travel
conditions are for much of the year very difficult and time-
consuming. Since almost all extension agents are male, they are
not likely to communicate directly to women when they go to
villages, nor can women come to them.

whenever Government wants to communicate to rural women, it now has access to their representatives (other women of their community, not their husbands) without having to go to individual households where male extension officers would still be likely to talk only to males. And co-operative leaders, by bringing the real situation of rural women to the notice of Government, can act to bring about changes in the kind of information, service and supplies Government will offer, if it wants to affect the behavior and lives of rural women. The development of a local or community-based institution for women may provide a way for Government to be able to be of more service to women, than if it simply increased the number of its agents, who go to villages or talk to the few women who come out of the village, but who are not seen as responsible to the community they serve.

The classes are held at the *Thana* Center where there is usually a room or auditorium large enough for a class of 50 women, though it may not have adequate facilities like blackboards. The classes include, though with variations from *Thana* to *Thana*, subjects like insect control, poultry raising, horticulture, family planning, co-operative structure, loan management, handicrafts, co-operative discipline, childcare, seed preservation, adult literacy, livestock care, fish culture, economic enterprises, and health care. The teachers are for the most part extension agents at the *Thana* Center and other resource people who may be located in the area. Sometimes co-operative members with special skills or training conduct the classes. The method of teaching is primarily lecture since it is the only model the extension agents have had, but in a few classes there is emphasis on practice or on discussion.

Results of Training: Let us look first at the positive results of this approach to training rural women and then at some of the problems that have come to our attention through feedback from rural staff and as a result of tour visits. Women have been coming to training very regularly and with high attendance. Groups who come together from ten villages of a *Thana* are usually quite varied in socio-economic background and literacy, so that a kind of social "mixing" takes place that does not often occur in the villages. One training class, for example, includes two Hindu groups, a group of Muslim potters, a Muslim group that is predominantly under 25 and one that is predominantly over 35.

What is it that these women are actually learning? As in all cases there is variation from *Thana* to *Thana* related mostly to the vitality of the whole project. We have "tested" their knowledge of some of the information communicated in classrooms and have found for the most part that they can repeat what they have been taught, a feat of concentration and memory since they are mostly unable to read or write. Those who have had good family planning classes can explain how a baby is conceived, and how pills and ligations work. One woman drew a picture to show how the tube is cut in a ligation so that the egg will not pass beyond a certain point. Those who have had good horticulture classes have explained how to prepare ground in the modern way for planting vegetables and how to care for them. They have explained basic co-operative laws. Some have learned by practice how to give poultry injections and make jute handicrafts. Some have been given vegetable seeds to distribute to members whom they teach by their method of planting the seeds and caring for the vegetables. Some have been given improved breeds of poultry to raise; they share the eggs with other members and teach them poultry-care by their example. Progressive projects have shown the most ingenuity in developing useful training, and the women have shown that they learn what they are taught.

Gaining modern knowledge about horticulture, poultry raising or family planning is often worse than useless if the services and supplies necessary to put modern knowledge into practice with some hope of success are not available or not on time. Most of the projects have been able to guarantee pills and condoms as requested. One has been able to distribute coconut and fruit trees, another improved poultry, and several have distributed improved seeds. Training materials for literacy classes have been distributed. These examples have shown that channels for services and supplies exist and function.

One experiment in training co-operative leaders is going on now which illustrates significantly the direction in which the project is able to develop. It is a nutrition training program being sponsored by the Nutrition Institute of Dacca and UNICEF who sought out access to co-operative leaders as a way to reach large numbers of rural women. The program involves: initial training in nutrition for rural staff at an in-service training conference; five-day training sessions at the *Thana* Centers for co-operative leaders; and concentration in one *village* of each *Thana* on training and support for commercial level vegetable growing, on the assumption that more food in the village and a greater chance for women to earn income, with the changes that brings about in a woman's life, will lead to better nutrition for the family. Women in areas where the water supply is

inadequate for such commercial growing will be sold tube-wells
on an installment basis and will be given intensive training in
repair and maintenance of them.

The co-operative leaders, in varying degrees, have been effective in managing co-operative affairs and taking on leadership
roles in representing co-operative members. In most groups of
co-operative leaders, each one has been given responsibility for
one aspect of co-operative activity: organization of co-
operatives, economic activities, family planning, literacy,
health and nutrition. Though all five attend all classes, they
have responsibility in only one major area of activity. This
makes their work more likely to be effective and makes them more
accountable to the members and staff. In one society, for
example, the co-operative leader in charge of horticulture brings
sick leaves of plants and trees at members' requests to the *Thana*
Center for advice from the horticulture officer. Many have made
sure that all members who wanted loans were able to get them and
that all loans were paid back. Many who are in charge of family
planning have ensured that women get supplies and information
often in secret from their husband or mother-in-law. Many who
were in charge of savings collected money from women who were
secretly members or who, because of *purdah*, could not attend
village meetings. Some take handicrafts that members have made
to the *Thana* Center to try to sell them. As far as communicating
information they have learned at the *Thana* Center to the members
of the co-operative, the general experience, with exceptions, has
been that to the extent they have understood what they were
taught, they have communicated their knowledge to others.

There have been increasing examples of co-operative leaders
speaking up as representatives of rural women. At a recent
assembly of co-operative leaders from one *Thana* called because
of an appearance by the District Commissioner, village women who
had never openly spoken to strange men before, explained with
assurance the economic activities of the co-operatives, the loan
policy, and the profitability of these loans. With regard to
family planning, one woman explained that there were many physical problems being faced by women who had had ligations and
requested that a doctor be posted at the *Thana* to attend to
these problems. One co-operative leader from the same *Thana*
sought nomination to the local government council and got it.
In another *Thana*, where co-operative leaders were convened to
hear a representative of a foreign donor but were not called on
to express their views and needs, they complained to a staff
member later that such proceedings in which their views were not

sought seemed very suspicious.

Most of the co-operative leaders help others get loans as well as taking them for themselves. Usually they take the maximum loan allowable, based on amount of savings. But there are exceptions. One co-operative leader, who is considered by staff to be an example of really good leadership, said she took a smaller loan than she was entitled to so that other members of her co-operative would not be angry at having to take less of the total amount allotted to the co-operative. She had to placate those who wanted larger loans than were available, telling them they might get a better share next time. A few co-operative leaders from better-off families have not taken loans, feeling that it was not appropriate. This behavior does not necessarily indicate a "do-good" attitude (which bodes ill), since in these cases the co-operative leaders are getting obvious material benefits from travel allowance or from selling handicrafts.

Leaders vary considerably, of course. One staff member described the best and worst co-operative leader in her *Thana*. They represent the parameters within which most of the co-operative leaders fall. The best, she said, holds weekly meetings, gives loans correctly, collects shares and savings properly, and follows project instructions carefully. She has a good attitude toward the other women and they listen to her. She seems to care about others and their interests and is not greedy. On the other hand, the one who is the worst does not hold weekly meetings or increase membership. She herself has taken sewing training that was available to only a few in the *Thana* and has also taken a job with family planning. Though she is educated, she has no influence on the members. She thinks only of herself.

As regards the problems, the first year or two of the training of co-operative leaders have, realistically, been most successful in suggesting potentials rather than in realizing them. They have provided at the same time a good sense of some of the immediate problems to be addressed if those potentials are to be fulfilled. It is from this constructive point of view that we wish to examine the problems faced in training co-operative leaders.

The training program for women co-operative leaders is analogous in structure to that of male co-operative leaders. The project for males has been running for four years and in many areas the training component of the project has lost its vitality, as evidenced by the fact that attendance at training is in many cases under 50%. It will be unlikely that such clear evidence will be available to show lack of vitality on the women's side, since women co-operative leaders are needier than their male counterparts and can get greater benefit than males from their trip out of the village and the travel allowance they are paid. The trip itself, a new chance to come out of the village, is something women will not forego easily. But loss of vitality is just as likely to occur if certain measures are not taken quickly.

Let us look first at criticisms of the training program (some of them made by rural staff), and then analyze the salient issues. One criticism is that frequently teachers, the extension agents, do not come to take class. Another is that when they do, they often lecture, using language that is too difficult for rural women to understand, measurements that they are not acquainted with, and scientific or English terminology that is totally incomprehensible to them. In general, appropriate methodology and materials have not been developed to make it possible for rural women to learn well enough to be able to communicate what they have learned to others even more isolated from the modern world than they. Whatever is at the root of the existing lecture method, it reflects a lack of confidence in the knowledge and experience of students and an authoritarian approach to learning, inappropriate in this kind of situation. Often the content itself is not relevant to the situation rural women actually face. Or if it is relevant, as in the case of poultry raising or vegetable growing or family planning, it is not worth learning because vaccines, fertilizer, insecticides, and contraceptive follow-up care are simply not available when needed.

The rural staff criticize the trainees as well as the teachers. They say that women are often bored, the children make noise, the young girls chat and some women, tired from their travels, sleep. Women who do not come to class explain that the roads are muddy, they are too busy and the trip is too expensive. Yet women who do come tend to be older women not young ones who would be less tired by walking. There are too few mature, educated women. As a result, some staff say, they are ineffective in transmitting information to co-operative members who complain in some cases that their representatives are not doing their job.

From our point of view, selection of co-operative leaders to come to training cannot really be altered much. Rather, emphasis must be placed on developing and disseminating materials, methodology and content that are appropriate to the situation as it is and therefore likely to be of *interest* to rural women, offered at the appropriate times and supported by the services and supplies necessary for making new learning of value. Many of the problems attributed to poor selection of co-operative leaders or their inability to learn or remember are really, we think, created by poor training.

This training was intended to be a continuing exchange of information and services through a two-way channel of communication between the *Thana* and co-operative women. For example, if women have received horticultural training for winter vegetables or fruit trees, they should transmit this training to the rest of the co-operative and as need arises, bring back questions about problems such as yellowing leaves, or demands they may have for fertilizer. If there is genuine two-way communication, content and schedule of classes can be evolved out of the information rural women bring to class about their needs.

Methodology must be appropriate for both getting and giving information, which means it has to reflect a respect for the knowledge of rural women. Such a methodology is also likely to develop more egalitarian attitudes about teachers and students. Since one purpose of the training is to develop group strength and self-confidence in solving problems, it must operate on the assumption that rural women already know a lot and that guided group discussion will pool their knowledge and enable them to express their needs and look for realistic solutions. An appropriate method would enable rural women to share with each other what they already know about a given subject, to formulate their needs, to get new inputs of information from available experts and to work out solutions to their problems with the help of services and supplies necessary from the Government. Appropriate materials would take into account the language of rural people, and their way of learning when they are illiterate. National codes that apply to them, as for example the co-operative by-laws, should be available in simplified language so that they can be understood.

Some of these problems could be worked out through the existing project structure *if* there were more Headquarters staff to develop materials and methods and provide additional training to rural staff. But rural staff of the project cannot and should not be expected to be experts in the many areas for which Government has created individual extension agents. Ideally

the material and methodology of extension agents should be made
more conducive to effective learning, but if that does not
happen, the project staff may have to "translate" their lectures
so that information becomes part of the whole communication
process that the project hopes to provide.

Problems arise in other forms of behavior of co-operative
leaders toward members beside the communication of what they
were taught at training. These are problems of leadership. For
example, in a few co-operatives, the leaders deny loans not just
to individual poor women who seem to be bad risks but to poor or
landless women in general. Since no-one in the co-operative can
get a second loan until the previous round of loans has been
fully repaid, this concern with likelihood of repayment is
natural, but if poor women are consistently denied loans, the
purpose of the co-operative, as seen by Headquarters, is defeated.
In men's co-operatives, the loan problem was just the opposite.
Wealthier members who took large loans and did not repay them
made it impossible for poorer members to qualify for loans. This
behavior is so far fairly rare and may differ from village to
village in the same *Thana*. For example, in one *Thana*
leaders of one co-operative did not give loans to any landless
women, while leaders of another divided the allotted money in
equal shares for every member of the co-operative. Obviously
these acts are the reflection of much more than the "fairminded-
ness" of individual leaders. They probably reflect the socio-
economic forces of the whole village.

Another problem that arises if the leaders are from more elite
homes is their inability to travel to the homes of poorer members
to look at vegetable plots or arrangements for poultry. Traditionally, visiting takes place only in the other direction.
Similarly when the leaders are young unmarried women or new
brides, they cannot move around the village as older women can.
Whether training alone can change this traditional behavior is
doubtful. The hope is that as groups develop a sense of identity and unity and find they are not getting access to resources
they want because of the behavior of their leaders, they may be
able to exert pressure to change behavior. In a few instances
co-operative leaders have "resigned" because they were not able
to carry out their duties well. This may have been a sign of
group dissatisfaction. Certain rural staff have been alert in
observing the behavior of co-operative leaders and recommending
changes. With their help, widespread trends can be anticipated
and policy modified to the extent possible to counteract
behavior if it is found seriously to threaten project objectives.

Even more constructive would be periodic conferences, by district or region, of co-operative leaders to enable them to share problems and get advanced training.

Membership

When the co-operatives first started and for at least six months, and sometimes up to a year, until they could be registered, they were not able to offer loans to members. They made demands on members to meet regularly, to deposit savings regularly and to send five women to training outside the village every week, but they did not yet offer economic benefits. This situation no doubt had an influence on who was interested and able to join at first and on the number of members.

To form a co-operative it was necessary that 15 women buy a share each and pay a small admission fee. Women were allowed to deposit small amounts toward the cost of the share and at the same time attend meetings and take training. However, once the co-operative was officially authorized, it was managed by the co-operative leaders and they could decide how to handle membership, within co-operative regulations of course. About a year after the co-operatives in the ten *Thanas* were organized, when some had started giving loans and some had not, a sample survey was taken of 14 co-operatives to collect some initial information about membership with regard to education, marital status, number of children, age, and profession of male guardian. The results were as follows:

> *Education:* 80% of the members are illiterate and semi-literate; among the literate 20%, almost half have been educated to high school matriculation or above.

> *Marital Status:* 88% of the members are married and living with their husbands; 5% are widows and 2% are divorced; 5% are unmarried girls.

> *Age:* 70% of the members are between 21 and 40; 18% are 20 and below.

> *Occupation of Male Guardians:* 43% are in farming; 13% are in business; 16% are in service; 6% are in respected village "professions", 12% are in low status village occupations; 6% are laborers; and 4% are unemployed. 70% of the male guardians are not members of male co-operatives.

Further studies of individual co-operatives have provided
additional information since the survey was taken, none of it
contradictory to the initial findings. In most cases individual
co-operatives include members of varying economic situations,
and of varying ages and literacy. As typical examples, one co-
operative has 42 members of whom ten are poor enough to be working in others' houses. Of the 42, only three are literate. One
co-operative has 25 members of whom 12 are poor; six are illiterate. One has 80 members of whom 20 are married to daily
laborers and the rest are in below subsistence farming families.
Although information about the socio-economic condition of co-
operative members is not detailed enough yet, it seems to indicate that the majority of members are from small-farming
families or landless.(7)

At the same time, there are often important differences among
co-operatives, probably based on differences in villages. With
regard to kinship, some co-operatives have members who all come
from the same *para* and are all related. In other co-operatives,
members may come from several *paras* and be strangers to each
other. More typically the co-operatives include women who are
known to each other because they live in the same area and are
related in "clusters" of twos, threes, and fours.

With regard to economic condition and status, co-operatives may
vary considerably. Sometimes all the members are of "good"
status, although the range of need will vary between poor and
middle-class. Sometimes the whole co-operative will be made up
of women who do what is considered low-status work, like potters
or fisherwomen. Sometimes the co-operative will be formed of
women from farm families, either with a range of neediness, or
mainly middle or mostly small farm women. Sometimes all the

---

(7) Problems in classifying the economic condition of rural
women in co-operatives with more precision are related not only
to the lack of time and personnel for collecting this kind of
information during the early stages of the project but as much
to the lack of clarity of the issue itself. Problems that exist
in defining the economic condition of rural families (see Adnan,
1977b) are compounded by the way status influences the economic
behavior of women in need and by the frequent difference between
a woman's economic condition and that of her family if she has
been widowed, divorced or deserted.

members are landless, in new settlements or business communities. With regard to other characteristics also, there are variations. In some areas, for reasons not yet clear, there are co-operatives with large numbers of very young women, many of them married and already divorced. In some co-operatives, most of the women have relatives in male co-operatives; in other cases, none or very few do. Some co-operatives include Hindus and Muslims; some have one group only. Literacy may range from almost none in a co-operative to almost all. Because there are so many variations of this sort among co-operatives, no one program can suit them all. That is why the emphasis must be on encouraging each group, within project guidelines, to develop its own way.

The size of co-operatives has been increasing probably as the result of loans being given. Most co-operatives started with the minimum 15 members. Now, the average membership of a society that is a year old is close to 40. Since villages vary greatly in size, the significance of the number of co-operative members comes from its relation to the potential number, that is the number of households in a neighborhood or village.(8) It is becoming obvious in some areas that the potential membership for a co-operative is related to the size of the *para* not to the size of the village as a whole, since many members cannot go to the compulsory weekly meeting if it means travelling to another neighborhood of the village. In addition one *para* may have a different economic orientation or level of need than another in the same village, or two *paras* may constitute two factions at odds with each other. The question of size is an important one. First, of course, present coverage must be understood, in terms of households, *baris, paras* and villages. It is in the process of being studied and evaluated. Then goals for optimal size, both for the functioning of the co-operative and for appropriate coverage of an area, can be worked out.

Meetings

Part of the discipline of the co-operative is the weekly meeting in the village. The meeting of groups of women not necessarily related, for business rather than for family or village functions, is a new experience.

---

(8) Co-operative law limits membership to one woman per household, i.e. *ghor* not *bari*.

Location of Meetings: Meetings are often held in the house of
a prominent member of the co-operative, whose status lends respectability to the co-operative and makes it possible for women
from other status-conscious households to attend. As indicated
earlier, in traditional villages, women from higher status
households do not visit the homes of lower status households.
In some co-operatives there are members who cannot attend meetings because of the strict *purdah* they maintain or because they
are not allowed to visit the place where the meeting is held.
Some of these women are from households the villagers refer to
as the *boro bari*, the big or important household, and may even
be "secret" members. When co-operatives are made up of women
who come from several *paras* the meeting place may be selected
for its convenience for most women. In a few cases, meetings
are held in public buildings.

Duration of Meetings: Meetings are, of necessity, short. They
may last for an hour or two which, if women have to travel at
all to attend, adds up to three hours away from the household.
Since women always have to worry about pleasing either mothers-
in-law or husbands with their work, they must be careful if they
are not very powerful in the household, or if there is not full
support for their involvement in the co-operative, not to antagonize anyone by their absence from their traditional place.
During harvest seasons, even three hours in a week may be
impossible to manage.

Content of Meetings: Several activities are part of every
meeting. Savings are collected from all the members and receipts
given; the receipt for the amount deposited by the co-operative
in the bank the previous week is shown; and women are advised how
much their total savings are. Since many women are illiterate
and unable to reckon figures, great probity, care and trust are
required in handling this aspect of co-operative activities.
Book-keeping with the supervision of project staff is necessary
to keep records clear. If there were mishandling or even mistakes in accounting for savings, women would quickly lose confidence in the co-operative. Part of the meeting is taken up
with the transmission of information that was learned at *Thana*
training. Horticulture, loan procedures, possibilities of
income generating activities, and problems to be taken up at the
Thana are among the topics discussed at meetings we have inquired
about. Distribution of family planning supplies, exchange of
information and further requests for supplies are also part of
weekly meetings.

Evaluation: The meeting has an important potential in the project as the opportunity for co-operation, collective strength and leadership to develop, as well as being the vehicle for exchange of information and supplies. It is to be expected, as with meetings of all institutions where attendance cannot be mandated, that there will be a tendency to neglect them. But, at the same time, the general vitality of the project, the quality of the co-operative leaders, and the extent to which the co-operative is valued by its members will exert a counter-tendency. In all cases these meetings of women have been accepted in the villages, an important step in itself. There are several co-operatives where attendance is regularly high. In many others, women on their way to the meeting call on others who, if they cannot come because of household duties or illness, send their savings along to be deposited. In many others, however, attendance is only 40% to 60%. A contributing factor to low attendance in other than harvest seasons is probably the ineffectiveness of co-operative leaders in making these meetings events of importance to women. They, in turn, are often victims of ineffective training at the *Thana*. The presence of project staff which probably strengthens the meetings at this stage and stresses regularity cannot always be assured because of their transportation problems. Some of these problems may be solved by emphasis on better training at the *Thana* Center, provision of transport for women staff and improvement of project services in ways that will lead members to put pressure on their leaders to assure them access. When women consider that the co-operative belongs to them and has value to them, meetings will be more important. High attendance is not necessarily the criterion for effective meetings. What must be watched is how well they serve as *two*-way channels of pressure and information.

Economic Program

A major focus of the Women's Program is economic. That is, a primary goal is to create opportunities for rural women to contribute regularly to family income. This is a new focus for a national rural development institution. It seems the appropriate one for any effort to reach rural women and bring about changes in their behavior in line with national priorities. The Comilla Women's Program, ten years ago, proved that the primary interest of women involved in that project was economic gain. Since then economic need has increased in rural areas and change in the direction of relaxation of strict *purdah* has been occurring. Still rural Islamic culture upholds the ideal of sheltered and

protected women even though women of all classes, some secretly
and some openly and for a variety of needs, are engaged in money-
making activities. Therefore, a project that makes economic
opportunity for women an overt goal must start in a way that
women are likely and able to respond to, and be flexible enough
to evolve pragmatically as women's responses to project resources indicate. In this project the *first step* involves institu-
tionalized savings and loans.

Savings: Members of women's co-operatives buy a share in the
co-operative when they join and then are required to deposit
weekly savings in the bank. The amount of money they can borrow
is based on the number of shares a woman has, in addition to her
savings, although with the exception of a few co-operatives, the
money they borrow does not come from their savings. Saving small
amounts of money collected from a variety of sources is, as
indicated earlier, a practice of rural women. Therefore it is
not surprising that most women have found systematic saving, in
a way that makes it difficult to dip into savings for routine
needs, to their advantage.

The amount of capital - shares and savings together - that 5,508
women have saved through 190 co-operatives up to May 1977 is
about 190,000 *taka*.(9) These figures do not tell us very much
about the rate and average amount of savings because they include
old and new co-operatives. Looking for a moment at the six
oldest *Thana* projects, one finds that about 2600 members of 71
co-operatives have collected about 113,500 *takas* over an average
of two years. That comes to an average of more than 40 *takas*
per woman and more than 1500 *takas* per co-operative. Records
of savings collected over the last two years indicate that
savings have been increasing steadily. How long and how much
women will continue to save in co-operatives remains to be seen.
What they will do with their money either individually or through
the co-operative will be an indication of the extent to which the
project is affecting their lives.

Loans: Borrowing and lending money and rice for high rates of
interest, including mortgaged land, is a familiar economic
activity in rural society. Women, as well as men, are involved
in such practices, though usually the amounts of money and rice
they lend and borrow are relatively small. However it is
exceedingly rare for rural women to take loans from a bank.

---

(9) See IRDP Women's Program *Third Report*, 1977.

There are basic differences between traditional lending practices and those followed by the co-operative. For one thing,
the co-operative loan has no interest rate, though there is a
service charge of 5%. For another, repayment involves group
responsibility. And third, the borrower must give evidence that
the money is being used in ways approved by the project sponsors.
The immediate project goal in giving such loans is to show women
and their families that there is a *direction* in which women can
move, through skills they already have, that will improve the
economic condition of the family. Another goal is to introduce
women to a more advantageous system of credit than traditional
money lending.

Certain procedures related to giving credit to co-operative
members are especially important. For the most part so far,
credit has been given to individual members for individual
projects(10) but the process for lending and repaying the loans
involves the co-operative as a whole. In order to qualify for
a loan the member must be in good standing and have a specific
amount of shares and saving to her name. With the help of the
co-operative leaders, who themselves are guided through training
classes and the support of the staff, members develop "production plans" which indicate how much money they want, what they
intend to use it for and when they will pay it back. No individual is able to get a loan until the co-operative can present
a group "production plan" specifying who is requesting a loan
and for what purpose and have the plan approved by project
staff. Money is then given to the co-operative leaders at a
weekly training class and they distribute it to members according to the plan. When the repayment date comes round, the
co-operative leaders collect the money and return it to the
Thana IRDP office. The members cannot get loans again until the
whole preceding loan of the co-operative has been repaid. Thus,
though the economic activities are determined and carried on by
members individually, the leaders have a responsibility to the
group and the group to each other.

The question of security for the loans has not been fully resolved. Until recently the members of the men's co-operatives

---

(10) On the assumption that collective economic projects with
shared gains involving women from separate families would not
work at this stage, there is no pressure from the project to
move in that direction, though if women were to choose to work
collectively, they would be supported.

all have land which provided the security for their loans. This is not a requirement for membership in women's co-operatives nor is it appropriate, if the project is to encourage a measure of economic autonomy for women, to require their male guardians signature as security for their loans. The question of how to secure their loans without the signature of a male relative is in the process of being addressed.

The project staff do not tell women *how* to use their loans. Rather, the project counts on learning from women what is feasible, what is profitable, what has growth possibilities, what is seasonal and so on. But it does provide guidelines. Because this is the initial stage of the project and because of the economic condition of many of the members, it is important for women to get returns on their investment of loan money fairly quickly. Therefore, they are advised to invest in what they already know how to do, with raw materials that are readily available in their area and for local markets that are guaranteed. They are advised that the project cannot support exploitative behavior like stocking commodities because it makes things worse for the poor rather than better, and that the loans are intended for production not personal affairs.

In preparation for giving loans, training classes at the *Thana* Center focused on explanations of loan procedures and production plans and discussions of productive and profitable uses of loans. There were discussions about the commercial possibilities of work women already knew how to do, and the comparative profitability of different kinds of ventures. Women were encouraged to think about profit and loss in more commercial ways than they had done before; to estimate, for example, the cost of buying a young goat, the cost of feeding it for several months, and the price it could be sold at. They were helped to use measurements and "weights" that were more appropriate for estimating profit and loss than those they used for domestic and village exchange.

Even before loans were given women began to engage in economic projects supported by the co-operative structure. One group hired a teacher to train them to make stools and tote bags using plastic. Many groups who had access to training in jute handicrafts made a variety of items which the *Thana* office bought to encourage continuing effort. In these ventures, as in attempts at sewing, the concept of a standard product for a competitive market was new and had to be developed. Many women began to consider poultry, ducks, and vegetables as potentially more profitable than they had traditionally been.

Although there is a basic policy for giving loans, there is variation between *Thanas* and sometimes, within *Thanas*, and between villages. These reflect differences in project staff and in relationships among co-operative members. The maximum loan is 300 *taka*. Sometimes each member is given the same amount, while sometimes the amount is determined by the type of project, or by the capital a member has invested in the co-operative. In some co-operatives, loans are not given to new members or to those who are considered bad risks. It is recommended that loans be given in kind to insure that they will be used for the purpose specified.

The results of the first series of loans were described in a "Report on the Use of Loans by Female Co-operative Members" written by Florence McCarthy in January 1977. Up to that time, 195,575 *takas* had been issued to 1,992 co-operative members in seven *Thanas*. The report analyzed the loan use of 70 of those members. It found that 22 of the 70 used their loans for processing paddy into rice, 30 bought poultry and livestock to raise and sell and 18 used their loans for some kind of small business like pottery, making bamboo mats, or cigarettes. Most of these activities are traditionally women's work. Those who took loans to process paddy into rice were probably poor women, since, as we have seen, this is the laborious, time-consuming work that poor women traditionally do in others' houses to earn food. As McCarthy points out, "this work provides immediate returns." In the right season, women can buy unprocessed rice, process it, eat some and still make enough profit from selling the rest to buy more unprocessed rice. Those who bought poultry and livestock probably had to have some land, even if it was just a homestead. It is hard to tell whether the women who undertook non-agricultural ventures were landless or not accustomed to doing agricultural work. It is important to note that most women used their loans for enterprises that were already familiar to them as rural women's work with its already established place in the rural economy. Loans are usually made for six months or a year. To the extent they have fallen due, they have been repaid almost 100%. Although there is not much data about the amount of profit women realize from these loans, the fact that they repay on time and are asking for increased amounts of loans indicates that women find this credit system to their advantage.

Looking at individual situations, one finds indications of developments in promising directions that need to be fostered as well as problems that need to be solved. On the positive

side, there are many examples. There are instances of women
taking loans for family enterprises, as in the case of a woman
whose husband, a trader, buys paddy which she processes into
pita (a pastry), or peanuts which she makes into sweets for sale
in the market. She took a 200 *taka* loan to increase this business. Other women took loans for family weaving businesses.
In most cases, however, women take loans for their own work,
often to support themselves because they are widowed or divorced
or to contribute to the family income through their work. One
woman with four children who was abandoned by her husband and
lives with her widowed mother took a 200 *taka* loan to husk rice
and was able to make 81 *taka* profit, 31 of which she put into
savings. Another woman, a widow with a grown son and daughter,
took a 100 *taka* loan to buy a goat which she says is her "future
hope". When the goat gives birth, she will repay the loan by
selling the kid. The mother goat will stay with her and give
birth yearly. This will be her source of saving through which
she will do something else in the future. Another woman has
added her own savings to a loan and bought a milking cow, a
steady source of small income. Another, who is a potter, has
taken a 200 *taka* loan to increase production. Several who took
loans for rice processing said they were able to stop working in
others' homes, where they work mainly for food, and can begin to
build capital. Usually loans are taken from the Government
credit but in one *Thana* where capital formation is very high,
women take loans from co-operative savings for special purposes.
For example, one co-operative borrowed from its own savings to
buy up a land mortgage that a member could not pay off so that
she would not lose it.

There are other types of loan behavior, not very common but,
nevertheless, a possible tendency, that have to be deterred.
One is the use of loans by husbands for their own purposes. One
woman said she took a loan and gave it to her husband for his
business. She said she at least got some respect for having
been able to get the loan. Another woman gave her loan to her
husband to lease in land and buy her poultry. He did the former,
but never bought her the poultry. Some women lie about how they
use their loans, pointing, for example, to chickens they had
owned before as evidence of what they spent the loan money on.
Some women stock commodities, usually rice, hoping to make a
profit at the season of scarcity. There is some amount of prestige in this, since it is a way of making money without work,
and poorer women may do it in imitation of better-off women. It
is, of course, much easier than labor, though usually riskier
and less profitable.

One can say that these initial loan activities have been successful, from the project point of view, in a number of ways.(11)
For the most part they are being used in food production, which
suggests that women will be likely to take advantage of chances
for increased food production through modernization when supplies and services are available. They are being used to help
women provide some base for themselves and their children on
which to build if they are without husbands or gain some stature
in the family if they are contributing to the household with the
profits they have made.

This first step is a big one, but still only a first step. Women
who took very small loans or paid them back too quickly to allow
maximum profit have perhaps developed more confidence in their
ability to produce and sell and will take more useful loans next
time. Co-operatives that have paid back a loan and are eligible
for the next probably have more confidence in themselves as a
group and will act more efficiently and creatively next time.
These experiences are creating better understanding of when loans
should be available for seasonal enterprises and how long the
repayment period should be for different kinds of enterprises.

It will be very important, after women have been using this
credit system for two or three years, to make a careful study
of prevalent loan procedures as they accord with the record of
women's credit behavior. At present women are taking loans
under the prevailing credit system with a few experimental
adjustments to enable them to use it. However, this system
involves some cumbersome, time-consuming and inhibiting procedures which have been considered necessary to prevent misuse
of credit. Some of these procedures may be found less appropriate for women both in relation to the ways they can make use
of credit and their behavior in paying it back. Because of
their socio-economic roles, women may be able to use credit
more readily and more productively, with less chance of waste,
than men and may be more reliable in paying back loans on time.
They may take fewer risks with their loans than men because
their reputations and status would suffer more from charges of
corruption. These, at least, are some of the assumptions that
lead one to think that a review of the credit system as it
involves women will be important, when enough time has passed

(11) One *Thana* did a sample survey of loan usage as a basis for
giving a second round of loans and found that nine out of 11
loans had produced profits.

to provide a good record of their behavior, as a basis for developing a more appropriate system. Strengthening and expanding
this system of credit for rural production will take time, but
thought must be given now to developments beyond small loans
for individual production. On the basis of limited experience,
one can see women using this system in several ways, that one
can perhaps consider as "stages".

The first stage involves putting credit to use for immediate
return to fill immediate needs as exemplified in their use of
loans to buy paddy and process it. The next involves building
up savings for investment in economic activities that provide
returns over a longer period of time, as exemplified in buying
goats or a cow. A longer range vision may be a collective project that will belong to the co-operative. It is difficult to
imagine under present economic conditions that such projects
for women, any more than for men, can develop and grow without
improved training, investment in larger schemes, improved technology, and special attention to marketing. One would like to
see investments in small-scale agro-based industries which are
developments of what have traditionally been women's areas of
expertise and which women would eventually own and manage through
co-operatives. It is likely, through their growing experience
with commercial enterprise in co-operatives, that rural women,
recently in traditional *purdah*, will be ready for such developments and in fact will take some of the first steps themselves.
To the extent Government wants changes in the rural situation
that involve women's spheres of knowledge and productivity, it
will find a mechanism for reaching them.

Recent Developments

New developments are already occurring among the co-operatives
as the result of the initiative of the members and the existence
of a vehicle for efforts to reach women in appropriate ways. In
one *Thana*, women are experimenting with fish breeding in tanks
which they and their families are digging. In the same *Thana*,
experiments are underway to develop commercial poultry-raising
with the limited modernization that is possible under village
conditions. To the extent these experiments are successful,
women from other project areas can come for training and can
carry these new techniques back to villages all over the country.
In other villages, new varieties of ducks are being raised and
several *Thanas* are developing "model" duck farms. Similarly
the villages which are involved in the commercial gardening

projects mentioned earlier can to the extent they are profitable,
serve as models for the other villages. In the cases of poultry,
ducks and horticulture, as with improvements in production in
other activities as they occur, new development can be maximized
through the network of co-operatives with their machinery for
credit, service and supplies.

One of the problems with small-scale commercial horticulture as
a women's activity in certain areas is lack of water which makes
it difficult to grow most winter vegetables without irrigation.
The recent effort of UNICEF to distribute hand-pumps had led to
strong demands by co-operative women for access to these hand-
pumps which will benefit them in commercial as well as domestic
efforts. There is no doubt that hand-pumps have status value
in rural areas as do sewing machines, but they have a much more
practical value, and it is a sign that co-operatives are at
least perceived as having a rural base when co-operative women
are seeking access to them. It is now up to project staff to
develop practical guidelines for distributing them.

We have already mentioned that a nutrition education program is
under experiment in several *Thanas* and has been linked with
efforts at commercial food production so that those who are
responsible for nutrition will be in a position to solve some of
the economic problems that *prevent* good nutrition. A program
for improved medical care through training of para-professionals
is under consideration. An adult literacy program involving the
services of trainers from BRAC, a non-Government community development institution, is underway. It involves training co-
operative members as literacy teachers and project staff as
supervisors, with support, supervision and evaluation at the
Thanas at regular periods by BRAC staff. Co-operative members
who work as literacy teachers will be paid on the basis of the
progress of their students. This co-ordination between a non-
Government and a Government institution can provide a much
needed service to the latter and enable the former to test its
system through better understanding of existing rural conditions.
These are some examples of the possibilities that co-operatives
offer Government to reach women who are in the process of change.

Specialized Training

In addition to training five co-operative leaders every week who
are expected to communicate what they learn at weekly village
meetings, the project has experimented with special training for

selected co-operative members in skills appropriate to rural
areas. It is assumed that this training may provide fairly
quickly to the rural areas women with advanced training in
economically viable skills. If these women are suitably supported with investment, supplies and services, they can become
models of economic enterprise and employment for other women
through their example and, in some cases, through the training
they provide for others.

These women receive more intensive training than the weekly
classes at the *Thana* Center. Their training is provided at the
institutions where the expertise exists as well as at the *Thana*
Center. The purpose of this experiment is to discover what
suitable training is available, how it can be adapted to rural
women's needs, which women can leave the village to take advantage of it, what benefits are derived from their exposure to
the world beyond the village, and what use it will be to the
women, the co-operative and the village.

Kinds of Training: In looking for kinds of training that would
be appropriate, there were several criteria. One was whether
the skill was suitable for rural women in terms of their cultural
and economic setting. Another was whether the skill was likely
to have economic and/or service potential in rural areas.
Another was whether there was training available that had already
proven itself competitively. Each of these criteria narrowed the
range of possibilities but perhaps the last criterion narrowed it
most. The kinds of training experimented with so far are those
which meet at least some of the criteria - jute handicrafts,
tailoring, duck raising, teaching, and horticulture. In looking
for appropriate training situations, certain problems came to
light that the project will have to find ways to deal with. For
example, a visit to a small-scale Government food processing
factory revealed that the equipment in such a production unit is
too modern to be replicated in the village so that training for
village women in such commercial processing would be useless.
Similarly, a visit to a Government poultry farm revealed that
its emphasis was home consumption and that there were no models
for small-scale home-based commercial ventures in poultry. Again
a visit to a renowned food research institute in India indicated
an enormous gap between commercial technology in food processing
and preservation and the conditions of rural life, which one
would have to bridge if one's goal were home or village or even
Thana-based commercial production. There seemed to be no acceptable model of production between home consumption and the
factory.

Kinds of Trainees: In general the criteria suggested by Headquarters for the women who would attend specialized training
included need and proven aptness in the skill for which advanced
training was being provided. The basic question, however, was
whether any village women would be allowed to travel long dis-
tances and stay away from home for long periods of time. The
response indicated that on the whole, women would be allowed to
travel for training. For the most part the prerequisite of
neediness was met. Of the women who came to training during
the first year, those who were not poor with regard to family
resources were likely to be in "marginal" positions, i.e. widows,
divorced women, or co-wives. The prerequisite of aptness was
met in perhaps 75% of the trainees. Most of the trainees were
married; most were between 20 and 40; most were illiterate or
barely literate; and most had not been outside their *Thanas*, or
at the farthest their district towns, before coming to training.

Travel and Accommodation: Women travelled to training sites far
distant from their homes accompanied by male relatives or project
staff or in a group unaccompanied by anyone else, in a few cases
bringing young children, and stayed away from home for periods
ranging from a week to seven months. In a few cases they stayed
with relatives. For the most part they stayed in accommodation
that was provided for them. Unlike men, for whom the provision
of room allowance might be all that was necessary since they
could find lodging for themselves, accommodation with suitable
shelter and food arrangements had to be worked out for the women
for all the training classes. These included: a small house in
a compound where a women's clinic was located, a separate block
of dormitory rooms in a hostel, and beds in the homes of women
who were giving the training. To the extent possible, modern
medical care was made available and encouraged. These women,
more than 100 in all, without any serious problem, conflict or
dislocation, experienced, usually for the first time, distant
travel, living with other women who were strangers, new foods,
new sights, new behavior on the part of women, and the responsibility of new opportunities.

Training: The mode of training varied considerably depending
on its source. Horticulture training has been given at two
different places, one involving formal classroom training as
well as supervised field work, one concentrating much more on
learning by doing and then teaching others how to do. Tailoring
training was a professional course in a women's institution that
had already succeeded in bringing women into this field competitively. Handicraft training was more like apprentice training,

in that women who were learning lived in the homes of women who were commercially successful in this work and worked along with them throughout the day at the various steps of this home-based industry, including marketing. This seemed the most appropriate mode of training for communicating a realistic attitude about marketable skills, since the "teachers" were basically no different from the trainees and were dealing with and overcoming successfully the same kinds of problems the trainees would have to face. The project is looking for other such training situations and may find them in the future in the homes of village women who have been successful in their new economic enterprises.

Along with the training, women have to be able to take back to the villages some of the equipment basic to their new skills and, in the case of modern practices in, for example, duck-raising or horticulture, to count on access to requisite supplies, like vaccines or hand-pumps. They must also be in a position to invest in necessary raw materials.(12) Ideally, the services of the project in their area should be able to reinforce their training in these ways. Unless it can, the women will not be in a position to make the best use of their training.

Results: Although it is too early to look for significant results, there has been enough experience to date to reach certain conclusions. One is that women will learn well what they are taught. Women who received jute handicraft training are able to make marketable products. Those who learned horticulture are following new growing practices. A second conclusion is that to the extent they are supported and considered a resource by the project in their *Thana*, the benefits of their training are extended. In some *Thanas* those who received handicraft training are teaching others at the *Thana* Center. In one *Thana*, a woman who received horticulture training has been employed by the project to travel to different villages to graft fruit trees. The woman who received tailoring training in that *Thana* is conducting classes for others. Another conclusion is that,

---

(12) Training in jute handicrafts proved useless for women in areas where it was difficult to procure good jute. Training in duck raising allowed women to take home the ducks they had raised during training period. Tailoring training is providing ways in which women can buy sewing machines on an installment basis. Horticulture training has included provision of basic implements and, when possible, a way for women to buy hand-pumps on an installment basis.

individually, women are benefitting in a variety of ways from
the opportunity to go for training, ranging from finding chances
for employment outside the project or saving expenses and travel
money to buy a goat. In short, one can see from what has happened so far that such a training program is feasible as far as
involving village women is concerned and will serve the goals
of the project to the extent appropriate training and project
support are available. Expansion and modification of training
in horticulture, duck raising, teaching and tailoring are well
underway. Experiments in commercial poultry-raising are being
supported in the hope that they will provide a base for training.

Case Studies of Co-operatives and Co-operative Members

The following description of three co-operatives from three
different districts illustrates concretely some of the ways in
which rural women are responding to the resources and guidelines
of the project. This kind of information is needed to understand how to develop and modify policy since it indicates to
what extent what the project offers and what women want have a
common basis. Unless the project remains aware of the responses
of rural women, it cannot hope to evolve realistic guidelines.

> *Case I:* One co-operative is in a village in the district
> of Tangail. Before 1947 the village was dominated economi-
> cally and culturally by Hindus. Muslims who lived here
> were poor farmers. In 1947 most of the Hindus left. The
> result is that the better-off Muslims in the village have
> acquired their assets recently; there is no traditional
> status barrier between better-off and poor Muslims in the
> village, nor is the village bound by tradition as one in
> which the leadership is older might be. The village has
> 110 households of 600 people and is predominantly agri-
> cultural. There is a men's co-operative with 74 members.
> The women's co-operative has 45 members. 25 of these
> women had been members of the men's co-operative and had
> left to form their own co-operative when the project was
> started in this *Thana*. All but three of the members have
> a male relative in the men's co-operative. Four of the
> members are widows. There are six well-to-do households
> in the village, related to each other. All of them have
> members in the co-operative. One of these women is the
> Manager. About 20 of the members are literate, among whom
> four have had some measure of high school education.

The Manager is a woman close to 40 with three daughters and
one son, all of whom she is educating to upper grades. Her
husband holds a similar position in the men's co-operative.
She has had a tubal ligation and is in good health. Her
house has a tin roof, her homestead is spacious, including
a deep well and a valuable plantation of supari trees. She
keeps chickens, has been to the training program in winter
vegetables, and has planted seeds according to modern
methods.

The training program for the leaders of this co-operative
at the *Thana* Center seems to have focused on economic projects and loan procedures more than any other subject. The
knowledge of members on subjects like family planning or
poultry-raising was not as good as that of women from other
Thanas. The primary interest of the women seems to be loans.
One round of loans has been given - 6700 *takas* to 36 members.
20 of these loans were for the combined projects of raising
poultry and contributing to the investment needed for growing rice. One woman took a 200 *taka* loan for the business
she and her husband, who is a trader, run by buying paddy,
processing it into food, and selling it in the market. There
are seven members in her family. One woman took a 200 *taka*
loan to buy paddy which she processes, taking advantage of
the men's co-operative-run mill, and sells. Another woman
took a 300 *taka* loan to use toward inputs for leasing out
land; while yet another took a 200 *taka* loan to lease in
land and hire a pump to irrigate it.(13)

The following are representative members. One is a woman
whose husband is a laborer who works regularly. They have
three daughters and one son. They have land of their own
that gives them food for three months and they are able to
lease in some land. A second is a woman whose husband is
a laborer. They have five sons and two daughters. They
have land enough for 2 or 3 month's food. A third is a
woman in a joint family of three brothers that has four
acres. She has one son and two daughters and uses the pill.

---

(13) This co-operative also provided examples of landless families whose men could not get credit from the men's co-operative
using the women's co-operative as a way to borrow money to lease
in land.

During a visit to a co-operative meeting we listened to
discussions among members on several issues. One on family
planning will be referred to later. Another was about how
best to use loans. One young woman, from a better-off
family, said she had given the loan money to her husband.
Another woman, older and less well-off, spoke up, saying
that it was not just the loan money that was of value but
how it was used, and that that required intelligence. She
said, "Today, if my husband says, 'I can't feed you', I can
feed myself. God has given me that much power. I don't
have to ask permission for everything." She went on to
explain that during the Liberation War when her husband had
to leave the village and the family was in difficulty, her
brother-in-law wanted to sell the land. Instead, she sold
the cow and saved the land. She told the others that a
woman who knows how to *use* her loan money has more status
in the family than one who just gives the money to her husband. This seemed to be corroborated for the group by the
fact that the young woman who asked her husband to buy some
poultry for her with the loan money she *gave* him, never got
the poultry. The members were eager to get hand-pumps,
though one or two requested sewing machines.

Case II: This co-operative is in a village in Dacca district.
The village provides easy access for men to urban and industrial areas where many of them work because there is only a
20 minute walk on dirt roads and across fields to a major
motorable road. The village is agricultural, with extensive
pineapple plantations. There are 1,100 people in 143 households. There is a primary school in the village as well as
a Red Cross facility and a co-ed high school in the next
village. Because many of the men work in modern occupations,
there is an acceptance of new ideas and change in the village, although the lives of women there are far from modern.

There are 42 members in the co-operative. All but one are
of the same *para*. They are mostly of the same status,
though there is a wide range of economic need. At least ten
of the members work for food in others' houses. Three of
the members are from *boro baris* or prestigious families and
cannot attend meetings because that would violate *purdah*.
Only two or three members are literate. The co-operative
leaders are the women responsible for having created the
co-operative. They had heard of a handicraft co-operative
making jute products in a nearby *para* and tried, unsuccess-

fully, to join it. They were told that a new women's project was starting under IRDP and they contacted project
staff to help them organize.(14)

One of the co-operative leaders, the Manager, is a daughter-
in-law of the village. Her father was landless and her
husband is a contract laborer. They have only homestead
land. She used to work on yearly contract also, but now is
able to work at home. She has six children and her sons are
contract laborers. She has 75 *takas* in shares and savings
and has taken a 200 *taka* loan. She goes to training class
regularly, which is eight miles from the village. She walks
and is able to save her travel allowance. With it she has
bought a shawl and lungi for her husband, to keep him happy,
she says, and to be sure she is allowed to go to training
class. Her husband, she says, used to call her a fool. Now,
he says, she is clever because she can talk and reply. He
pays more attention to her.

Another co-operative leader is a daughter and daughter-in-
law of the village. Her husband is postman and they have
one-sixth of an acre of land. They have two daughters and
three sons, of whom two are mill workers and one is in Class
Six. The girls were married when they were 12, having
studied to Class Four. She herself studied to Class Four.
She is about 41 years old and has been using family planning
for many years. She owns three shares in the co-operative
and took a 200 *taka* loan for poultry. When questioned on a
variety of subjects taught at training she answered expertly.
She took six months tailoring training in Dacca.

A third leader is younger, about 28. She is also a daughter
and daughter-in-law of the village, and was married at 13
after studying to Class Four. Her husband is a farmer who
studied to Class Five. They have an acre of land on which
they raise one crop of high yielding variety rice and pine-
apples. They have two sons who are studying in Class Five
and Two. She attends training regularly, has 43 *takas*
invested in the co-operative and took a loan of 200 *takas*.
With what she learned at training about poultry, she was
able to invest in chickens and a goat. She repaid the loan
by selling eggs and chickens, with the rest of the money

---

(14) This is a good example of a co-operative being organized
on the village women's own initiative.

added by her husband. Now she owns outright the goat, which
is pregnant.

The following are representative members: One is a woman
whose husband sent her home to her widowed mother when he
took a second wife. He kept their three sons but she has
the daughter with her. Her husband does not support her.
The Manager lent her money to join the co-operative. She
has taken a 200 *taka* loan and bought rice from the market
to husk and sell. She is making jute handicrafts and grows
vegetables in the hope of making money. She hopes she can
get a hand-pump through the project. She is now able to
feed her sons and offer them special treats when they come
to visit her. A second is a widow with three daughters and
one son who is living at home with her widowed mother. She
cannot afford to send her children to school. She joined
recently because she did not have the money for joining
earlier. She deposits a *taka* a week by selling puffed rice.
She supports herself by husking rice and making quilts for
others. She joined too late to be eligible for the first
round of loans. A third woman, who is about to join, has
little land and six children who are all studying. She has
been trying hard to save enough to join, but kept spending
what she saved before she could buy a share. Now she has
made two jute handicraft items and sent them with the co-
operative leaders to be sold at the *Thana* Center. With
that money she expects to join.

All in all 3500 *takas* were given as loans to 18 members.
The money was used for rice processing, poultry and jute
handicrafts. The village meetings seem active. At a recent
meeting, the member who went for training in winter vegetables distributed seeds and explained how to plant them.
She has been requested to bring insecticide from the *Thana*
to treat the young plants. The women recognize that they
have a water problem that makes winter vegetables difficult
to grow and are eager to get hand pumps.

Case III: This co-operative is in the district of Barisol.
Its members are not village women but women of a rural
bazaar area almost all of whom have moved here with their
families recently because their husbands or fathers lost
their land to the river. They were formerly agricultural
people in better economic condition than they are now.
There are 32 members, some Hindu, some Muslim. They come

from several areas around the Bazaar and are for the most
part not related. A few have male relatives in the men's
co-operative. 24 of the members are married. Five have
had high school education, 15 have studied to Class Five,
and the rest are illiterate. Nine were already engaged in
economic activities, including shops, before they joined
the co-operative.

The Manager is a young woman, about 24 years old. Her
family is well-off. Her father is a member of the men's
co-operative. She has two brothers who have good jobs and
the other six brothers and sisters are studying. Once they
were *zamindars*, but the river took their land; now they own
some again. She has been divorced twice. She goes to
training regularly and conducts village meetings at her home.
She has saved 85 *takas* in the co-operative. She went to
Dacca for jute training and is trying to sell jute handicrafts. She saves her travel allowance to buy and store
rice. She did not take a loan but made sure that others got
them and repaid them, even lending one member money to repay.
She likes her job and is getting attention from others for
her efforts. Her grandmother who used to scold her for being
involved in the co-operative now herself has joined.

Another co-operative leader, who is in charge of family
planning, is a Hindu woman. Her husband is a homeopathic
doctor and she also knows a lot about indigenous medicine.
Her husband is in the male co-operative. They lost their
land to the river but have been able to buy three or four
acres which they lease out. They have one daughter and two
sons. She uses the pill. The daughter is entering for her
high school exam. The mother attends training classes regularly although she had never left her home before she joined
the co-operative. Her husband is very supportive. She is
exceptionally knowledgeable about family planning. She says
women come to her to find out about family planning when they
do not want their mothers-in-law to know what they are considering. She distributes pills to women and condoms for
their husbands when the women are nursing. She has 130
takas invested in the co-operative. She took a 250 *taka* loan
to store commodities and made a 250 *taka* profit. With the
travel allowance she saved, she paid her daughter's matricu-
lation fee and bought supari nuts to process and sell.

The following are representative members: One is a woman
with four children surviving out of seven whose husband is

a bus driver. They have no land. Their children are all
studying and she is hopeful that she can educate her son far
enough so that he can get a good job. Her husband earns 300
taka on his job which is not enough for their needs. He is
in the male co-operative, but they are in debt. She and her
son run a *pan* business in secret from her husband. She has
not received much benefit from the co-operative. She took
a 75 *taka* loan from the co-operative and wasted it, she says.
She needed her husband's help to pay it back. She would like
to take another loan for stocking commodities which she can
keep secret from her husband. If her husband knows she is
making money he will give her less from his salary. She does
not know what else to do since she cannot raise goats or make
household items. She has not received much guidance from the
co-operative. A second is a woman whose husband has a gro-
cery shop. They had land before but now they have only one
sixth of an acre, including coconut and supari trees. They
have three sons who are studying and three daughters. She
took a loan of 60 *takas* which she invested in her husband's
business. She has paid it back. She says there is value in
this kind of loan because it gives her some say in the business. A third is a woman, the wife of a high school master,
who is considering whether or not to join. It depends, she
feels, on what other kinds of women join. If they are not
genteel, it will affect her own status to join.

At a meeting convened recently for visiting Headquarters
staff, the discussion focused on what women in their situation could do with loans besides stocking goods. For
reasons specific to this project, guidance through training
classes had not been adequate in dealing with these issues.
The women discussed the fact that there was certain work
they could not do because they had no land, other work they
had no background in because of the way they had been raised
and other work which was not appropriate to their status,
even if they knew how to do it. They realized that theirs
was a difficult problem which might be solved by some kind
of joint venture involving everyone producing something which
could be sold outside the area, some kind of craft or business. One woman thought of jute handicrafts, a problem
because raw jute was not locally available. Another woman
·who had developed a skin medicine thought it might be something the group could produce for city markets. The issue
was not resolved, but the meeting pointed up the need for
addressing the issue.

One of the important results of this kind of information has
been the realization that the formation and development of co-
operatives vary greatly from one village to another depending
on the particular socio-economic situation of the village, even
though a primary interest of most women from village to village
is to improve the economic situation of their families. These
variations are further support for giving continuing attention
to the training of field staff so that they can respond with
initiative and creativity to the specific directions women are
taking in different places.

CHAPTER IV

FAMILY PLANNING

We are devoting a separate chapter to the family planning component of the project for two main reasons. One is that the
project came into existence as part of a large population project and is administered by the Population Control and Family
Planning Department as well as by the ministry in charge of
rural development and co-operatives. From its inception, therefore, the project has been concerned with family planning education and distribution of supplies in liaison with the Government
family planning program. We think it necessary, in terms of a
case study approach, to describe how it began this aspect of its
work within the constraints of available services, available
kinds of contraceptives, and its own organizational structure.
The other reason is our belief that what was learned from the
response of rural women to these efforts has significance to
those concerned with family planning programs and other development efforts involving women if they are to bring their programs
in line with the needs of rural women.

It is expected that the project will have both immediate and
long-term impact on lowering fertility. The long-term impact
cannot of course be measured yet, although one can see examples
in individual women's lives of what one expects to happen on a
large scale. The long-term impact on fertility is expected as
a result of having created for women and their families, over a
generation or two, alternatives to having a large family that
are economically and culturally preferable and feasible. One
project alone cannot create such a cultural change. It must be
part of an integrated program for rural women.

The immediate impact is more easily described and demonstrated, though one should not, for that reason, consider it the more important impact and neglect the careful modification and expansion of the project to serve the needs of more women. Otherwise the immediate impact, which may seem impressive at first, will be limited to women already motivated who are taking advantage of opportunities to use contraception that were not available before - opportunities for better information, better access to family planning services, supplies, health services with follow-up care, as well as discretion and support. These are some of the important services of the project that women can take advantage of as co-operative members. However, women seem to be joining co-operatives out of economic need, not for better family planning services. It is very easy for planners to set increased contraceptive practice as the priority in their zeal to control population growth from the perspective of the future. But it is a mistake to think that this is the substance of the program, since rural women, acting on data from the present *and* past, usually put their *clearly economic* priorities first. The family planning component of the project, which serves men as well as women, is an extension of the national family planning program to the co-operatives under IRDP. It depends on the Population Control and Family Planning Department for services and supplies and works in co-operation and co-ordination with family planning officers at the *Thana* level. Its major emphases are education about contraception and access to services.

Let us look for a moment at the cultural situation that makes such an approach seem practical. As mentioned earlier, rural men and women rarely discuss sex or family planning with each other. If a young village woman uses contraception and has problems with it, she is in a very difficult situation. The person who speaks for her if the outside world is involved is her mother-in-law who will hear from her son that there is a problem. The young woman must therefore have their prior approval in order to go to them, and even then there is likely to be embarrassment. If there were no problem *within* the household, the woman in difficulty is still faced with the real problem of getting adequate attention because there is likely to be no one really knowledgeable about family planning *in* the village; because travel to a clinic is culturally and physically difficult or costly; because services may not be adequate even at a clinic; and because dependable health care relevant to family planning needs may not be available at all. In addition, going out for help reveals the problem to the whole village and the men of the family are subject to ridicule for allowing such a situation to occur. It is not hard to understand why, in this setting, many women who may be motivated or interested in contraception, will not take the risk of trying it, or if they do, will stop as soon as they encounter difficulties. It may be genuinely less difficult and even less costly to have another child.

The national family planning program has made great progress in the few years it has been in existence. But because it is young, it is not yet in a position to provide personnel well informed about contraception and to whom women in the village feel free to talk without shyness or adequate follow-up health care with a base in the village. It has found many acceptors but it has also created demand and interest beyond the services it can offer to satisfy them adequately.

Modern methods of contraception or sterilization inevitably produce periods of discomfort or side-effects that may be mild and simply require patience, or severe enough to require medical attention. Since rural women are isolated from sources of information about what these discomforts or side effects may indicate, and from medical attention, they inevitably run into difficulties that become examples to other women of why not to use contraception. With the I.U.D. there may be heavy bleeding and cramps; with the pill and injectibles there may be, in addition to nausea, breakthrough bleeding or lessening of menstrual bleeding; with ligation there may be pain and infection. Without adequate information or follow-up services, women in these situation will stop taking the pill, remove the I.U.D., or not take the next injectible, and, in general, will serve as examples to discourage others from undergoing the same difficulties. Indigenous doctors who know what resources are available to rural women often advise against these modern methods. As a result the program does not advance as smoothly as it could, resistance is incurred, and a variety of unrelated health problems are attributed to contraception.

In this context, it has been felt that the family planning component of the Women's Program can be most useful by making available to women *in* villages through a village-based institution adequate information about: what bodily reactions to expect from the use of contraception and why; what problems require medical attention; and where and how to get medical attention. Through new ways of bringing village women together it provides necessary protection from mothers-in-law or husbands or other village males, as well as new support groups for changing behavior. Through its training program for co-operative leaders, it supports women in villages who have regular access to Government services, supplies, and information but who are part of the village community and responsible to it because they live there, not women whose responsibility and allegiance are seen to be to the Government as family planning workers and who therefore may not be readily accepted or trusted. The family planning component makes the services and supplies that the Government provides more accessible to village women and is an important source of information to Government about what other services are needed to improve its program.

Training in Family Planning

In the section on staff training (pp.116-138), there is an explanation of the role the project staff play in the family planning component of the Women's Program as well as a brief review of their training and the personal and professional changes that result.

Co-operative Leaders: The co-operative leaders receive training in family planning at the weekly *Thana* training classes. They bring the questions and problems of members to the class for discussion and advice and carry back to the village supplies requested by co-operative members and other village women. Their training classes are conducted by family planning and rural health personnel, when possible, and are supplemented by the work of the female staff. Teaching generally includes an explanation, and when feasible a display, of available contraceptive methods.

The presence of 50 village women, of varying ages, both unmarried and married, in a classroom to learn about contraception and discuss their problems represents a great change in rural mores and offers an important opportunity for Government to reach large numbers of rural women and to improve its services to them. The results of these classes have been promising. Women are getting more accurate information than was generally available before and, to the extent that they are responsible leaders, are advising other village women, reporting their problems, and escorting them for medical attention. One especially responsible leader reports: "Those of my members who can conceive are all taking birth control pills though they objected at first because of fear of their guardians. Now they take pills without telling their guardians. Even non-members are taking the pills." Another, who is a hard-working farm wife with three daughters and a son, all of whom she is trying to educate, says, "I have used family

planning for three years. I advise the members of the co-
operative and even my relatives to practise family planning. I
distribute family planning medicine at weekly meetings and give
instructions about using them." Many of the co-operative leaders
are using family planning, whether ligation, the pill or ayurvedic medicine. Where the teachers are available and competent,
the level of information among the co-operative leaders is very
high. Where the classes allow for participation, the problems
village women face in using available contraceptive technology
are becoming apparent. This aspect of the problem of the *Thana*
training program faces the program as a whole (see pp.159-162).
The recommendations for improving training are basically the
same.

It is especially important in relation to family planning that
materials be developed for teaching illiterate rural women how
contraceptives work in the body so that they will understand
what to expect and how to respond appropriately to real problems.
The traditional emphases have been on "motivation", on the two-
child family or on simply "accepting" contraception, none of
which are of great relevance to village people. They have
assumed that providing more detailed information was not neces-
ary or appropriate for uneducated rural women, or that telling
them about problems they might face would frighten them. *Given
the cultural setting of these women, they need information.* Not
that informed co-operative leaders will supplant family planning
personnel or paramedics. Rather they will enable village women,
in their isolated situations, to have a basis for making decisions about how and when to call on these resources. Such
leaders will be accountable to the women they advise and therefore likely to demand the services that are lacking.

The methodology of teaching has to allow for input from the
women so that the information addresses their situations realistically, but even more it should forward the project goal of
increased autonomy for women by treating them in the classroom
as people capable of autonomy. And, as mentioned several times,
the services and supplies requisite to modern contraceptive
behavior must be made available.

Co-operative Members: Both at weekly meetings and through the
traditional channels of communication in the village, the co-
operative members gain new resources for controlling their
reproductive lives. Information and supplies are available now
in their village from local women; discretion is made possible
through new patterns of association; support for new behavior,

even the possibility of new behavior, is fostered by the presence of the new modernizing institution directed toward women.
Access to services outside the village is made easier through
the mediation of co-operative leaders.

Co-operative meetings are forums for a variety of points of
view about contraception. At meetings visited by Headquarters
staff, women have presented openly and frankly their personal
support for, concerns about, or disapproval of family planning.
One meeting in particular stands out for the way in which two
opposing points of view were so clearly expressed. A young
women was talking about her experience of the pill, which she has
has been taking since her first child was born. She said she
was unwell for three months but, except for fatigue, has been
alright since then. Her mother-in-law spoke up, saying that
there would be time for her to have more babies later. Another
member of the co-operative, an older, less modern woman with
seven sons and two daughters, replied that it was too early for
this young girl to take the pill, that she had not even started
childbearing yet, that she had better wait until she has had
at least two children. In response, the young woman said: "You
don't *raise* your children, you just *have* them. You would have
babies even if you took the pill. If you can't have a good
child, it's better not to have one at all." It seemed clear
that in this group, contraception was under trial and evaluation,
and that those who were inclined in that direction would be
supported by the positive experience of others.

At another meeting women who were taking the pill compared
experiences. One had three periods in one month at first, then
her period became regular although she gets cramps now; another
talked of heavy bleeding at first which has lessened; another
said her period has been reduced to one day. But all three are
continuing to use the pill. At this and other meetings there
has been high consciousness of contraceptive alternatives and
an acceptance of varied responses to the alternatives.

Results

Records of family planning acceptors are being kept by project
staff. Information was collected from 14 *Thanas*, old and new,
in March 1977. This information, reported in the Third Project
Report, indicates that 40% of the 1750 members of five old
Thanas, 47% of the 850 members of three newer *Thanas*, and 30%
of the 1100 members of six newest *Thanas* have accepted contra-

ception. About 60% of all acceptors use the pill, 15% use
condoms and 12% have had ligations.

This data is hard to interpret for several reasons. One does
not know how many of the rest of the members are not in need
of contraception, i.e. divorced, widowed, unmarried, sterile,
etc. One does not know how many non-members motivated through
the project have been included in or excluded from these numbers.
And one does know how difficult it is to verify continuing use
of contraception unless all one's energy and resources are
directed toward that end. Still, the findings are in line with
the results published by the Research and Evaluation Cell of
the Family Planning Directorate which find, from a sample survey
of 14 *Thanas*, that 38% of 486 Co-operative women who were interviewed were contraceptive users.(1)

The project staff are being trained in collecting and recording
such information accurately, but there is a concern, at the same
time, that such research and evaluation by project staff should
not hamper the wider reach of the project. Since more sophis-
ticated enumeration is being done by the research cell of the
Population Control and Family Planning Department, project staff
are perhaps more appropriately deployed in making sure that all
co-operative members at risk of conception have access to family
planning information, good services and supplies.

There is no doubt that women's co-operatives are an effective
way of spreading the use of contraception. Some representative
examples of members who have adopted family planning illustrate
this statement. One woman whose husband will not allow her to
use contraceptives, receives pills secretly from her mother-in-
law who is a co-operative member. Another young woman is able
to use contraceptives secretly because *she* is in the co-operative.
While yet another woman, a widow, living with her son, a laborer,
and her daughter-in-law who already has three children wants her
daughter-in-law to use contraception: "I can't tell her directly,
being a mother-in-law, but I advise other neighboring women to
tell her, because she can't feed her three children properly or
give them medicine in time of illness. So I think it is better
for her not to have any more children." When asked where she
learned about contraception, she said, "From the Manager. The
first day I did not understand anything but later she made every-

(1) "Some observations on Women's Functional Literacy Program
and Use of Model Farmers and Co-operative Managers" (Akhter, 1977).

thing clear." Another woman, 26 years old, educated and reason-
ably well-off with four children, said she had tried the pill a
while back but stopped when two other family members who were
using it had irregular bleeding. She feels the instructions on
pill use were not clear. Now through the co-operative she has
learned how to use the pill correctly and is taking it again.

There is no doubt that increasingly women in co-operatives are
able to consider contraception from a vantage point of knowledge.
In villages where there are no co-operatives or they are just
beginning, the staff reports that resistance to family planning
is expressed in statements such as "It's a sin" or "My husband
won't allow me." Where co-operatives have been active for six
months or a year, women are more likely to be discussing instances of break-through bleeding and how they were treated, and
comparing cases of those who have and have not had side effects
from the pill. In other words they are no longer completely
fatalistic about the possibilities of controlling family size.

However, the main theme in feedback about those who are unwilling
to try contraception or have tried and given it up is fear of
risking ill health, which is not only a matter of one's physical
well-being but of one's economic and social well-being also.
Many women say it is easier and less costly, given the available
alternatives, to have another child. The following are typical
stories heard at co-operative meetings:

> One woman of 26, a laborer's wife who herself works as a
> laborer in other's houses, has three sons and three daugh-
> ters. She tried the I.U.D. but had trouble and removed it.
> Now she is using the pill which is not really satisfactory.
> She wants a permanent method but is afraid of the "operation"
> - i.e. ligation - because she works in other's houses to
> survive. She has heard that women with the operation cannot
> perform hard work. If that happens to her, she says, she
> and her children will die for lack of food and money.

> Another woman, very poor, with seven children, said she
> tried the pill, but got her period two or three times a
> month and felt continually dizzy. She told the "doctor"
> what she felt, but got no response from him. She says,
> "we are unable to get medicine. We have to spend money
> [to alleviate discomfort]. Can we afford to pay? I don't
> want to increase my *diseases* by taking the pill." She is
> now pregnant with her eighth child.

A young woman, pregnant with her first child, has been
hearing about family planning through the co-operative.
When asked if she would use it, she said: "I don't know.
It depends on my husband. The women in the neighborhood
who took it are suffering. They menstruate a lot, their
bodies are weak, and they can't work. It frightens me. I
always get information from those who are trying it."

A 30 year old woman, the wife of a schoolteacher, has four
daughters and a son. They have enough land for four months
food. She is trying to give her daughters some education.
She has taken the family planning injection. Everyone is
telling her how dangerous it is, so she is wondering whether
she'll take the next one. "We are poor," she said. "Who
is going to help us in our distress?" She is seeking advice
for a better method. She does not want any more children.

Another woman with seven children whose husband owns a rickshaw is trying to stop having more children. She has used
the I.U.D. for the last three months. Her husband did not
agree at first. He said it was a sin. Then, finally, he
said, "Do what you want. If you have a problem, then you
will understand." Now she is having heavy bleeding and is
feeling weak. Her husband is angry and she is thinking of
removing the I.U.D.

A woman with four surviving children out of seven started
taking the pill a year and a half ago. At first she was
alright. Then when she started receiving a different kind
of pill, a square one, her health became bad. She felt
weak and dizzy; she got her period three times a month; and
she bled after intercourse and while processing rice. She
stopped taking the pill and tried medicine and then the
local hospital, to no avail. Finally she had to travel to
a distant hospital for a D & C and is now alright.

Perhaps the most telling illustration is the story related by a
woman, visiting her home village because her father died, who
attended a co-operative meeting at which Headquarters staff were
present. She had not heard of the Women's Program and asked the
staff member if she was from family planning. "No," the staff
member answered. "Do you have a problem?" The woman responded
by telling the story of her sister-in-law who had taken the
I.U.D. and suffered severely from bleeding and infection. She
had the I.U.D. removed, but the heavy bleeding did not subside
and she died. The young woman spoke movingly to the staff

member: "This is why women don't use it. Don't we understand
that we're poor? Don't we understand that we have too many
children and can't feed them. We understand. But what can we
do? Whatever caused this woman's death, we had no facilities
for helping her."

It would seem then, from what rural women are indicating, that
if one is concerned with encouraging rural women to take advantage of family planning services, it is imperative to improve
contraceptive technology and to provide good follow-up care
for women who are accepting contraceptives and health services
for all women. To quote Dr. McCarthy in the Third Project
Report:

> The paramount problem facing the family planning program
> is the lack of adequate medical facilities for village
> people who adopt family planning. There is neither prelim-
> inary medical examination before some contraceptives are
> prescribed, nor is there any follow-up care for people who
> have difficulties after adopting some method. What results
> are numerous situations where women in ill health begin
> using contraceptives when they are physically not fit. This
> causes further health complications in the client, and
> whether accurate or not, the contraceptive is blamed for the
> illness, and women cease using family planning.

With support from the health and family planning departments
and in co-ordination with them, the project could be a vehicle
for bringing improved services, as they are created, to women
in the village. Certainly the project provides an excellent
opportunity to learn quickly about the responses of women all
over the country to services as they exist, as a basis for
bringing about appropriate change.

Reasons for Accepting or Opposing Contraception

Those women who are unwilling to use family planning give a
variety of reasons. The following are representative of the
reasons reported by the staff or heard in interviews:

> One woman with eleven children is married to a *mulvi*
> (village religious leader) and keeps strict *purdah*. Her
> daughters do not study at all. She will not consider
> family planning. She says children are God's gift. She
> thinks the family planning program is shameful for allowing

unmarried girls to talk about birth control and conception.

A woman with eight sons is not worried about having more children because "all the boys can work. Children are the only support which we can rely on in time of danger or in old age."

A poor woman says she does not have to worry about the cost of children since she only has to feed them until they are ten or 11 and then they can take care of themselves. "It is not worth committing a sin," she concludes.

One woman says, "You can stop childbirth, but you cannot rely on only two or three children. If you have more children they can work and help earn money for the family." Another says, "I have only two children. If they die, what will I do?"

A young woman with four children who plans to use contraceptives gives an unexpected reason: "Unless I adopt it, there is no other way. If we have children every year, my health won't be good. I cannot maintain the family. In that case my husband might marry again. As long as women can work, men are good but as soon as they can't work they are beaten, and men marry again. With fewer children our health is better and we can work." The interviewer interjected, "Not only will your husband be good, but with fewer children in the family you can feed them well without trouble." To which the woman replied, "I don't worry about feeding them. Whom God gives, He provides for." In addition, there are a series of religious objections one hears in various places:

"The babies that are stopped might have been prophets or doctors."

"God gives and God takes away."

"God gives children and gives them food. He gets angry if you try to stop them. The problems that women are facing from pills are due to the curse of God."

The following are a few pages from the diary of a staff member, Gita Rani, recording her intensive self-initiated efforts during her field training to promote family planning. It tells a great deal about the responses of women though it leaves unanswered the question of *why* individual women made the choices they did.

1st week: First, the number of couples in the village was determined. There were 309 couples. Among them, the "eligible" and "ineligible" were categorized as follows:(2)

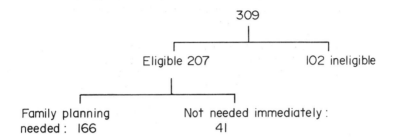

The "campaign" was started with 166 women. They were asked if they had any headaches, eye troubles, irritations, injuries, nervousness, etc. None of them had these problems. Different systems of family planning were discussed with them. They were told about pills, condoms, the plastic coil, the operation [ligation], vasectomy, foam, etc. They were also told, "A small family is a happy family. All of you are mothers of three to nine children. No more children are desirable. You should all start practising family planning." Only six of them agreed after listening to me. The rest said that they would give their final verdict after talking to their husbands.

After asking their husbands they brought back the following types of objections:

God will be angry. It is anti-religious.

The peace of the family will be disturbed.

It is not possible to take pills every day. We cannot remember it in our daily work.

---

(2) These categories are important. "Ineligible" includes those who are too old or who have problems of sterility. "Eligible" couples who do not need family planning immediately include those who were just married, those who are already practising, those who have just lost a child, those with one child who want a second.

After taking pills, the period stops and there is stomach ache.

Pills cause headaches and the body becomes weak.

God has given us this wealth. If there are no human beings, who will be able to eat?

We will not be able to do hard work afterwards, so we won't undergo the operation.

You can stop child birth, but can you give a child to one who does not have any?

The side-effects will definitely happen.

My father-in-law studies Quran sharif. He will not let me use medicines.

But others said:

We have seven or eight children. We would be relieved if we did not have any more. Please give us good medicine.

I have nine children. I feel like going to the woods and leaving them. We would be obliged if you could give us medicine so that we had fewer children. Due to family problems all the time I can't attend the weekly meeting of the society.

After listening to them I did not give up, but rather started explaining to them again. We discussed the uses of pill, condom, foam, plastic coil, etc. After the discussion nine of the women took pills and condoms and left.

2nd week: We, along with the family planning workers, went to the houses of the women who did not want to take up any of the methods. The need for and utility of birth control was explained to the husband and wife together. We spent about seven days on these "encouraging" visits to the houses of the other 157 women. Later, another 31 of them agreed to take pills and condoms.

3rd week: The users of condoms started bringing some problems to me: The children play with the condoms as balloons. They destroy one and ask for more. As a result two or three

condoms were spoiled this way. If the used condoms are
thrown in the woods others see them and they feel ashamed.
They were told to keep all these birth control articles in
a box which no-one except the husband and wife can open.
It should always be kept away from the children's reach.
The used condom should be dug under the ground. Thus nobody
can see anything. With great patience we kept encouraging
the women. Two women came forward and said that they would
use coils. I told them that I would manage everything
regarding the coil and if necessary I would provide medicine.
That day many women took pills and condoms and a total of 79
women accepted family planning.

4th week: This week I went to every woman's house to enquire
if they had any problems whatsoever. All said that they were
using the methods properly. In one woman's container of
pills I saw that she had started eating them from the opposite side of the right way and had finished 11 tablets. The
only reason for this mistake is that the woman is illiterate
and cannot count. She cannot say how many tablets she has
eaten or how many tablets were there in the container. Many
other women faced such difficulties. In the fourth and
fifth week I taught them to count up to 30.

Women have had various troubles with taking the tablets.
They have to take one tablet every night for 21 nights and
the other seven they have to take during the day. But many
of them make mistakes in taking the tablets. One woman
forgot to take the tablets for three consecutive days. She
was told to give up the tablets for the time being and start
using condoms. By the fourth week only 80 of 166 women
could be brought under family planning even after much
effort. All the rest come when I call, they listen to what
I say but they don't take up any of the methods. Many have
the need and even want to, but they won't agree. The women
are reluctant due to social fear, shame, etc.

5th week: In the fifth week five more women took cycles of
tablets. Two women who wanted to use plastic coils were
told by their husbands not to use them. Then I met their
husbands and after explaining to them they gave me their
word that they would agree. It was decided that on the
third day of the sixth week the coil would be inserted.
But two days later a small child of one of the two women
caught fever. Her husband said, "God is displeased. There
is no need of that system." From working in the village

for family planning, I could see that the men also have
superstitious beliefs along with the women. They are not
willing to move with the pace of the progressive world.

6th week: On the third day of the sixth week the two women
came to the agreed place. They will use coils even if their
husbands do not agree. I was present there while the coils
were inserted by the health inspectress. And they went off
happily. Later information revealed that their husbands
did not say much about it.

7th week: We got together all the women on the concluding
day of the seventh week. All the 166 women were present.
With my effort 82 of them accepted different methods of
family planning. Even if the rest did not accept there was
a change in their outlook. They had started realizing that
family planning is important for them. Women who are taking
tablets report vomiting tendencies, headaches and increase
in their periods, but they are patient and are willing to
work hard at it for three or four months.

SUCCESS

Period of Work	Number Aimed At	Number of Women Accepting Methods	Plastic Coil Users	Tablets Users	Condom Users	Number of Women who have not accepted
6 wks	166	82	2	53	27	84

It is evident from the above data that education about
family planning should be expanded to reach women. To make
family planning successful no force can be used. The advantages should be pointed out by explaining, reasoning,
encouraging and by solving immediately the problems arising.
Only then, human confidence can be gained, and they will
respond to our calls.

Ultimately it is hard to know what the reasons some women express
for not accepting family planning really mean to them and why
other women in similar situations accept family planning. One
only knows that women who accept do so because it seems *worth* the
health problems, the religious risk, and the criticism of neighbors, whether out of the desperation produced by extreme poverty,

the hope produced by upward mobility, or because the weight of
a variety of factors specific to individual situations make
contraception seem the obvious choice. It is really not clear
yet what percentage of rural women would use contraception if
the technology and follow up care were adequate to their needs
and what percentage would still not see contraception as a
rational choice because of factors in their socio-economic
condition.

CHAPTER V

THE PARADOX OF WOMEN'S PROGRAMS

The basic work of the Women's Program administrators is to
identify and attempt to solve problems related to providing
services to rural women and to evolve policy that is realistic
in terms of the priorities of rural women and of national development. In addition, much of the time of the administrators is
directed to training and support of field staff. Unfortunately,
a disproportionate amount of time must be directed to the demands
for reports, meetings and paper work from the larger administrative bodies of which this project is a part. Probably these are
aspects of project work that all administrators cope with to
varying degrees on a day-to-day basis.

However, because this project is directed toward women through
a rural development institution it has faced problems of a
special sort at the institutional level that divert energy from
the real work of the project at the village level. It is important, we think, to call attention to some of these problems
because those who are not in a position to experience them may
not know that they exist as an obstruction to project work. It
is also important to stress that there have been significant,
though rare, exceptions to the attitudes and behavior described
in the following pages, without which the effort to carry out
the work of the project might have been too burdensome. Recently,
support at the highest levels of Government for efforts to reach
rural women has added weight to the project which has helped it
withstand the difficulties it faces as a project for women.

Since the project faces problems because it is identified as a
women's project, it has had to question continually the need for

a separate component for women within an institution for rural
development and for separate women's co-operatives as the instrument of the program.(1) The Women's Program is institutionally
integrated in IRDP, in the sense that its recruitment, administration, and, increasingly, its evaluation needs are served
by the relevant sections of IRDP, and in the sense that all its
staff and the program itself are under the authority of superior
IRDP officers. Structurally, it uses the same approach of
village-based institutions. But the evolution of the women's
program at this stage is in many ways different from the regular
program, which up to now has reached only men.

There seems, at present, to be no alternative to a specific
women's project. It is impossible to imagine in this development
context that resources would reach rural women in ways they could
effectively use them without a special women's focus. Resources
have not reached them in the past and as a result there is already a "modernization gap" between men and women that tends to
be self-perpetuating - i.e. there is a feeling of impatience with
the lack of modernity in women's lives that further isolates them
from opportunities for change, through training or better technology.

This frustrating situation involves a paradox that has to be
addressed and understood if it is to be resolved. The work of
rural women is and always has been integrated in the household
and rural economy. But, as we have seen, the women themselves
are, for the most part, sexually segregated; their work is based
on a sexual division of labor; and they are isolated from improved resources except through male intermediaries. To reach
them and support the work they are doing in the rural economy it
is necessary to have a "sheltered" approach that rural families
can accept and that at the same time directly addresses women in
terms of their expertise and spheres of control. Although one
may hope for integration, in the sense of interchangeability of
kind of work performed by men and women, in the future, it is not
possible to begin in that way. The need for separate co-
operatives for women has a similar base in rural culture and an
additional rationale in that such co-operatives provide a better
opportunity for women to develop as leaders than if they were

---

(1) We are not considering here the issue of a separate department or ministry for women. To our way of thinking, this would
create a degree of isolation from the already established
ministries that would be too difficult to overcome.

members of mixed co-operatives, since their culture stresses obedience and submissiveness in the presence of men.

As mentioned above, rural women are integrated in the rural economy. But those who make policy and administer institutions are unaware of or indifferent to this fact (which becomes most evident to those who are in contact with rural women *through a project*). Aspects of the culture and development process that make it necessary to have a women's component in a rural development institution operate at another level to produce resistance and criticism of such an approach. Because there is little awareness of the work of rural women, many men who are the policy-makers, planners, and experts in the field of rural development have been unable to accept it as a "serious" program worthy of their support. Thinking that rural women do nothing, or nothing *worthwhile* in terms of development, they consider a program for rural women without substance and irrelevant to an institution for rural development. Since there is no alternative to a separate component for reaching rural women, their lack of support for a women's program, in fact, rejects *any* approach to women.

Lack of support has been experienced in terms of negative attitudes and behavior. Let us look first at the most persistent attitudes expressed in response to the project over the last three years. They have been expressed for the most part by educated urbanized males, upon whom the project depends in some way for its performance, as justification for their lack of confidence in the aims of the project and what it may be able to accomplish. Village men have, so far, been much more supportive. This lack of confidence may unfortunately be self-fulfilling, in that lack of support by Government officers of a project for women in a male-dominated culture will certainly have a negative effect on its performance. Where there have been instances of support among Government workers, their positive influence in performance has been extraordinary.

We are presenting the attitudes encountered most persistently in the following list, not to indicate frequency or importance, but simply because there seems to be no conceptual framework that makes sense for organizing them in any other way:

> There is no need to increase women's influence in family decisions since they are already in control and have more than enough power in the household.

There is no need to provide economic opportunities for women since they are already cherished and maintained by their husbands. The only problem is women beggars and of course something should be done for them.

There is no use introducing any program for women until they are educated. Their main problem is that they are ignorant and illiterate and this is the problem that must be addressed. If there must be economic projects let them be taken up as hobbies.

If there must be a program for rural women, let it be *home* development with an emphasis on better management of resources, education in better child-care, sanitation, nutrition, etc. Perhaps there can be opportunity for "a little gain."

If women have opportunities for earning income there will be conflict in the family. Such a program will hurt the family, not help it.

Economic opportunities for women will take jobs away from men.

If women earn money, their husbands will stop working.

It is too hard to organize women. They will not co-operate. They will be jealous and fight with each other.

Women do not have time for economic ventures.

Since women are not in agriculture, a program for them is not relevant in the context of rural development.

Nothing will help women unless there is a revolution, so why waste time.

The problems of rural women can be solved by changes in the law to prohibit dowry and provide maintenance after divorce - and by handicrafts.

There is no use starting a project for women unless you already know what the specific program is.

One thing one recognizes immediately about these attitudes toward the project is that they display a *complete lack* of knowledge of the situation of rural women. They cannot be the basis for the analysis and criticism of the project that one genuinely desires. Rather, they indicate the ignorance of the persons expressing them. There has, of course, been a legitimate basis for such ignorance but it is unfortunate to find it continuing among people of influence in rural development. One would hope to see it acknowledged as ignorance and eliminated through available opportunities for new information. But this has happened all too rarely. More commonly, we have found, even among those involved in or responsible for the program, for whom access to information is easiest if they wanted to know, a refusal to learn what it is about. One such person sums it up after three year's association as "a sewing project"; and another, though he supports the female staff, dismisses it by saying, "What is it? It won't last! Why waste money?" For many, it can only be explained as some superior's whimsy.

It is important to recognize that the source of these attitudes in many people is not a simple lack of knowledge that can be corrected by new information, but a deeper resistance to change in the condition of women. No one has yet, in all the literature about women, been able to explain fully the cause of such resistance but it has been well-documented as a wide-spread phenomenon, occurring in countries as varied as China and the United States. Many of the attitudes expressed about this project, though they are culturally specific, seem to be manifestations of that resistance. It is extremely frustrating as one's knowledge of rural women increases through the project to confront such self-assured ignorance. Recognizing the wide-spread nature of these attitudes is distressing, of course, but at the same time it allows one to avoid wasting time or energy on rational explanation where one sees it to be irrelevant. Still, one hopes that those who have influence and are not resistant to change will confront these attitudes, as they encounter them in others, for what they are.

Another aspect of the problem faced by the Women's Program is the *behavior* of males with whom it is associated institutionally. It is obvious that the presence of women in a male-dominated institution is both physically and symbolically an embarrassment for some men. The presence of women in their offices makes some men uncomfortable. They find it difficult to discuss serious issues *with* women and at the same time one knows they will never raise development issues *involving* women if women do not bring them up. References to women, if made at all, are bound to lack seriousness. One administrator told us quite frankly that he

did not want to be associated with a Women's Program function
because his colleagues would laugh at him. It seems to be a
problem to an institution engaged in "serious" work to have
women associated with it. Again there is a paradox. Neither
men nor women feel comfortable unless the physical spaces for
men and women are clearly demarcated. But separate women's
space, which provides a sense of shelter, contributes to the
invisibility that many in the institution have seemed to want
as the next best substitute for absence. Even such invisibility
and segregation have apparently not been enough since there have
been moves, from time to time, to relocate the Women's Program
to a completely separate building.

Even the concept of a Women's Program in rural development has
been difficult to integrate within other relevant institutions.
Either it has been dealt with in isolation from all other issues
of rural production or, as in one seminar on rural development,
it finds itself represented as the last item of a list of topics
as "Women and miscellaneous". One can, of course, be understanding and sympathetic toward this problem of a new conceptualization, even among men in the field of rural development who
are expected to understand the rural culture and economy, but,
in this case, such sympathy cannot extend to the point where it
is obvious there is no interest in integrating the issue in men's
thinking even if it means ignoring aspects of agricultural production that women are involved in, until perhaps men take them
over. The relevant institutions, after four years, continue,
for the most part, to exclude consideration of women's role from
their evolving programs.

In addition to lack of understanding of the rationale of a
women's program, there has been skepticism about the ability of
female staff to administer it. Female field staff have been
told they should be in family planning, not rural development.
Their supervisors have *assumed* they would not be able to handle
certain responsibilities of the job. Their male colleagues have
assumed they could handle a woman's program better than the
women. The female staff have been criticized for faults that
are ignored in males. The special problems they face in the job
because of the culture, problems of transportation to the villages, the need for talking to male colleagues, as well as to be
appropriately sheltered from them, have led to criticism of their
behavior rather than to sympathy or understanding for their
difficult situation. As one man said, "*I* treat them like equals,
but they don't behave that way."

As indicated earlier, the project cannot function well without the support of male officers on whom the women must depend. When it is given, the project develops rapidly. But unfortunately there has been more indifference and neglect than support. One likes to think these responses are changing. There have been several examples of conversion from skepticism to support as a result of personal contact with village women involved in the project. One might say that there seems to be a lessening of opposition rather than an increase in support. One can probably not find at the moment any man in rural development who will support the Women's Program with the enthusiasm he would express for a tube-well project.

It has been our experience also, over the last four years, that the attitudes of those in the international community whose support might have expedited the work of the project, have, instead, in many cases, stood in the way of support. Fortunately this has not always been the case. The International Women's Year, itself created by new pressures and concepts, has focused attention on the importance of allocating resources to women in new ways in order to promote national development. Material and "moral" support of the kind that recognizes the significance of directing resources to women but does not prescribe how such work is to be carried out in another culture has come forth from a number of individuals and their institutions. The earliest support was the result of individuals having enough conviction about the issue to influence their institutions to support the Bangladesh initiative. In recent months there has been increasing movement in this direction as, for a variety of reasons, the climate of opinion has become more favorable, but there have been and continue to be attitudes and behavior from the international aid community that run counter to constructive support. In order for these attitudes to be confronted we will mention some we have experienced directly in relation to the project or indirectly in relation to policy that affects the project.

One problem is that many representatives of the institutions in the international aid community express attitudes about rural Bangladeshi women that are clearly inaccurate. Rather they reflect the assumption, unstated and probably unconscious, that what one knows or *thinks* one knows about women in one culture and economic setting is true of women in another. In many cases there has been no understanding or hint of curiosity about the situation of rural Bangladeshi women as the basis for preferring one program approach to another. Rather there has often been a lack of interest in what has been learned about women through existing projects and worse, at times, a denial of what has been learned. Such refusal to deal with new information or concepts may be the result of an individual's lack of awareness of his or her own assumptions about women or development and a consequent inability to analyze them in the light of new information; or it may be the result of an institution having little flexibility to deal with new concepts. Whatever the reason, the result is a frustrating gap in communication, and worse.

The kinds of objections we have heard to an economic program for rural women, analogous or parallel to men's, are illuminating. One institution's representative would not consider hearing about separate co-operatives for women because his institution "does not support segregation." A representative of another institution maintained that women are already too busy and unable to take proper care of their children, and therefore one should not introduce additional work. At the same time there have been frequent objections to the presence of babies and young children at training classes for rural women, because they are seen as a hindrance to training. Some international personnel who were able to accept the notion of co-operatives for women simply could not accept the fact that women would receive credit from *banks* as men do. The project was frequently advised that women should take loans from their own savings.

In fact, there has been a persistent reaction by international donors against programs for women that have an economic base. One large influential institution continues to support a western home economics approach as *the* appropriate approach to rural women, with a preference for keeping them in the home, in spite of the explanations from women in developing countries, who are working with rural women, that this approach is inappropriate. Many institutions continue to find "home management" the only rationale for a women's program and deny that profit may be a motivating force in women's behavior, though it is accepted in understanding men's behavior. Improved methods of poultry care or vegetable growing or sewing are included in such programs with a view to encouraging more production for a woman's family, without the recognition that these new methods are more expensive than the ones she is already using, and therefore from her point of view, likely, if she is not well-off, to be of questionable good to the family. Some foreigners pull back from *supporting* economic programs for women on the grounds that such support may seem like cultural imperialism when, in fact, their cultural values *prevent* them from seeing that rural women are already economically motivated and active and that their families are in need of new sources of income.

To the extent international donors *do* accept the idea of economic programs for rural women, most of them think of finding or creating work for destitute women and women who are heads of families. But the concept of opportunities for socially rewarded work for all women as a development goal or the idea that rural women's work is already socially valuable, but without recognition in terms of resources and training, is rarely understood. Donors have tended to think of handicraft production when they think of economic programs for women, but for the most part they have failed to recognize that a significant economically viable handicraft industry requires many years of heavy investment.

Additional weight in favor of economic programs for rural women has come from the apparent correlation between jobs for women and lower fertility. In our experience, however, where lowering fertility has been the primary consideration for support of a program, there has been little concern or understanding of the *process* of evolving a viable program for rural women. A prevalent attitude toward women themselves in such a development context is reflected in one individual's assertion that one might have success in lowering fertility (by raising marriage age) if one "could just find some way to keep these girls busy." The "way" unfortunately may ignore both the reality of women's lives and the socio-economic condition of the nation.

Another program approach to rural women that some international donors promote involves various sorts of education - health education, child-care education, sanitation education, nutrition education, and literacy education. When this is the only or primary content of a women's program it has seemed to be based on an assumption that rural women are behaving in ways inappropriate to development because they are ignorant, and that once they know the "right" way to behave they will change. It tends to ignore the reasons rural women have for their behavior and fails to address those reasons in trying to bring about change. It also tends to give women no credit for the ways they are already coping with serious problems, but rather rejects those ways as backward. It is difficult, of course, to seem to be speaking against education programs. However, one can truly be in favor of communication of new information in ways that enable it to be used, but at the same time very skeptical of approaches to rural women that are without an understanding of what resources are available to them and what cultural factors affect their access to resources.

The involvement of the Women's Program in providing family planning education to men and women co-operators has brought it into contact with members of the international aid community whose primary interest is promotion of family planning. The lack of support for the Women's Programs approach has been disappointing, especially because the Women's Program, like other projects directly involving rural women, was a rare source of information about the family planning needs, experiences and responses of rural women. As indicated earlier, contact with rural women suggested that many women were already motivated to control family size but were unwilling to try modern contraception for a number of reasons, including lack of clear information about how different methods of contraception work in the body, their predictable side-effects, and problems that require medical treatment, as well as access to service and supplies, etc. Unfortunately, there was almost no one in the international aid community to whom this concept was explained who was able or willing to accept it as valid family planning education. Rather, in contradiction of Women's Program experience, donors asserted that such information was too technical for staff and too shocking, too worrisome for village people, although staff who had used such material during training were requesting copies to be supplied at *Thana* Centers and village women were already discussing such matters frankly and openly. The Women's Program was advised to use more conventional motivational materials, illustrating in colored pictures the desirability of a two-child family although experience with rural women made it clear that pictures were not likely to motivate them and the idea of planning to have only two children was not likely to be taken seriously by the majority of rural women.

In summary, it is important to repeat that there have been significant exceptions to these examples of behavior and attitudes that have diverted time and energy from the work of the project. Obviously there has had to be support for the project to enable it to accomplish what it has. But for the most part the reception of the program by village women and their families has been far more favourable than its reception by policy makers, planners, officers and staff of Bangladesh and foreign institutions. *With* their support the program would be able to accomplish much more.

PART THREE

OVERVIEW

OVERVIEW

Even during this initial period when much of the effort of the
project has involved organization and training at the administrative level, the indications are that the project is moving
in the direction of its goals. Villages are accepting an institution that openly supports the participation of women in economic activities. Women are using the institution to save money
and to take loans for production in work of importance in the
rural economy. They are using the credit institution, which is
completely new to them, successfully. Unlike male co-operators,
they have been repaying loans on time. They are using profits
to increase their and their families' control over their own
lives. They have new access to various kinds of training and
information relevant to their lives. They have improved access
to existing services in family planning and are taking advantage
of it; they are indicating how health and family planning services can be improved. Because the instrument of these changes
is a community-based institution, there is a chance for group
responsibility and leadership to develop and, in older groups,
there are clear examples of their emergence. In other words,
the project has entered villages where the scope for women was
extremely limited and has developed a *base* on which it can
build toward its long-range objectives. The project has also
been exploring ways to learn about itself and rural women and
to record its progress and problems.

On the basis of this experience we would like to point to some
of the issues that seem central to us and which we think should
be taken into account by policy-makers, rural development
planners, and project and extension workers who are concerned

215

with the participation of rural women in the attainment of national development goals.

Efforts to carry out programs for rural women are more likely to succeed, in spite of initial difficulties of acceptance, if they are *integrated in already existing rural development institutions* which have requisite organization and experience, than if they are inaugurated as separate "women's" institutions. However, within these existing rural development institutions, rural women may be organized separately from men, especially where there is a rural pattern of social segregation and sex-specific work roles, responsibilities and time allocation, where women are expected to be quiet in the presence of men, and where a modernization gap already exists between men and women.

There are definite advantages in organizing rural women at the village level in *village-based organizations*. In this way one can build on existing patterns of co-operation and accountability among rural women in ways that are culturally acceptable. In addition, the existence of a sanctioned group enables individual members to choose new options appropriate to their situation, which they could not have risked in isolation. If the group is able to develop cohesiveness and strong leadership, it can speak for the community of women in requesting resources and services women will be able to make use of.

The designs of projects or services intended to reach rural women are more likely to take hold if they address the *priorities* of rural women and their families and the village. In learning what these priorities are, several issues have to be considered. Firstly, it is important to keep in mind that, while normative descriptions of women's behavior and belief systems or social ideology concerning them serve an important function in rural society, actual behavior often differs considerably. Both must be recognized and taken into consideration. No project for women can enter or remain in the village without at least tacit acceptance of village leaders. But women will not respond as project designers may hope unless they see its resources as useful. Project design must be based on the understanding that women choose rationally among existing options to meet their

(1) Although social ideology about rural women's behavior does change when new options make change advantageous, the *potential* for such change may not be obvious when alternatives are not yet apparent to village people.

priorities and that the socio-economic setting which creates and delimits their options differs from that of men. To the extent possible, a project's long-term goals should address the forces that delimit women's options.

Secondly, in many situations, existing dependency relationships (feudal, male, in-law) through which women meet family needs are the only context in which new options can be offered. This means that options have to be introduced in ways that women who need them, of whatever class, will consider safe and appropriate to respond to in their present situation. Only if the new options prove to be clearly advantageous can women begin to shift from depending on unfavorable arrangements to self-reliance. Women who are the poorest, i.e., totally dependent for survival on their daily labor, may not be able to respond until a project has created opportunities that meet daily survival needs. These take time to develop.

Thirdly, project design should address women's most pressing priorities which are often economic, but they should also recognize that health and family planning services and improved technology for their routine work are an integral part of women's needs. Rural women do not usually distinguish between their economic, maternal and domestic roles.

The specific evolution of a project cannot be predicted. The objectives and approach derive from national policy and institutional framework; the design and guidelines reflect village reality. Still, when first steps are taken, it is the response of women that will determine in what direction the second and third steps will go and at what pace. For example, the nature of the response of women to supervised credit points the way to exploring the possibilities of small agro-based industry and better access to technology like hand-pumps and threshers. Their response to information and improved access to family planning service highlights their health needs and points the way to developing improved services. As new steps evolve, the project must continually modify its guidelines and monitor the direction of change so that it remains in line with project goals and national priorities. If a project is vital, *this process of change* never stops. As one set of problems is addressed, the act of change itself uncovers or creates new problems which may be anticipated but are not totally predictable. One need not be afraid of problems or see them as a sign of failure if there is enough flexibility in the institution to allow the project to continue moving in the direction of its goals.

A project has need of several kinds of *information*, some, if
not all, of which it may have to collect and provide itself, in
the absence of other resources. One kind is the action-oriented
research of Part One which seeks to understand the perspective
that rural women have on their situation. Another is project-
feedback that indicates fairly quickly how villages and village
women are responding to new resources. These two kinds of
information address issues raised by the project. For example,
co-operative membership has been open to all women, but an
understanding of who is joining and who is using which resources
(feedback) and why (action-oriented research) will determine
what policies are needed to attract members from a wide range
of backgrounds or to improve chances for equitable distribution
of resources. A third kind of information a project needs to
collect and provide is a record of its own process of initiating
change, a case study that will help the project and others
understand where it started from, where it is going and how.
Such a record, of failures as well as successes, is an important
knowledge base on which others will be able to build.

One of the critical dynamics of a project for rural women is the
interaction between rural women and rural or field *staff*. If a
project is administered centrally but operates throughout the
rural areas (which, as we have seen vary considerably from village to village), it must depend on the initiative, responsibility
and commitment of field staff to enable women of each area to
evolve in the direction their circumstances dictate. This staff
needs training, encouragement and support (including adequate
pay, travel facilities, and accommodation) appropriate to their
critical role in the success of a project.

The progress of a project for rural women depends on the quality
of relevant *support services*. Extension workers in agriculture,
health, family planning, and other services need to know what
women are already doing and why, so that they can build their
services on what is practicable. If they are advocating modern
practices, they should be able to guarantee the essential
supportive services.

For communicating new methods and practices to rural women, they
should evolve a methodology based on respect for rural women's
expertise that will support the requisite two-way communication.

With regard to *family planning* services, it is our experience
that many more rural women want to limit family size than are
able to, because of social, economic, and health risks they see

219

in the existing pattern of services. An understanding of conditions under which these motivated rural women could use services and the development of services in that direction would increase the response of rural women.

Internal evaluation must be an ongoing part of a project through staff conferences, records, field visits, and reports. *External evaluation* is undertaken from time to time by interested institutions for varying purposes which determine their specific approach. However, there are several general issues which we think should be taken into consideration in external evaluation. Firstly, since the objectives of a project are determined by the national context in which it is operating, it cannot change aspects of the social system that are supported, tacitly or explicitly by national policy. Evaluation should distinguish whether a project creates or reflects social ills. Secondly, the approach a project can take is determined by what is acceptable in a rural context. Evaluation should be based on an understanding of the rural context. Thirdly, evaluation should take into account the realities of implementation, including training, transportation, acquisition of material inputs, and availability of relevant Government services. Fourthly, in order to measure progress, it is necessary to have an appreciation of the base from which one starts. Baseline studies should include such information as the available options for village women with regard to commerce, employment, family planning, health, horticulture, etc., before the onset of a project. Case histories of women involved in the project will record the variety of ways, many of them unanticipated, in which women use the opportunities provided by a project. Lastly, the long-term national benefits anticipated in setting up a project are not the main indicators by which to measure progress in the early stages of a project. After a project has been working in rural areas for a few years, it can begin to develop a realistic timetable and intermediate objectives for reaching its long-term goals and to identify appropriate performance indicators to measure progress toward intermediate objectives. For example, although the use of credit is not a long-term goal of the Bangladesh project, village women's use of what is a new institution for them is perceived as a step toward economic self-reliance. Therefore an evaluation of women's use of the credit system at an appropriate stage indicates progress toward an *intermediate* objective.

The period of *expansion* beyond the pilot phase is an exceedingly critical time in the evolution of a project. The pilot phase does not produce a replicable package that can be set in place in new areas. What is being expanded is not a finished product but a guided process moving in a certain direction at a certain speed that will now involve more people and more places. The period of expansion requires even greater support and attention than the beginnings. Adequate staff to administer a large program and an adequate budget to support rural women as they undertake larger enterprises are essential at this stage to give a women's program of the kind discussed here a reasonable chance of success.

GLOSSARY OF ABBREVIATIONS AND VERNACULAR WORDS

Bari   - a homestead, usually a group of houses belonging to the same family built around a central courtyard
Bepari   - a pedlar
Bidi   - a kind of cigar
Bigha   - a land measurement of about a third of an acre
Borga   - a sharecropping arrangement, returning a certain amount of the yield, usually 50%, to the owner
B.R.A.C. - Bangladesh Rural Advancement Committee
Burkah   - an overgarment covering a woman from head to foot
Chula   - an earthen stove
Dai   - a local untrained village midwife
Dheki   - a wooden implement for husking rice
Dhokan   - a village shop
D.P.O.   - Deputy Project Officer
Ghor   - a small house, often woven or thatched with local fibers
Gram   - the village
Hakim   - a local village "doctor"
Haram   - prohibited by religion
I.A.   - Intermediate Arts degree, indicating satisfactory completion of two years of education after high school
Kabiraj   - a local "doctor"
I.R.D.P. - Integrated Rural Development Program
Maund   - a weight measurement of 82 pounds
Moulvi   - a local religious leader
Naior   - a visit to the parents' home by the daughter after marriage
Paddy   - the name for rice in the field and during processing
Pan   - a mild stimulant of betel nut, lime and spices wrapped in a leaf
Para   - a neighborhood within the village, often made up of related families
Pir   - a saint
Purdah   - the veil; the seclusion of women
Seer   - a measurement of approximately two pounds
Sutki   - a kind of dried fish
Taka   - a unit of currency, of about six or seven U.S. cents (1979)
Tabij   - an amulet worn to ward off evil spirits
Thana   - an administrative district
Zamindar - a very large land-owner

APPENDIX A

SAMPLE QUESTIONNAIRES

The following are some of the questions used in group and individual interviews of rural women under appropriate headings:

Basic Family Background

What is your name?

What is your husband's name?

What village do you come from?

What is your father's name?

Are your parents living?

How many brothers and sisters do you have? How many are older, how many younger?

How many times has your mother been married? Your father?

What work does your father do?

Does your father own land?

How much education have you had? Where?

How old were you when you married?

222

How old was your husband at marriage?

How many in his family?

What is his work?

How many children do you have? How old are they?

How old are you?

Menstruation

How old were you when you had your first period? Was it before or after marriage? Was there a special ceremony? Describe it.

Did you know about menstruation before your first period? If yes, how? If no, who explained to you about menstruation? What did she say?

Can you say why we have menstruation? Why does it start? Why does it stop?

Do you know anyone who didn't menstruate? Can you have a baby before menstruation starts or after it stops?

What different names are used for menstruation in your village?

After how many days do you get your period? Do you feel pain before and/or during menstruation? What other feelings do you have? How many days does the bleeding continue? Does it happen this way every month? If not, do you know why?

How do you keep yourself clean during menstruation?

Is there any prohibition in food, movement, daily activities, and religious activities during your period?

Pregnancy

Do you have children? How many?

What is the age of the youngest? Of the oldest?

Did any babies die? How many? Of what? Any miscarriages?

What were the causes?

When you first got pregnant, how did you know you were pregnant?

What words do you use for pregnancy?

Are you told to eat any special foods during pregnancy?

Do you have any special ceremonies during pregnancy?

Do you get any special instructions about how to behave during pregnancy? If yes, what and from whom?

Childbirth

How old were you when your first child was born?

How old were you when you got married?

How many years after marriage was your first child born?

Whose house did you give birth in - your mother's or mother-in-law's?

Which room in the house was the child born in, the main room, side room or other?

How long were the labor pains with your first child? With the next child?

Who was present during labor? During delivery?

Sometimes the baby's navel or the mother's womb get infected after childbirth. What was done in your case to prevent infection?

Did you have an infection after childbirth? If yes, how did you take care of it? Who prescribed the medicine?

Did your baby have an infection after childbirth? If yes, how did you take care of it? Who prescribed the medicine?

How was the baby born? Were you lying down, sitting up or in some other position? Can you show us?

To make the baby come faster, lots of things are done. What was done in your case?

Immediately after childbirth, what were you given to eat?

Did you take any medicine? If yes, what?

Think about what you ate for the first forty days after childbirth. What did you eat a lot of? What were you not allowed to eat?

To dry up the birth canal did you get special foods? Did you get special foods for producing milk?

To dry up the baby's navel quickly, what was done?

How long after childbirth did you have to stay in the same room?

Then how long did you have to stay within the *bari*?

What prohibitions were there about moving about after childbirth?

Could you move about at any time of day or night?

Did you nurse all your babies?

When did you start nursing after childbirth? How frequently do you nurse your baby? How long did you nurse your first baby? Your last baby?

How long were you bleeding after childbirth?

When did your period start again after the first child? After the last child?

How many more children do you want?

Have you ever heard of Family Planning?

Have you ever used it? What kind? Did you have problems with it?

Sex

Village girls know about sex before marriage. How old are they
when they know? How do they know? Don't girls talk about the
comings and goings from the husband's room? What do they say?
When you got married, did you know about sex? Who told you?
What words are used among village women to discuss sex? If
there are sex problems, who do the girls talk to? Who does
your husband talk to about sex problems?

Divorce

How common is divorce in your village?

Mention some cases that you know of.

What were the causes?

Who initiated the divorce?

What happened to the wife?

What happened to the children?

Abortion

Many women don't want more children after they have had seven
or eight. Perhaps they can't afford to feed and clothe more
children or they have some other reason. Do you know anyone
who has had an abortion? If yes, why? How? What method was
used? Did the husband or family know of the abortion?

Are there doctors of any kind who give medicine for abortion?

What other methods do you know of for abortion?

Do you know anyone else who had an abortion? Describe the case.

What other reaons might there be for abortion?

What do villagers and village leaders think about abortion?

Do you know cases of premarital sex, of unmarried mothers, of
relationships with men other than the husband?

Village Code

Who is considered to be a beautiful girl in your village? What does she look like?

Who is considered to be a good girl? How does she behave?

Who is considered to be a bad girl? What has she done? Do you think she's bad?

What happens to a bad girl in your village?

What do you consider to be a good husband?

What is *purdah*? Do you keep it?

What does the *moulvi* think is a good girl? Do you believe the *moulvi*? Does your husband?

Rice Processing

Who parboils and dries rice in your *bari*?

Why do you parboil rice?

How long do you parboil it?

How much heat do you use?

How do you know when it is finished?

How can you tell when the rice is dried?

Do you get a lot of broken rice?

What causes *Cheeta dhan* (spoiled rice)?

How do you store the rice seed?

Do rats and/or insects spoil the seed? Why? Why not?

Why do some seeds *not* germinate?

How much rice do you get from one *maund* of paddy?

How much *koi* (a different form of rice)?

How much *morri* (a different form of rice)?

Do you get better rice from a *dheki* or a mill?

Do you use the mill? Why? Why not?

How much does the mill charge?

How much time does it take for one woman to process ten *maunds* of paddy?

Agricultural Production

How much paddy land do you own?

Where are your plots?

How many crops did you grow this year? Last year?

How much yield did you get this year? Last year?

When were the crops sown this year? When were they harvested?

How much paddy did you sell this year? At what price? How much last year?

How many laborers did you hire this year? How many days did they work?

Do you have irrigation?

How much did you pay for seed?

How much did you pay for fertilizer?

How much did you pay for insecticide?

How much is your land worth?

Livestock Care

How can you tell if a cow, bullock or goat is of good breed?

What do you feed your animals?

How do you care for them?

What diseases do they contract?

How do you treat them?

Earning and Saving

Do you know women who are earning money? Tell about one.

What do you think of her?

What is her attitude toward her husband, in-laws, family?

Do villagers appreciate her behavior?

Do villagers object to her earning?

Some women save money. How do they do it? Tell about one.

Where does she keep her money?

What does she do with her savings?

Does her husband know she has savings?

If she wants to do business, how much interest does she charge?

If she lends her savings, how much interest does she charge?

If she hoards paddy, how does she arrange it?

If she lends goats, what are the arrangements?

230

Spending

Who decides how to spend the money you earn?

Do you give your earnings to your husband?

Have you bought land with your earnings? In whose name?

Did you buy ornaments for your sister's marriage? Did you have
to take your husband's permission?

How do you spend your earnings?

APPENDIX **B**

THE BASIC STRUCTURE OF THE PROJECT

Supervision: The Women's Program is supervised and evaluated by two ministries - the Ministry of Health, Population Control and Family Planning, and the Ministry of Land Administration, Local Government, Rural Development and Co-operatives.

Duration: The life of the *pilot* project is three and a half years.

Staff: The project is administered at IRDP headquarters by a Joint-Director, an Assistant Director, two Statistical Assistants, an Accountant and a Junior Officer. At each *Thana* where the project is working, there are three female staff - a Deputy Project Officer, appointed by Headquarters, and two Inspectors, appointed at the *Thana*. *Thana* staff receive intensive pre-service training and continuous in-service training.

Coverage: The project is set up to operate in 19 specified *Thanas*, one in each of the country's 19 districts, where IRDP is already operating a program of co-operatives for farmers. Its coverage is phased over the duration of the project so that ten *Thanas* are covered in the first two years and nine in the last year of the project.

Method: In each *Thana*, ten women's village co-operatives are organized. To join the co-operative, women buy a share and pay a small admission fee. As members of co-operatives, which are nationally regulated, they are obliged to follow co-operative discipline, which includes depositing savings weekly in the bank. As members in good standing, they are entitled to credit for

VWB - Q

231

economic projects and have access to training and services in
health, family planning and literacy. Five women from each co-
operative attend weekly training classes at the *Thana* Center
and transmit what they have learned to the rest of the co-
operative at weekly village meetings. An additional, more
intensive kind of training is offered to selected co-operators
either at institutions that can give market-oriented training
in skills suitable to the village or in special courses at the
Thana Center.

Results: In numerical terms, the results as of December 1978
are:

1. 598 co-operatives have been organized in 28 *Thanas*
   throughout Bangladesh;(1)

2. Membership in the co-operatives is 23,300, an average of
   38 members per co-operative;

3. 1,100,000 *taka* have been collected in shares and savings
   or about 47 *taka* per member;

4. 1,400,000 *taka* have been given in loans in amounts of 100-
   300 *taka*;

5. The percentage of family planning acceptors among members
   is 35-40%.(2)

Unfortunately these figures are not very clear since they
include both *Thana* projects that have been functioning for two
years or more and others that have been functioning for only
one year. It is important to keep in mind, also, that although

---

(1) The project has expanded more quickly than originally
intended in the pilot stage as the result, in part, of pressure
from the original *Thanas* to increase the number of co-operatives
and adjoining *Thanas* to be included in the project. At present,
then, it covers rather more than the original 19 *Thanas* and may
include up to 30 co-operatives rather than ten in each of the
original 19 *Thanas*. The second project plan is now being considered and anticipates expansion by 1985 to 50 villages in
each of 50 *Thanas*.
(2) The percentage would be higher if only those members who
are from eligible couples were considered, but these figures are
not available.

233

the project was almost four years old in December 1978, the *full range of inputs* necessary for the program at the *Thana* and village level has not been in place in any *Thana* for more than two years, *if that long.*(3)

---

(3) Analyses of IRDP Women's Program monthly reports as of December 1978.

REFERENCES

Abdullah, T. 1974. *Village Women as I Saw Them*, Ford
    Foundation, Dacca. (First published as "Palli Anganader
    Jemon Dekhechi", Comilla, PARD, 1966).

Abdullah, T. and Hoque, N. December 1970. *Women's Education
    and Home Development Program, Fifth Report, July 1968 -
    June 1970*, Comilla, PARD.

Abdullah, T. and Zeidenstein, S. 1976. *Finding Ways to Learn
    About Rural Women: Experiences From a Pilot Project in
    Bangladesh*, Ford Foundation, Dacca.

Abdullah, T. and Zeidenstein, S. May 1977. "Some Health
    Practices of Rural Bangladesh", *Sishu Diganta, A Child's
    Horizon*, UNICEF, Dacca.

Adnan, Shapan and Village Study Group. June 1975. "The
    Preliminary Findings of a Social and Economic Study of Four
    Bangladesh Villages", *Dacca University Studies*.

Adnan, Shapan and Village Study Group. November 1975. "Social
    Structure and Resource Allocation in a Chittagong Village",
    Dacca.

Adnan, Shapan and Village Study Group. March 1976. "Land,
    Power and Violence in Barisal Villages", Dacca.

Adnan, Shapan, Rushidan, Salem and the Dacca University Village
    Study Group. March 1977a. "Social Change and Rural Women:

234

Possibilities in Participation", *Role of Women in Socio-Economic Development in Bangladesh*, Bangladesh Economic Association, Dacca.

Adnan, Shapan and Village Study Group. April 1977b. "Differentiation and Class Structure in Village Samaj", Dacca.

Ahmad, Nafis. 1968. *An Economic Geography of East Pakistan*, 2nd Ed. London, Oxford University Press.

Ahmed, Tahrunnessa. 1965. *Women's Education and Home Development Program of Comilla Academy 2nd Report April 1963 to June 1965*, Comilla, PARD.

Ahmed, Tahrunnessa. December 1966. *Women's Education and Home Development Program. Third Annual Report, July 1965 to June 1966*, Comilla, PARD.

Ahsan, Ekramul and K. Azharul Haque. April 9-11, 1975. "Appropriate Technology for the Cultivation of HYV Rice and Their Socio-Economic Implications". Paper 39 at Bard-Ford Seminar on Socio-Economic Implications of High Yielding Variety Rice Production.

Akhter, Farkunda. 1977. "Some Observations on Women's Functional literacy Program and Use of Model Farmers and Co-operative Managers (Second Phase IRDP Baseline Survey)", Dacca.

Alamgir, Susan. June 1977. *Profile of Bangladeshi Women: Selected Aspects of Women's Roles and Status in Bangladesh*, USAID Dacca.

Arens, Jeneke. 1975. "The Double Exploited". Unpublished manuscript, Dacca.

Aziz, K.M. Ashraful. 1976. "Kin Terminologies and Family Structure of Muslims and Hindus in Matlab Thana and Neighborhood, Rural Bangladesh", M. Phil.Thesis, Rajshahi University.

Bangladesh Bureau of Statistics. 1978. *Statistical Pocket Book - 1978*, Statistics Division, Ministry of Planning, Government of Bangladesh, Dacca.

Bangladesh Bureau of Statistics. 1975. *Statistical Yearbook of Bangladesh - 1975*, Dacca.

236

Bertocci, Peter J. December 1972. "Community Structure and Social Rank in Two Villages in Bangladesh", *Contributions to Indian Sociology New Series*, VI.

Cain, Mead. October 1976. "Demographic and Socio-Economic Profile of the Study Village: Results from the Census", *Bangladesh Development Studies*.

Cain, Mead T. 1977a. "The Economic Activities of Children in a Village in Bangladesh", *Population and Development Review*, III, 3.

Cain, Mead T. February 1977b. "Household Time Budgets", Village Fertility Study Methodology Report #1, *Bangladesh Institute of Development Studies* (Mimeo).

Chen, Marty, and Ruby Guznavy. 1977. *Women in Food-For-Work: The Bangladesh Experience*, World Food Programme, Dacca.

Ellickson, Jean. 1972. "A Believer Among Believers: The Religious Beliefs, Practices and Meanings in A Village in Bangladesh". Ph.D. Dissertation, Michigan State University.

Ellickson, Jean. 1975. "Rural Women", *Women for Women*, Dacca, University Press Ltd.

Faaland, Just and J.R. Parkinson. 1976. *Bangladesh: The Test Case for Development*, London, Hurst.

Farouk, A. and M. Ali. 1975. *The Hardworking Poor - A Survey on How People Use Their Time in Bangladesh*, Dacca Bureau of Economic Research, Dacca University.

Huq, M. Nurul. 1973. *Village Development in Bangladesh*, Comilla, BARD.

IRDP Population Planning and Rural Women's Co-operatives Reports, 1974-77. IRDP, Dacca.

IRDP Reports. 1974-77. IRDP, Dacca.

Islam, Mahmuda. 1975. "Women at Work in Bangladesh", *Women for Women*, Dacca, University Press Limited.

Jahan, Rounaq. 1975. "Women in Bangladesh", *Women for Women*, Dacca, University Press Limited.

Khan, Akhter Hameed. February 1967. "Speech of Akhter Hameed Khan at the Third Women's Rally Held on March 6, 1966". Comilla, PARD.

Khan, Ali Akhtar. April 1968. *Rural Credit in Gazipur Village*, Comilla, PARD.

Khan, Azizur Rahman. 1972. *The Economy of Bangladesh*, London, McMillan Press Ltd.

Khatun, Saleha and Gita Rani. December 1977. *Bari-Based Post Harvest Operations and Livestock Care: Some Observations and Case Studies*, Dacca, Ford Foundation.

Khatun, Sharifa. March 1977. "Equal Educational Opportunity for Women: A Myth", *Role of Women in Socio-Economic Development in Bangladesh*, Dacca, Bangladesh Economic Association.

Khatun, Tahziba. June 1975. *Women's Education and Home Development 1970-73*, Comilla, BARD.

Lindenbaum, Shirley. 1965. "Infant Care in Rural East Pakistan", Dacca, Cholera Research Laboratory.

Lindenbaum, Shirley. 1975. "The Value of Women", *Bengal in the Nineteenth and Twentieth Century*, East Lansing, Michigan State University Asian Studies Center, Occasional Papers, South Asia Series, No. 25.

Martius-Von Harder, Gudrun. 1975. "Women's Role in Rice Processing", *Women for Women*, Dacca, University Press Ltd.

McCarthy, Florence E. April 1963. *Women's Education and Home Development Program, First Report, January 1962 through March 1963*, Comilla, PARD.

McCarthy, Florence E. 1967. "Bengali Village Women: Mediators Between Tradition and Development", M.A. Thesis, Michigan State University.

McCarthy, Florence E. 1977a. "Reports on Use of Loans by Female Co-operative Members", Dacca, IRDP.

McCarthy, Florence E. June 1977b. "I.R.D.P. Pilot Project in Population Planning and Rural Women's Co-operatives. Third

Report. June 1976 - May 1977". Dacca, IRDP.

Mernissi, Fatima. 1975. *Beyond The Veil: Male-Female Dynamics in a Modern Muslim Society*, Cambridge, Mass., Schenkman.

Pakistan Master Survey of Agriculture, 1968, Government of Pakistan karachi.

"Problems in Field Work with Village Women", November 1964. Comilla, PARD.

Qadir, S.A. 1960. *Village Dhaniswar - Three Generations of Man-Land Adjustment in an East Pakistan Village*, Comilla, PARD.

Salimullah, A.B.M. and Shamsul Islam. April 1976. "A Note on the Condition of Rural Poor in Bangladesh", *Bangladesh Development Studies*, IV.

Sattar, Ellen. 1974. *Women in Bangladesh: A Village Study*, Dacca, Ford Foundation.

Sattar, Ellen. June 1977. "Universal Primary Education in Bangladesh, Annual Report, Meher Panchagram Universal Primary Education", Comilla, Bangladesh.

Senaratne, S.P.F. 1975. "Micro Studies, Employment and the Strategies of Development", unpublished manuscript, Sri Lanka.

Sobhan, Salma. 1978. *The Legal Status of Women in Bangladesh*, Dacca, Institute of Law, Dacca University.

Women for Women. 1975. Dacca, University Press Limited.

Zeidenstein, S. October 1975. "Report and Commentary on IRDP Women's Program, The First Year", Dacca, IRDP.

Zeidenstein, S. June 1976. "Report on the First Two Years of the IRDP Pilot Project on Population Planning and Rural Women's Co-operatives", Dacca, IRDP.

RELATED READINGS

Abdullah, Abu, Mosharaff Hossain and Richard Nations. 1976. "Agrarian Structure and the IRDP - Preliminary Considerations", *Bangladesh Development Studies*, IV, 2.

Abdullah, T. and S. Zeidenstein. 1974. "Socio-Economic Implications of HYV Rice Production on Rural Women of Bangladesh". Bard-Ford Seminar of High-Yielding Variety Rice Production, Comilla, BARD.

Abdullah, T. and S. Zeidenstein. March 1977. "Rural Women and Development", *Role of Women in Socio-Economic Development in Bangladesh*, Dacca, Bangladesh Economic Association.

Abdullah, T. and S. Zeidenstein. June 1977. "Livestock Care in the Village", *ADAB News*, Dacca, IV, 6.

ADAB News. June 1977. Dacca, IV, 6.

Ahmed, Nizam Uddin. 1973. "The Life-Cycle of the Individual and the Developmental Cycle of the 'Domestic Group' in Three Villages in Bangladesh". Paper prepared for IX International Congress of Anthropological and Ethnological Sciences.

Ahmed, Sufia. 1974. *Muslim Community in Bengal 1884-1912*, Bangladesh, Oxford University Press.

Alamgir, Mohiuddin. 1975. "Some Aspects of Bangladesh Agriculture: Review of Performance and Evaluation of Policies", *Bangladesh Development Studies*, III, 3.

Alamgir, Mohiuddin. 1976. "Economy of Bangladesh: Which Way Are We Moving", Bangladesh Economic Association, Second Annual Conference.

Aziz, K.M.A., A.K.M. Alauddin Chowdhury and Wiley H. Mosely, "Patterns of Marriage: A Study in Rural Bangladesh", Dacca, Cholera Research Laboratory.

Bangladesh Bureau of Statistics. 1976. *The Yearbook of Agricultural Statistics of Bangladesh 1975-76*, Dacca.

240

Bangladesh Rural Advancement Committee Newsletters and Reports.
1974-77. Dacca.

Barkat-e-Khuda. 1976. "The Importance of Work Done By Children
in a Bangladesh Village", Dacca, unpublished mimeograph.

Bertocci, Peter. 1974. "Rural Communities In Bangladesh:
Hajipur and Tinpara", *South Asia: Seven Community Profiles*,
ed. C. Maloney, New York, Holt Rinehart and Winston.

Bertocci, Peter. 1976. "Rural Development in Bangladesh",
Rural Development in Bangladesh and Pakistan, ed. Robert D.
Stevens, Hamza Alavi and Peter J. Bertocci, Honolulu,
University Press of Hawaii.

Blades, Derek. 1975. "Non-Monetary (Subsistence) Activities
in the National Accounts of Developing Countries", Paris
Development Center of the Organization for Economic Co-
operation and Development.

Blair, H.W. 1974. *The Elusiveness of Equity: Institutional
Approaches to Rural Development in Bangladesh*, Ithaca, N.Y.,
Cornell University Press.

Boserup, E. 1970. *Women's Role in Economic Development*,
London, Allen and Unwin.

Chaudhury, Rafiqul Huda. 1974. "Labor Force Status and
Fertility", *Bangladesh Development Studies*, II, 4.

Chen, Lincoln et al. 1974. *Maternal Mortality in Rural
Bangladesh*, Dacca, Ford Foundation.

Chen, Lincoln ed. 1973. *Disaster in Bangladesh: Health Crises
in a Developing Nation*, New York, Oxford University Press.

Chen, Lincoln, Sandra Huffman, and Penny Satterthwaite. 1976.
*Recent Fertility Trends in Bangladesh: Speculation on the
Role of Biological Factors and Socio-Economic Change*, Dacca,
Ford Foundation.

Chen, Lincoln and Rafiqul Huda Chaudhury. 1975. *Demographic
Change and Trends of Food Production and Availabilities in
Bangladesh (1960-1974)*, Dacca, Ford Foundation.

Chen, Lincoln and Monowar Hossain. 1976. "The Transfer of Population Technology", paper presented at Bangladesh Economic Association Second Annual Conference.

Chinas, Beverly L. 1973. *The Isthmus Zapotecs: Women's Roles in Cultural Context*, New York, Holt Rinehart and Winston.

Choudhury, Alauddin, Sandra Huffman and George Curlin. 1976. *Malnutrition, Menarche and Marriage in Rural Bangladesh*, Dacca, Cholera Research Laboratory.

Choudhury, A.K.M., Atiqur Rahman Khan and Lincoln Chen. March 1975. *The Effect of Child Mortality Experience on Subsequent Fertility*, Dacca, Ford Foundation.

Chowdhury, Anwarullah. December 1975. "Social Stratification in a Bangladesh Village", *Journal of the Asiatic Society of Bangladesh*.

Clay, Edward J. 1976. "Institutional Change and Agriculture Wages in Bangladesh", *Bangladesh Development Studies*, IV, 4.

Das Gupta, Monica. August 9-13, 1976. "Ladies First", paper presented at Fourth World Congress for Rural Sociology, Torun, Poland.

Eglar, Zekiye. 1960. *A Punjabi Village in Pakistan*. New York, Columbia University Press.

Ellickson, Jean. December 1972. "Islamic Institutions: Perception and Practice in a Village in Bangladesh", *Contributions to Indian Sociology*.

Epstein, T. Scarlett. 1973. *South India Yesterday Today and Tomorrow*, New York, Holmes and Meier.

Fernea, Elizabeth Warnock. 1969. *Guests of the Sheik: An Ethnography of an Iraqi Village*, New York, Anchor Books.

Germain, Adrienne. 1966-77. "Poor Rural Women: A Policy Perspective", *Journal of International Affairs*, XXX, 2.

Gonoshasta Kendra. 1974-76. Progress Reports.

Hossain, Mahbub. October 1973. "Farm Size and Productivity in Bangladesh Agriculture: A Case Study of Phulpur Farms", Dacca, BIDE.

Hull, Valerie J. August 9-13, 1976. "Women in Java's Rural
Middle Class, Progress or Regress", prepared for the Fourth
World Congress for Rural Sociology, Torun, Poland.

Hunter, W.W. 1974. *A Statistical Account of Bengal 1876*
(Volume VIII), New Delhi, Rakesh Press.

Hunter, W.W. 1975. *The Indian Musalmans* (Written in 1871),
Dacca, W. Rahman.

Huq, M. Ameerul ed. 1976. *Exploitation and the Rural Poor*,
Comilla, BARD.

Islam, A.K.M. Aminul. 1974. *A Bangladesh Village, Conflict
and Cohesion: An Anthropological Study of Politics*, Cambridge
Mass., Schenkman.

Islam, Shamima. March 1977. "Women, Education and Development
in Bangladesh: A Few Reflections", *Role of Women in Socio-
Economic Development in Bangladesh*, Dacca, Bangladesh
Economic Association.

Islam, Sirajul. 1974. "The Bengal Peasantry in Debt 1904-45",
Dacca University Studies, XXII (Part A).

Jack, J.C. 1927. *The Economic Life of a Bengal District*,
London, Oxford University Press.

Jacobson, Doranne. 1970. *Hidden Faces: Hindu and Muslim Purdah
in a Central Indian Village*, Ph.D. Dissertation, Columbia
University.

Jahan, Rounaq. 1972. *Pakistan: Failure in National Integration*,
New York, Columbia University Press.

Jain, Devaki ed. 1975. *Indian Women*, New Delhi, Ministry of
Information and Broadcasting.

Kabir, K. et al. 1976. *Rural Women in Bangladesh: Exploding
Some Myths*, Dacca, Ford Foundation.

Khan, A.R. March 1976. "Poverty and Inequality in Rural
Bangladesh", Working Paper in World Employment Program
Research, Geneva, International Labor Office.

Khan, Akhter Hameed. July 1963. "The Role of Women in a

Country's Development", Comilla, PARD.

Khan, Akhter Hameed. February 1971. *Tour of Twenty Thanas*, Comilla, BARD.

Khan, Atiqur R., Douglas H. Huber, Makhlisur Rahman. September 1977. "Household Distribution of Contraceptives in Bangladesh - Rural Experience", Dacca, Cholera Research Laboratory.

Khan, L.R. March 1976. "Some Conflicts in Rural Institutions", Dacca.

Khan, L.R. November 1974. "Rural Communication and Farmers Education in Bangladesh", Dacca.

Lindenbaum, Shirley. June 1968. "Women and the Left Hand: Social Status and Symbolism in East Pakistan", *Mankind*, VI, 11.

Lindenbaum, Shirley. 1974. *The Social and Economic Status of Women in Bangladesh*, Dacca, Ford Foundation.

McCord, Colin. 1976. "What's the Use of a Demonstration Project", Dacca, Ford Foundation.

Mia, Ahmadulla. October 1976. "Problems of Rural Development: Some Household Level Indicators", *Benchmark Survey Report Series, No. 2*, Dacca, IRDP.

Murphy, Yolanda and Robert Murphy. 1974. *Women of the Forest*, New York, Columbia University Press.

Nations, Richard. 1975. "The Economic Structure of Pakistan and Bangladesh". *Explosion In A Subcontinent*, ed. Robin Blackburn, England, Penguin Books.

Pala, Achola O. June 1974. "The Role of African Women in Rural Development: Research Priorities". Institute for Development Studies. Discussion Paper 203, University of Nairobi.

Palmer, Ingrid. January-February 1977. "Rural Women and the Basic-Needs Approach to Development", *International Labor Review*.

Papanek, Hanna. August 1971. "Purdah in Pakistan: Seclusion and Modern Occupations for Women", *Journal of Marriage and the Family*.

Papanek, Hanna. 1973. "Purdah: Separate Worlds and Symbolic Shelter", *Comparative Studies in Society and History*, L, 3.

Papanek, Hanna. Autumn, 1977. "The Integration of Women in Development: Women's Work and Development Planning for Women", *Signs*, III.

Pastner, Carroll, McC. May 1974. "Accommodations to Purdah: The Female Perspective", *Journal of Marriage and the Family*.

Planning Commission of Bangladesh. June 1974. "Integrated Rural Development Program: An Evaluation", Dacca.

Proceedings of the International Seminar on Socio-Economic Implications of Introducing HYV In Bangladesh. November 1975. Comilla, BARD.

Qadir, Sayeda Roushan. 1975. "Bastees of Dacca, A Study of Squatter Settlements", Dacca, Local Government Institute.

Rahim, S.A. April 1970. *Farmers Opinions on Selected Topics*, Comilla, PARD.

Rahman, Khandker Mahmudur. August 1975. "The Experience of Marketing with Regard to Small Farmers in Bangladesh with Particular Reference to Comilla Rural Development Program", Comilla, BARD.

Raper, Arthur F. 1970. *Rural Development in Action*. Ithaca, Cornell University Press.

Rizvi, Najma. December 1976. "Food Avoidances During Post-Partum Period Among Muslim Women in Bangladesh", *Shishu Diganta: A Child's Horizon*, Dacca, UNICEF.

Rizvi, Najma. May 1977. "Appropriate Nutrition Technology", *Shishu Diganta: A Child's Horizon*, Dacca, UNICEF.

Role of Women in Socio-Economic Development in Bangladesh: Proceedings of a Seminar Held in Dacca, May 9-10, 1975. March 1977, Dacca, Bangladesh Economic Association.